The Crumbs off the Wife's Table

The Crumbs off the Wife's Table

Hilda Ogbe

Spectrum Books Limited
Ibadan
Abuja • Benin City • Lagos • Owerri

Spectrum titles can be purchased on line at
www.spectrumbooksonline.com

Published by
Spectrum Books Limited
Spectrum House
Ring Road
PMB 5612
Ibadan, Nigeria

in association with
Safari Books (Export) Limited
1st Floor
17 Bond Street
St Helier
Jersey JE2 3NP
Channel Islands
United Kingdom

Europe and USA Distributor
African Books Collective Ltd
The Jam Factory
27 Park End Street
Oxford OX1, 1HU, UK

© Hilda Ogbe

First published 2001

All rights reserved. This book is copyright and so no part of it may be reproduced, stored in a retrieval system, or transmitted, in any form or by any means, electronic, mechanical, electrostatic, magnetic tape, photocopying, recording or otherwise, without the prior written permission of the copyright owner.

ISBN: 978-029-317-5

Front Cover: Hilda and Tommy on their wedding day.

Printed by Meg-Comm Network, Tel: 090-403-444

DEDICATION

Dedicated to my wonderful mother,

Gertrude Gerson

and

my dear brother

John Gerson.

CONTENTS

Dedication — *v*
Acknowledgement — *ix*
Prologue — *xi*

Chapter One:	Escape and War	1
Chapter Two:	Peace, Career and Marriage	58
Chapter Three:	Arrival and Early Life in Nigeria	89
Chapter Four:	The Silver Business	154
Chapter Five:	The Nigerian Civil War	184
Chapter Six:	The Crumbs, The Slice and The Whole Cake	200
Chapter Seven:	Freedom From Pain	234
Chapter Eight:	Sickle Cell Counselling	256
Chapter Nine:	A Fulfilled Life	261
Chapter Ten:	Widowhood	271
Chapter Eleven:	Astrology, My Crutch	278
Chapter Twelve:	Epilogue	285
	Index	291

ACKNOWLEDGEMENT

My thanks go to Dr. Nina Mba, (historian) for her encouragement and advice during the writing of this, my life's story. Without her this book may never have been written, and she supervised its progress step by step.

So too Chief Joop Berkhout, M.D., Spectrum Books Limited, helped to set the ball rolling when he asked me three years ago at a function in Lagos: 'When are we going to get *your* story?' I am also greatly indebted to my adopted family of Hon. Justice Victor Omage J.C.A., his wife Christine and their children who have supported me in every way since I took the big step freedom from pain. My thanks also go to the indefatigable typing efforts of Mr. A.O. Ariemugbovbe, who typed several versions of this book until my computer got tired and gave up. Even his daughter, Mrs. Anne Egwali, a teacher in Computer Science, had a hand in producing the final copy.

Last but not least, my thanks go to my good friend and "sister"; Mrs Susan Iyoha who gave last minute help when NEPA failed. May all these people's dreams also come true.

PROLOGUE

A tapestry is made of thousands of different coloured stitches. This is how my brother Johnny saw my life when I sent him an audio tape describing my daily, monthly happenings in Nigeria. He replied on audio tape from New York: 'Thank you for letting me share the rich tapestry that is your life.'

My husband, late Prince Tommy A. Ogbe Esq. was a large part of it of course. And as he always stated that he would not want to be forgotten after his death, I hope that this book will help to keep him alive.

"When you write your autobiography, the main thing is that you should be truthful", I was advised. I cannot be anything other than truthful, so may I be forgiven for not adhering to the norm: "Do not speak ill of the dead."

This book was planned long before my husband, Tommy A. Ogbe, died. He was an individualist, eccentric and contrary in the extreme – and proud of it. "I don't care a bogary what anybody knows of me, thinks of me, hears about me. I believe in freedom. Freedom of thought, speech and action. Nobody will ever hold me to ransom." He seemed to be fearless in all situations, and he carried his outrageous statements and deeds with aplomb.

Chapter I

ESCAPE AND WAR

"Ah! Today is your birthday," said the immigration officer as he stamped my exit visa into my travel papers. "Congratulations."

Yes, it was my eighteenth birthday the 31st July, 1939, but I did not react. Inside me I thought bitterly: "What is the use of your trying to be friendly now when for years you and your ilk have tormented and persecuted us Jewish citizens without mercy? When you have burnt our synagogues, when you have smashed our shop windows, when you demoted and dismissed all Jewish officials in high places, when you have driven Jewish children out of your German schools and have sent their fathers, their uncles into concentration camps. When you made us live in fear and resentment, as second-class citizens, we were now no citizens at all anymore. You took away our German passports and gave us a 'Nansenpass' which meant a travel document stating our identity but not our nationality. We are now called 'stateless'." I kept these negative thoughts to myself and I entered the gangplank leading to the ship that was to take me to England. I was exultant. I was free! The thought of freedom bubbled inside me. Even the thought of my mother still left behind in Germany did not, at that moment, dull my excitement.

I was embarking on a journey from my home-town of Hamburg, and as soon as I came aboard I met other young people who were on the same voyage as I. My brother John, sixteen years old, had already been sent to England one month earlier. It was the only chance we had to get out of Germany. Although we had applied for immigration to the USA where a distant relation had stood surety for us, there was a long waiting list for German Jews to enter that country. There was a quota system of so many thousand refugee immigrants apportioned to each country. Other European countries also had refugees from Nazi oppression. According to the size of their country of origin, America gave that country a quota. The German quota was the largest, and it was brimful. This meant several years of waiting, and my mother thought that it was just not safe to wait in Germany.

To enter another country as a refugee, one had to deposit the sum of fifty English pounds in a bank overseas, to guarantee that the refugee in question would not be a liability to the country he was entering. The snag was that in Germany it was strictly forbidden to own foreign currency. It did not matter however secretly one tried to arrange such a bank account by writing, every single letter leaving Germany was opened and censored. The regime was so strict and so efficient, that even if one posted from another town in Germany they would trace the writer of the letter and send him or her to concentration camp immediately. This was a risk nobody could take, but good old England offered an alternative.

England was short of domestic servants. She consequently offered, through Jewish welfare organisations, that she would take in women who were qualified in housework to be employed as domestics. We were lucky that my mother and I found a home, which employed the two of us at the same time. So, I was going to be a domestic servant and my mother would do the same work, once she had tied up loose ends in Hamburg. She would then follow me and we would be reunited. My father did not fancy the idea of being a butler, gardener, or footman. He was a superbly tall, handsome, and impeccably dressed businessman who looked like a film-star. He decided that he would go to France to relations there and would from there connect to us in England. Perhaps he thought he could bring money from there into England and build a different kind of existence for all of us.

My brother had been found a position on a chicken farm, because farmers too were short of hands to work on the land or with the animals. The children's transports were arranged again by another Jewish welfare committee. I was glad that at least I would meet my brother in the not too distant future, and confident that our mother would soon join us.

Little did we know what lay in store for Europe and the world. In 1939, there were no death camps yet as far as we knew. It was true that two of my uncles had been sent to different concentration camps for what we and they did not know. They were just picked up in the street for their Jewish looks and we never saw them again. But we lived in hope, and when you are eighteen years old, your life lies before you and your heart is full of expectation.

As I entered the ship, the smell of engine oil and the dark brown linoleum which carpeted all the gangways hit me. But soon I met with other young people and together we were excited and joyful to be going to England. It was an overnight voyage. By the time we disembarked at Southampton, even the memories of what we had seen or heard or eaten on the voyage had faded.

EMPLOYMENT

I was met by a member of the committee which had organised our employment. They were from Surrey where our jobs had been found in the home of two old ladies in the Surrey town of Reigate. This meant a train ride from Southampton to London now and a change of trains from London to Surrey. The member of the committee turned out to be a very distant relation of ours which I had not known before. So I felt lucky and protected and trusted her implicitly to deposit me safely at the home of my employers. This relation was of Russian descent. She and her husband had fled from the Russian revolution in 1917 to France where they had lived for many years before coming to settle in England. Her English was very funny. She spoke with a thick Russian accent which I recognised even though I was not very proficient in

English myself, but I had an ear for language and heard her hard accent and rolled 'Rs' to be foreign to the English language.

We arrived at the home of the old ladies which was an imposing traditional English country home — a storey building. The Misses Dunn and Donkin were politely welcoming but lacked the warmth that I was used to in my family. Of course, I was an employee, I was not a relation of theirs; and I vowed that I would do my best to satisfy their requirements with gratitude and goodwill. I arrived late in the evening, so there were no duties for me immediately. I was told to go to bed and start my work the next morning.

Going to bed was the first chilling experience I had since my immigration to England. Chilling it was literally. As I climbed between two seemingly damp cotton sheets, I wondered whether there was any way in which I could make myself more comfortable. It was only July, the height of summer, and I did not know that the island of Great Britain was permanently damp. I had not yet learnt that British people were a hardy race who believed in fresh air anytime of the year and kept their windows open day and night; nor had I discovered the secret of the hot water bottle. So I lay shivering between what seemed clammy though white and clean sheets, curled into a ball and hastily withdrawing my foot if it stretched to investigate further points in the cold bed.

The next morning, I was shown what my work would be. I was given a large white apron and told to wear a plain dress beneath it. I was a little embarrassed, because I had no plain dress. Contrary to what one would expect, I had a suitcase full of fashionable clothes. In those days, the horrors of refugees driven from their homes with nothing but the clothes they stood up in, which is now such a familiar picture all over the world, had not yet applied to refugees from Hitler's oppression who, though robbed of their homes and valuables, had nevertheless been able to conduct a civilized exodus from their homes.

From our household in the lovely suburb of Hamburg, where everything valuable had been auctioned off for very low sums of money, we had moved into a small apartment in town, getting ready for our emigration. Even then, we still had many belongings and at that time we were allowed one of the small containers that were called "lifts" for each household. We were still allowed to take out our wedding rings of gold but no other gold jewellery or precious stones. Of our family silver cutlery, we were allowed two sets per person: two knives, two forks, two serving spoons, two soup spoons, two teaspoons each. So, my employers were taken aback that I had much finery with me, and somehow I had to concoct a dark skirt and a darkish blouse to make up a plain dress to wear under the big apron. I was shown how to scrub and polish first of all — floors, staircase, — the dark brown linoleum was now a familiar floor covering to me but I did not know that it had to be scrubbed and polished with Mansion Polish until it shone. Both activities were then carried out on one's knees. No long handle scrubbers in those days nor polishing machines.

Understanding instructions was not as easy as I had thought. Although I had done six years of English lessons at school and had always come out with an 'A', I found that the idiomatic and fast spoken English of my two ladies was often beyond my comprehension. Little words like 'underneath' floored me, because the one word I knew for that location was 'under'. However I was not daunted, I knew I would soon pick up.

My main concern now was the arrival of my mother. She had said she would come by the next boat, but two weeks had passed and no sign of her. In the end I summoned up courage and asked my employers if I might use their telephone. I wanted to telephone our distant relations in Dorking, Surrey to ask about my mother's arrival. The two ladies raised their eyebrows in unison. I suppose, it had not sunk in with me that I was a domestic servant who was not entitled to use the telephone. But they relented and when I got through to our contact, I was delighted to hear that my mother was on her way. She arrived by the same route as I had done, having been met at the boat and chaperoned to Reigate. Our reunion was ecstatic. But we soon controlled ourselves because we felt instinctively that too much show of emotion was not to the liking of English people, especially if they were employers.

We went to sleep that night in our servant quarters. I had earlier warned my mother, by letter, of the damp bed sheets and she had brought her electric heating pad with her. She had always kept it in Germany because she was suffering from sciatica. Unfortunately, the plug did not fit the English system. So without a hot water bottle which I had not yet purchased, we had to cover the bottom sheet on which she was to lie with some clothes and put more clothes on top of the blankets which in no way kept us as warm as the German featherbeds had done. We talked in whispers until late into the night.

We really did not mind any hardship. We were so glad to be free, so glad to be together. My mother had the greatest affection for the British people, and to illustrate their kindness she related a moment on her arrival when a porter had helped her with her luggage down from the ship and she had given him a two shilling piece. The porter knew that all those disembarking were refugees from Hitler's oppression and he said: "Are you sure madam, you can spare it?" She was so touched by this sympathetic gesture, but it did not stop her from giving him the shillings.

The next morning it was I who introduced my mother to her/our duties. She was of course an experienced housewife and sweeping, dusting, polishing, washing plates, washing clothes and ironing held no problem for her. Where we both failed miserably was with the laying and lighting of fires in the grates. Every inhabited room was warmed by an open fire. We had no experience of this, and I had not really become proficient in the art, even after two weeks of working as a domestic. I had been shown how to roll balls of newspaper, put them in the grate, make a pyramid of sticks of wood above it, light the paper until the wood caught and crackled and then put coal around and on top of it when the sticks were burning sufficiently to hold and ignite the coal. It always took me a long time to grapple with this duty, and my mother was no better at it. In Germany, we had had central heating in every house or flat we had lived in. My grandmother had iron stoves in every room of her apartment. These were better constructed than open fires, because they had a draught regulator.

One lit them from a flap in the bottom, closed the flap and put coal or wood through a top flap. The stove then kept burning and warming all day. One could even roast apples and groundnuts on its top.

Now, these open grates were a different challenge. Not only did they have to be cleaned out first from ashes of the previous day, but one had to bring up into the house heavy scuttles of coal and firewood to light the coal, and newspaper to light the firewood. I did the heavy part of it, of course, but somehow we were sorry for one another, with each chore that we had to perform. My mother often said to me, "I am so sorry for you children. You have no childhood." But I replied merrily "Oh but Mumsie, this is fun. This is different. This is exciting, and do you know, if it had not been for Hitler, I would not be speaking English now."

We did not do any cooking, but there were the many small meals to be arranged on trays and served to the ladies in different rooms.

7:00 a.m.: Early morning tea with one biscuit

9:00 a.m.: Fried breakfast of bacon and egg, toast and marmalade

11:00 a.m.: Tea

1:00 p.m.: Lunch

4:00 p.m.: Afternoon tea

7:00 p.m.: Hot supper

11:00 p.m.: A cup of coffee served in the daintiest, brightly coloured china cups, cups and saucers gold edged, one brilliant blue, one bright red, another emerald green.

That some of them were cracked and lovingly repaired with some kind of staple across the cracks did not seem to disturb the ladies as it did disturb me. Washing up and putting away the coffee cups was the last chore of the day, before we fell into bed, exhausted.

Our situation changed very soon. Mother had arrived in the middle of August 1939. On the 3rd of September that year, we were called to the radio to listen to an important broadcast, and we heard the account of how Hitler had marched into Poland and then the voice of Prime Minister Chamberlain said in sombre measured tones: "Britain is now at war with Germany."

We looked at each other, trying to fathom what this could mean for us. We felt safe among the British, but we also knew that a war would now sever all contacts with Germany, and we did not know what would happen to the large family we had left behind. My mother thought of my father of course and then of her old parents whom she had had to leave behind. They were eighty-four years old. She had left them all the money she could spare, but she felt guilty at having escaped to safety when she did not know what would happen to them. Of course as the law of nature would have it, her duty to her children came first, and she had followed that law. My father had made his own choice. But now that Hitler was also marching into France, would he still be able to carry out his plan?

A few days after the announcement of war, the ladies Dunn and Donkin called us to say that they were very sorry but with the advent of war they could no longer afford to keep us. They would, they said, find us new employment.

In due course, my mother was sent to a family with one child. They had also taken in a Scottish couple with one child as evacuees. When Britain realised the danger that war could mean to her major cities, they organised immediately, that all school children from those cities should be evacuated to the country, for greater safety. With the children of course they had to evacuate the schools and with the schools the teachers. So it came that a

Scottish couple who were teachers were staying with the new employers who had accepted to employ my mother.

Her fondness for the Scottish people stemmed from those days. She found the evacuees friendly and warm-hearted. The teacher, Mr. Anderson, always helped her to bring up the wood and the coal, and was very concerned when, one day, she was so dizzy that she fell, face forward, into the grate which she was cleaning out.

In my own case, I was redirected to a small hospital 'croft home' whose matron was a friend of the two ladies with whom we were now living. The matron was very kind to me. Although I was to do domestic work, instead of housing me in the servants quarters she billeted me with the nurses, and I had my meals at table with the nurses, waited on by the domestic staff. The nurses too were very friendly, though the British were not used to making overt signs of friendship. Yet whenever I looked up from my plate at mealtime and met somebody else's eyes they would instantly smile at me. I was sharing a room with a much older nurse who taught me much English by telling me of her failed love story, with a man who had gone to South Africa and not sent for her as he had promised. I think I was company for her, and she was as willing to teach me, as I was keen to learn.

Most of my duties in the croft home consisted of scrubbing and polishing, and if you have ever seen the length of hospital corridors and hospital stairs, you'll have an idea of what this occupation meant. Besides, as I polished along on my knees, the draught from under the doors of the small wards left and right of me did not make my work more pleasant. The open windows in each ward and the gap under the doors which had never seen draught excluders certainly brought fresh air. The cross-ventilation might have been healthy for my lungs, but my back objected. After a few weeks of this work, I was seized with severe back pains and was actually hospitalised in this same hospital, unable to continue the work.

I felt very ashamed to be a burden to these kind people and as Christmas was approaching (I had now been in that job for three months), I thought of what present I could possibly give to the kind matron. I cannot now remember how I managed to buy a film for my camera with my poor earnings of fifteen shillings a week, but it seems I did buy a film or maybe two, and took shots of every single employee in that hospital — every nurse, every sister, doctor, domestic, and even the gardener. When the photos were developed, I made an album of them and for each staff I wrote a little poem to be pasted under their photo. This I packaged nicely and gave to matron on Christmas day. It is now on looking back that I can understand the look of total amazement on her face as she leafed through the album. She actually did not know what to say. I must have been an odd fish in her eyes, a refugee who had a camera and wrote verses in a newly acquired language. I remember one of the verses that was pasted under the cleaning lady's photo.

> Every morning at half past eight,
> Old Mrs Lacey comes through the gate.
> She works so quietly at her hard job,
> And maybe sighs sometimes,
> All this for a few bob.

After Christmas and the New Year of 1940, the British government realised that the war was going to last longer and be more serious than they had first thought. A law was released to say that foreign domestic workers were now to be allowed to do any other work that helped the war effort. As my back problem took a long time to heal and I was no longer fit to scrub and polish, I discussed with matron that if my mother could find war work for us, I hoped she would not be offended if I left her and the hospital. Of course she did not object.

Again, our relations in Dorking came to the rescue. They found a job for my mother and my brother in a factory making military uniforms. This factory was in Dorking and we were relocated to that small pleasant town and found ourselves a flat that nobody wanted, because it was near an overhead railway. We did not care. We moved into No. 8 Lincoln Road without any furniture.

To begin with, we acquired a few orange boxes and tea chests. Both were made of wood and in different sizes. The orange boxes served as chairs and the much larger tea chest was our table. We covered them with pieces of cloth or clothing or pillow cases. I do not remember how my handy brother knocked shelves into the recesses of the wall beside the fire place. In front of those shelves, he fixed a rod on which we hung a blanket.

Each of us had a blanket, and so we had a semblance of cupboards. In the evenings we would take down the blankets and cover ourselves with them. My mother now went daily to the factory to hand-sew with very fine stitches the elegant lapels of officers' uniforms. My brother was employed as an errand-boy carrying bales of cloths and braids and any other equipment that was needed for the work. He also trundled away big trolleys full of finished uniforms. Because of my back I was unable to sit for long to do the sewing. For the time being, I ran the home, hoping that I would get much better and then be able to do the same work my mother was doing.

In the meantime, we, as aliens had to report to the police once a week to show our presence and to have our alien registration book stamped. I asked permission to be allowed to do a freelance manicurist job until I was fit enough to do something worthwhile. I had a medical certificate to support my application, and it was granted. Before leaving Germany, and after I had taken and passed my Abitur, with nine subjects which entitled me to direct entry into university, I had very much wanted to study modern languages. But which of us Jewish youngsters could think now of further education when the priority lay on saving one's life and making a living?

I had left school at Easter in 1939. Between that time and the time of my departure, which was July 31st, I had not only worked mornings as a domestic in order to get a certificate that would qualify me for a post in England, but in the afternoons I had taken a course in beauty culture which included manicuring. For that too I got a certificate. It was my aunt's suggestion.

My mother's sister had had the good fortune of being sent to England for further education after she had finished her schooling in Germany. My grandparents thought that it would enhance her prospects of marriage. My aunt was a very romantic person who lived in a world of novels which she read avidly. From these novels and also from her experience in an English boarding school, she concluded that Britain was peppered with lords and ladies and advised my mother to let me train for beauty culture which would give me a chance to work in a beauty salon in Bond Street where a handsome lord would discover me and marry me.

I had to laugh at this naive idea. But at the time, all would-be emigrants strove to learn some skill which would stand them in good stead in their future country. So I took the course in beauty culture. My mother took a course in millinery. The art of making ladies' hats seemed a desirable one, and she learned, together with a few other friends, how to drape felt hats over steam and onto a block, the shape of a head; how to make the brim separately and sew it neatly onto the crown of the hat; how to fix ribbons; bands, flowers, feathers and other decorations to the finished hat to make it into a desirable creation.

As I mentioned earlier, manicuring was part of beauty culture. I could not set up a salon with all the paraphernalia of reclining chairs for the customers, creams and lotions and brushes and make-up, bands for the hair to keep the creams out of it or glass cupboards with jars and bottles to impress customers. The circle of customers in Dorking who needed manicuring was very tiny, not to say non-existent. I had one or two ladies who indulged in this treatment once a week but the money they paid hardly covered my transport fare to their homes.

In the meantime, I kept house for my mother and brother but money was very scarce. We had moved into that empty flat in January and February proved a bitterly cold month. While John and mother were at the factory, I wanted to do the washing in the house but found to my dismay that there was no water in the pipes. My neighbour kindly helped me to find a plumber who told me that the pipes had frozen solid and there could be no running water until the cold eased up. For this advice, the plumber charged one shilling and I burst into tears. I did not have one shilling in my purse. It was the end of the week and my mother and brother had not yet brought home their pay packets. The plumber took pity on me and said I could pay later.

Some of the time when there was a little money, I would go to the cinema to while away the time. For six pence I could sit through two performances of the same main feature film.

One day as I opened the cheapest newspaper, the *Daily Mirror* I saw on its centre pages *The Smiler*. An article beneath the heading invited the public to send in jokes for this page. Every joke published would fetch ten shillings and the best joke of the week carried the prize of five pounds. I sat down and wrote the joke somebody had not long ago told me. 'A French man is invited to an English Golden wedding. As the celebrations begin he nudges one of the guests and says: "What does it mean this golden wedding?"

"Well you see", the guest answers, "the man and the woman have lived together for fifty years, and now..."

"Ah!" interrupts the Frenchman, "and now 'e is going to marry' 'er. Bravo, bravo."

I sent this joke to the *Daily Mirror,* and could not believe my eyes when after a few days, I received a postal order for five pounds, the prize for the best joke of the week.

Five pounds were a fortune. Now I did not need to feel guilty anymore. I could contribute equally to the household as my mother and brother did, and I could allow myself little luxuries here and there. Even so, the money lasted for three months.

In the meantime, there had been dreadful bombing of London and other major towns, by the Germans. The British must have felt that they had been too generous, allowing so many foreigners into the country without being absolutely certain that they were genuine refugees. Consequently, tribunals were set up all over the country where foreigners had to present themselves. Each case was judged on its merits, categorizing the immigrants as friendly aliens or enemy aliens. My brother, John, had to go back to the village where he had worked on the chicken farm, because that was where he and his work were known. My mother and I had to go to the tribunal at Reigate for the same purpose. It would have appeared that much depended upon the personal view of the magistrate who judged us, because my brother was judged to be a friendly alien, whereas mother and I were classified as enemy aliens. We thought nothing of it at the time, but then one day my mother came home alone from work at a very early hour, accompanied by a man and a woman in plain clothes. Her voice shook as she said to me, "Hildchen, we are being interned. These people are police. They tell me we shall be away for only two or three days so we should pack only the essentials for such a time, but Johnny is to stay behind." My mother then said: "I have given him all the money I had for his own upkeep and I hope we shall really be back in a short while."

Well, we hastily packed some warm clothes, some night clothes and toiletries, and then followed the policeman and woman to an assembly point where we met a few other refugees who were going on the same journey. We were put on a train to London and from there on a train to Liverpool. It was a long journey. The train was crowded with refugees who were now being interned. Each compartment had a policewoman sitting with the occupants. Many of them were elderly, and the one who sat with us very soon nodded off as the train started moving. Of course, we were all anxious to know what was going to happen to us but I for one did not feel the terror I had felt in Germany whenever I saw a uniformed person coming towards me. My mother was anxious about my brother and wondered how he would manage on his own and when we would be back with him.

In Liverpool, we were all led into a sports arena. It was in fact a boxing ring with the boxing platform and ropes all around it in the centre and rows of seats all around the boxing ring rising in amphitheatre fashion around the boxing platform. We sat on tip-up seats, and soon after arrival, we were served a hot drink. To this day I do not know whether it was tea or coffee, Horlicks or Bournvita, but it was hot and sweet and very welcome. We spent some hours in this arena without being able to glean any information as to our future from any of our attendants. After a whole day, we were finally told we would be going on a boat trip. Again, no one knew where to. Most of us were new to the country and not very familiar with the geography. The biggest, nearest island we could think of was Ireland, but as it turned out later, we were headed for the Isle of Man.

On the boat, we all sat on deck, that is, where there was room to sit. I was very worried for my mother because of her sciatica. I knew she could not possibly lie down on the floor, or she would not be able to get up again. So I made every effort to secure a seat for her on deck. I was extremely tired. I lay down on deck with a life saving ring to lay my head on and fell asleep.

It was not a long trip. Very soon the ship bells clanged. We had arrived at the Port of Douglas. From there we were now divided into two groups of men and women. When it became known that we were going to different camps, there was a great outcry and clinging together of couples, then weeping of women when the men were taken away to stay in the Douglas camp while the women were taken to Port Erin and another town called St. Mary's.

If we had had any fears of concentration camp barracks, they were soon dispelled. It became known that we were going to be housed in seaside hotels, because the three places mentioned were seaside resorts. My mother and I were directed to the Golf Links Hotel. We were still numb with the mystery of it all, and especially with the uncertainty of what would happen to my brother John. This was my mother's greatest concern. Myself, I was once again bubbling with anticipation. "Only a few days" I thought to myself, "by the seaside in this beautiful hotel couldn't be so bad," and I was sure I would make the most of it. My mother had struck up an acquaintance with a Viennese woman called Lizzie, and I had made friends with a Viennese young girl called Irene. She told me she was a ballet dancer which immediately caught my imagination, but she was alone in England, as her parents had stayed behind in Vienna. It now appeared that we were to share hotel rooms four at a time which meant two women in each of two double beds. We had a beautiful view over the sea. We had beautiful tiled bathrooms to use. We had three regular meals a day, which were cooked by the inmates of the hotel who either volunteered for the job or were selected for it because of their previous experience.

But, of course, there were always some who were discontented, who found things to be disgruntled about. Coming from many different countries and backgrounds, it was difficult to please everybody where the cooking was concerned. For some; it was too rich, too fatty, too many dumplings; for others vegetables were overcooked, yet others complained that the food was skimpy; while the lean ones mentioned that the portions were too heavy. What a sin it was to have complained then, when we never went hungry at all, and when our meals were punctual and something to look forward to. Some women, with nothing to do, sat by the fireside in the sitting room and fought over the best armchairs. What a contrast with the refugee camps of today!

We had a view over the sea and its white sandy beaches; on which we could sun ourselves rubbing each other with oil to get a darker tan, and dip into the sea, but when this novelty wore off, time began to hang heavy on our hands.

After a while of course, we realized it was not just a three-day stay. We now had to occupy ourselves. We had the freedom of the town, which was a large village you might say with all the usual shops, and those who had money could buy whatever they wanted.

There were fishing ports all around the Isle of Man. Everywhere, swarms of seagulls circled and screeched overhead, ready to pounce on any tasty morsel of fishy prey.

I think the Isle of Man must have the best kippers in the world. I have mouth-watering memories of waking in the camp to the aroma of kippers frying for breakfast. This could be rivalled only by the smell of frying bacon. We, the inmates, got only small portions of each, but we did get such luxurious foods. One day, on a stroll with my mother, through the village, I saw in the fishmonger's shop a row of succulent kippers. They were smoked to a golden brown, their aroma irresistible. I bought one, and walking out into the street, began to eat it as it was, picking it with my fingers, enjoying the juicy flesh. There was really no need to boil or fry it. The smoking had cooked it done already. My mother was nonplussed that I should be eating in the street, but I thought, did one have to be so particular in an internment camp? One of the seagulls evidently shared her views, for it swooped down like lightning, snatched the whole heavy kipper from my hand and flew off with it. Mother said that all through her long life she never forgot the look of surprise on my face, as I stood there, with my mouth open, my now empty hand still held in the air.

The village was surrounded by barbed wire, but we never saw it. We had a stay of freedom, companionship, sunshine and beach, fresh air, and apart from missing the relations left behind or married women missing their husbands, we had nothing really to complain about. But time hung heavily on our hands until ingenious members created a service exchange. It was like a labour exchange where you could go and offer any skills you had and for those skills you were paid in cardboard tokens because money, real money, was not in circulation. There were teachers and dressmakers, hairdressers and artists, doctors and nurses who all offered their services. There were actors too, albeit amateur actors, and soon the whole camp was buzzing with activity.

I had volunteered for acting and teaching French and English. I had a passion for foreign languages. By now I had been in England seven months, and felt I had progressed sufficiently to teach others. I always felt that anything I knew, I could teach, I could pass on to somebody else. I loved the French language, and certainly was able to teach the rudiments of it, so I had no compunctions about offering my services. We now put up notices that English and French classes would be held in the church hall on different dates.

My preoccupation was with the pronunciation of English to begin with. I hated the German accent when spoken in English and made it my mission to correct the mal-pronunciation of the 'th', 'w' and 'r'. The people most in need of correct pronunciation were of course the older generation. It was hard for those who had never learnt English before, to get their tongues around the new sounds. My class was full of elderly ladies, but I was confident that I could improve their English if only they were able to drop their inhibitions. I went from pupil to pupil asking them to repeat the following sentence: "Well said the old woman. We shall very soon find out." The German pronunciation of this sounded somewhat like "vell, said ze old voman, ve shall veghy soon find out." As I passed in front of each pupil, their excuses became many. "Oh, you see", they explained to me in German that they could not say these sounds properly because of false teeth, because of not hearing them properly, because of not understanding the difference between the sounds and so on, but I let no excuse pass. I kept repeating the sounds and made the pupils move their lips to imitate them. The 'th' was not difficult really because, I said to them, when your child speaks with a lisp (and I called it 'lithp'), you know he puts his tongue between his teeth instead of behind them. Now you can copy that and you will have the correct sound of the 'th'. The 'r' proved to be more difficult, because the 'r' in German is a guttural one spoken at the back of the throat, whereas the English 'r' is spoken with the tip of the tongue curling behind the front teeth, touching the roof of the mouth just behind them. I suggested they should say a fast double 'd' like 'veddy' and they would soon have the correct sound. It worked.

I do not know where my ideas came from, but they were just inspirations because I was not taught the method of teaching in school. However, we began to have fun in the classes. At one point the village showed the film, *Pinocchio*, in which there was a song. "If you wish upon a star"

> If you wish upon a star,
> Makes no difference who you are,
> Anything your heart desires
> Will come to you.
> Fate is kind,
> She brings to those who love
> The sweet fulfilment of

Their secret longings...(repeat)

Most of us had been allowed to see the film and I now began to sing the song in the classroom. Whilst singing, the pupils learned the words that appeared in the song and also began to imitate the correct pronunciation. I took these classes twice a week and noticed that every time they grew larger, more and more people wanted to take part until the whole church hall was filled. This became more difficult to control. It seemed that many elderly ladies came for the entertainment rather than the study of English. I had to walk down the aisle of the hall from time to time to discover that their bent heads were not bent over any exercise books but that in fact the ladies in the back rows were knitting. I assumed a stern countenance and said: "ladies, the needle work classes are held elsewhere. Will you please go and join them." Looking back now, I felt I had quite a cheek at eighteen years to control these elderly pupils in this manner, but did they go to the needle work classes? No. They came again, but this time without their knitting.

The French classes were held in the vestry, because it was expected to be a much smaller group. They were held only once a week and we began with about fifteen pupils. The following week they rose to approximately twenty, then thirty, and when I came again to teach the following class, there was a queue waiting outside hoping that there would be enough room for them. There was not. The camp management now decided to give me another day in the vestry to teach a second batch of pupils who wanted to learn French.

I have to this day a typewritten testimonial from the Camp Commandant who said upon my release that I was a trained teacher of languages, that I had taught large classes of English and French, which had been among the most popular in the camp.

Another activity was forced upon me, when people began to complain that their roommates were snoring and that they could not sleep properly. One of the complainants was a young, brilliantly gifted pianist who was of a very sensitive nature. She had been so desperate about the nightly noises that she had put plasticine in her ears and could not get it out again. She had to have medical treatment, first to have the plasticine extracted. It had meanwhile gone brittle and disintegrated, and had made her ears very sore.

I felt something needed to be done for such people. My mind went back to my mother who also had had to endure my father's heavy snoring, and who had been unable to sleep well. She had discovered a kind of ear stopper in Germany which was called Oropax. I had played with it once or twice and felt that it was a waxy object which would soften between one's warm fingers and stay in the ear, shutting out all noise. Now, on the Isle of Man, I remembered this object and put to use my experience in beauty culture, where, apart from facial treatments, we also had learned how to make face creams. These involved bees wax and paraffin wax, almond oil and other ingredients. I now thought of the bees wax and found that the chemist in the village had some in stock. I also got some cotton wool and now melted the wax, dipping small cotton wool balls into it and letting them harden. At first attempt I saw that the bees wax was too soft and would leak into the ear. My next step was to get the harder paraffin wax. This too I melted but found that when I soaked the cotton wool in it and let it harden it was too hard to be squeezed into the ear. Putting two and two together the solution was obvious. I had to mix the bees wax with paraffin wax and finally obtained the right mix.

I called this product 'Nosound' and advertised it for six pence a pair. In the meantime we had been allowed to receive money from outside the camp, but this money was held in trust by the management and dished out to us in small amounts as weekly pocket money. I went to the service exchange and asked for an artist who would be willing to paint some posters for me against tokens which I had earned for my language classes. Yes, such an artist materialized. She drew for me and later painted in water colours four different very beautiful large posters which we pinned up in the lobbies of the four biggest hotels. I had given her instructions of how the Nosound ear plugs would not only keep out unwanted noises, but would also stabilize one's balance on a voyage, preventing sea sickness. Don't ask me where I got this idea from, but it proved to be correct. I was now earning real money in six pences by selling the pairs of Nosound ear plugs at six pence each.

The other activity for which I had time alongside my teaching and producing of ear plugs was amateur acting. There was, among us, a school teacher from Berlin who had a wonderful sense of humour. She got together a group of would-be actors and each of us had to pass an audition. I recited a dramatic passage from Goethe's "Faust". I gave my most heartrending performance of Gretchen "On Her Knees", but drama was not really my strong point. I was rejected, later to be reinstated for comedy.

In any case, our director Miss Goldberg, felt that we needed to laugh more than cry. She chose Oscar Wilde's "The Importance of Being Ernest", in which I played the dowager aunt. In another play "Midsummer Night Dream" by Shakespeare, I was Thisbe. We also had a variety show in which each actor invented his own script. I designed a scene in which my friend, Irene the ballet dancer, would pretend to be a wooden doll which had to be wound up in the back with a large key to set her in motion. She would then dance in wooden short hard steps. I was dressed as a clown with the conventional pointed hat, heavy red nose, painted face, ruched collar, baggy shirt and baggier trousers. I would now imitate the doll's steps, jerkily moving my arms and hands as she did, my knees and feet as she did and then I would make a mistake in my dance and fall down to make people laugh.

They laughed all right, but I did not. Not being a trained actor with experience of falling the right way, I had bumped down on my seat and created a dreadful backache for myself. The camp doctor was called to our room because after dragging myself there I could no longer get up from that bed. The camp doctor was of course, one of our inmates, a Viennese lady doctor who thought I had lumbago, prescribed a rubbing lotion and ordered bed rest. It was not until years later that an X-ray showed that I actually had a tiny fracture in my lower vertebra, and my back since then has gone from bad to worse.

Despite this handicap, I was on my feet again in a week or two and resumed life as normal. My friend and roommate, Irene, was very kind and concerned and did a lot of fetching and carrying for me. Indeed, we had struck up a close friendship as had my mother with her companion Lizzie. I cannot remember whether the latter had offered her services for any occupation but my mother had volunteered to be the toilet attendant in the very elegant downstairs toilets of the hotel. This was her function in case official visitors came to inspect the camp. We, the inmates, were given a certain number of sheets of toilet paper to last us a week each, but for the visiting VIPs my mother was put in charge of a whole toilet roll. The downstairs toilets were as elegant as the whole hotel. They were tiled in a beautiful green with lovely wash basins and separate cubicles and they were kept pristinely clean. The inmates were not allowed to use them.

For some time now it had been possible for the camp inmates to receive not only money but personal belongings sent from the mainland. Everything was censored and examined of course, but so long as a package did not contain prohibited goods, all was delivered intact to the rightful owner. We had no one to send us money, but what do you think awaited us one day, when we were called to the Commandant's office? There it was, embarrassingly large, — our "lift" (container) from Germany. It had arrived in Dorking in the meantime and had kindly been forwarded by the Refugee Committee (which ought to have known better). This "lift" had been packed in our house in Hamburg, under supervision of a grim-faced Nazi officer who observed our every movement to make sure that we did not wrap money, gold or precious stones with our permitted belongings.

Prior to that, Hitler had demanded that Jews hand over all their precious jewellery to the government. My grandmother had a lot of diamonds — diamond rings, diamond ear rings, diamond pendants; but she was too nervous to keep back any of them. She was then eighty-four years old and my mother did not want to burden her with a guilty conscience. But my mother herself thought she would rather lose her jewellery in the post than give it over to the government, and so she posted many precious rings and earrings to our relations in France. She simply sent them boxes of chocolate, unwrapped the chocolate from the foil, wrapped up a ring instead and put them back in the box. Maybe she risked two or three rings in one box of chocolates. When she heard from the relations thanking her for the chocolates and saying that they liked the hard centres, she knew they had arrived safely. She also sent some brooches, which were too long to be wrapped in chocolate wrappers, in a tin of talcum powder. I did not know of this until many years later because she did not want to burden me either with such a secret.

As it was, Hitler soon invaded France and our relations had to flee for their lives. The nearer Hitler came over the German border, the farther they fled down to the south of France and lived underground. Such was their loyalty and reliability, that they took my mother's jewels with them wherever they went. Many years after the war ended, we finally got this jewellery back from them through a traveller who travelled from France to England.

I had a young friend, who was learning to be a photographer. He had taken many photographs of me when I was doing beauty culture. They were excellent large portraits, and we both felt sure that he had a good future cut out for him whenever he left Germany. Before the official came to supervise our packing, this boy had begged me to pack his camera with my things so that it would get out of Germany safely before he could be reunited with it. It was a 35mm Leica. I was a little nervous about his request because the Leica had his name engraved on it, and I feared that the official might notice it. But all went well. I put the camera upside down into the packing so that the name would not be noticed. It was quite small and probably did not look as valuable as it was. He was gassed with a lot of other young Jewish people from Hamburg. Unfortunately, the poor boy did not survive the death camps. He was gassed with a lot of other young Jewish people from Hamburg. I kept his camera for many years afterwards in the hope that I would still hear from him or see him. It was not to be.

But I am digressing. When we had finished the packing, the officer sealed the case with the official seal of the Third Reich and gave us a document to clear our goods. What were we to do now with an almost complete household of dinner services, bed and table linen, cooking pots and kitchen utensils?

We could not even lift the thing and apologized to the Commandant for the inconvenience it caused. Although we were delighted to be reunited with our possessions, my resourceful mother decided that we would have to sell the breakables and with the money so earned, buy suitcases in which, eventually, to carry away the bed and table linens, and other soft belongings.

There was a beautiful coffee service of the purest white Meissen porcelain, gold edged and decorated with fabulous red roses. It was a set for twelve people and had been given to me by my romantic aunt, my mother's sister, as a present towards my trousseau. It was a wrench to part with it. We sold a dinner service too and some precious crystal dishes and glasses from Czechoslovakia, famous for such luxuries. Yes, we realized enough money for suitcases, with plenty to spare. My careful and wise mother held on to it for the future, in care of the camp authorities.

By now news had reached us that after all, the government had decided that even the previously classed "friendly aliens" were to be interned so as not to run any risk of espionage among the foreigners. So my brother also joined the men's camp in Douglas, and there was the occasional mail from Douglas to Port Erin or the other women's camp St. Mary's which we of Port Erin never got to see. My mother was now quite happy because John was near us and once a month a meeting of relations of both camps was arranged. How very kind and thoughtful the British were! They transported the women to Douglas where in a large hall, husbands and wives, mothers and sons and sisters and brothers could meet for an hour's chat. Of course, there was greater yearning among the married couples, and when they clung together on saying goodbye after that one hour, the camp guards would say good naturedly, "Come along now, leave a bit for next time".

My brother told us that he was in accommodation with other musicians, and as he himself was very musical (at that time he played the piano and the accordion), he was totally happy. There was one roommate who played the flute, another who played the violin, and a third who played the guitar. After their release, these men would meet for many years after and play chamber music together. Now that my mother saw that my brother was content, she stopped worrying about him.

Meanwhile though, bombs continued to rain on London: this time it was fire bombs which set the town ablaze. There was mumbling and grumbling among the citizens that while they were facing danger daily, we the foreigners were sitting pretty and secure on the Isle of Man. Whether this had anything to do with the decision of the government to release us, or whether they had meanwhile satisfied themselves of the true identity of the genuine refugees, they began releasing the friendly aliens. My brother was among them, and once again my mother had cause for concern about his well-being and whereabouts.

Luckily he was brought back to Dorking into the care of the refugee committee, and found a job as errand boy in a grocery store. He was also given accommodation in a hostel for refugees. He had stayed only six months in the Isle of Man but my mother and I had completed ten months, when our turn came to be released. Both Lizzie and Irene opted to go with us when we were given the chance to go back to Dorking also. So it happened that in 1941 we were back from internment, none the worse for it, but the richer for the experience.

In Dorking, Johnny had made arrangements with the manageress of the grocery store where he worked as an errand boy to introduce his sister to her, in case she could find employment for me. The manageress was a delightfully funny woman. An elderly spinster, short, dumpy with permanently watering eyes, but with speedy and capable movements, she took one look at me and nodded.

"When can you start?" she asked.

"Tomorrow", I said, and did start the following day. I had to wear an overall of my own, it was pale green with a zip from neck to bottom, down the front. A grocery store is the old fashioned equivalent of today's supermarket. In those days nobody helped himself. Every customer was waited on by a salesgirl or man. It was the time of food rationing, which had started in the early weeks of war by the government and was superbly organised. Everybody was issued with a ration book. This consisted of a booklet that was divided into weekly columns for the whole year, and the entitlements for each of the columns were 2 ozs of butter, 2 ozs of tea, 2 ozs of sugar, 8 ozs of meat per person. But there was also another booklet, a pink one, which was divided in squares that were called points. For some of these points one could get tinned food or luxuries like chocolate. These points were issued for the whole month. So, if you had a sweet tooth, you could eat the month's chocolate ration in one go. Or, if you fancied tinned meat, such as Spam, you could have that all in one go. There lived in Dorking, the famous composer Vaughan Williams, who possessed many Siamese cats. He fed these darlings on his precious points with tinned salmon. We got this information on authority from his cleaning lady. As a bonus, she added that he was also a heavy smoker, and that, in the mornings when she came to clean up, his study where he composed music was strewn with burnt match sticks.

Back to the grocery, which was a very old building that deserves to be described. It was an eighteenth century old time pub which Dickens used to frequent. It had the traditional bay windows with small leaded glass panes. It also had thick floor boards which were so worn, that we could look into the cellar between them. It was almost as if we were working in the Old Curiosity Shop. It had a lovely character for the romantically inclined, who also had to take the rough with the smooth or the smooth with the rough in the shape of rats.

Dorking was a small town of wealthy people who lived in large manor houses and had dozens of evacuees billeted with them. Consequently, their orders for weekly rations posed a problem for us in the store. When you have one order of sixteen times 2 ozs of tea, sixteen times 2 ozs of butter, sixteen times 2 ozs of sugar and so on, it takes a long time to prepare. The psychology of such orders was that, in fairness, everybody should have his own allocated share in front of him. So there was no way we could dish out sixteen times 2 ozs of sugar and make it thirty-two ounces. It would not have been fair!

We had very little time during the day to carry out these orders which came by written lists and would be delivered to the respective homes by my brother John on his bicycle. In the daytime, we had to attend over the counter customers who came in droves with their ration books which had to be stamped for every item, with a symbol which showed that the ration for that particular week had been given to them. So we were kept on our toes from eight in the morning until six in the evening when the shop closed. Then, after closing, the real work began. We now weighed and cut and patted the butter, the bacon, the sugar, the tea, until after eleven o'clock at night. We were on our feet all day. In the evenings when no more deliveries were being made, John also helped in the shop except for Thursdays when he was allowed to be off duty to play the accordion in the local dance band at the town hall.

On one such evening, when Johnny was playing in the band at the "Odd Fellows Hall", I went home alone after closing at 11.00 p.m. I took a shortcut to the hostel, passing a row of low houses. From the corner of my eye, I saw through the street-level window flames flickering and thought there was a fire burning in the grate. I passed by, but then went back a few steps to look properly. It was not a fire in the grate, but a pressing iron left on, on the wooden ironing board. The board had caught fire. Flames were licking around the iron, and in a short while I knew the little house would go up in flames, spreading to the neighbouring houses.

I banged on the door shouting "fire, fire" but no one came out. I dashed into the main street, colliding with a policeman on patrol. "Fire," I shouted. "Please come quickly." I led him to the small house where the flames were now consuming the whole ironing board. "Easy, easy, young lady," said the policeman "I'll get help," and he swung himself on his bicycle, dashing away to get the fire service.

Dorking was a small place. He did not have far to go before he returned with the fire engine clanging its bells, and waking up the whole town. The men and their hose set to work, wasting no time in breaking the window to insert their jet of water. They had come just in time to prevent major damage. When the owner of the tailoring shop (for that is what it was) came out of a neighbouring house, the policeman said to him: "you're lucky, mate. If this'ere young lady 'ad not raised alarm, all your property would 'ave gone for a Burton." The tailor thanked me and asked me to come and see him the following day. It was midnight now, my mother would be worried. I ran home as fast as I could, scrambled up the steep rise to the hostel and, breathlessly, told my story.

During my lunch time the next day, I called on the tailor who asked me what he could do for me to show his appreciation of my prompt action to save his house. "I need an overcoat" I said, to which he replied "if you bring the material, I will make it for you." Hmm, tall order. I had no clothing coupons left, and where was I going to get the money to buy cloth, anyway? My mother came to the rescue with an old off-white blanket. I had it dyed dark red and went to the tailor with it. He really did make me a smart overcoat from it and even supplied the lining, all free of charge.

As the work in the grocery was mounting, we felt it was time to suggest to Miss Marshall that she might need help with her bookkeeping and we had just the right person for her. Yes, you have guessed it, we had in mind our little mother. Miss Marshall liked the idea, accepted it, but suggested that for the sake of diplomacy, our mother should go under a different name. So she was called Mrs. Jones, later affectionately abbreviated to "Jonesie". Jonesie sat in an office upstairs surrounded by tea chests and boxes full of rice and flour. One day, she was serenely engrossed in her bookkeeping, which she kept in perfect order, when she was disturbed by rustling in the flour bin. She went to look at what was the matter and saw a large black rat looking at her quizzically.

She raised alarm and Miss Marshall ordered rat traps to be set up in the whole of the upper floor. It was lucky that the fashion for shoes in those days was suede upper leather and thick rubber soles, because one day we heard something clomping down the stairs. It was Jonesie, our poor mother, whose foot had got caught in a rat trap. Luckily the trap did not pierce the suede leather or the crepe soles, so that to our relief, we were able to laugh at Jonesie's peculiar footwear.

I, in my ambition to prove that I was as good as the male shop assistants, used to carry wooden boxes of tins of sardines from the cellar up the stairs into the shop, and though I earned the admiration of my colleagues, it was not really a good thing for me to carry a 'hundred-weight'.

Not everything was packaged as nicely as things are now in the supermarkets. Biscuits, for instance, came in large tins and were sold loose. If any biscuits were broken in the tins they would be sold cheaply. Sometimes an old pensioner would come and ask for broken biscuits, and if there were none, John or I would dip into the big tin and break a few before bringing them out to be weighed for the poor customer. Miss Marshall never got to know of this, but she was a bit of a cheat herself. There were in Surrey camps of gypsies, who would troop into the shop with their large families and equally large number of ration books. After attending to them and sighing with relief when she had finished, Miss Marshall would add the figures of the date of the day to the bill of groceries which she now presented to the customers. They seemed to have plenty of money, or they were careless enough never to check the bill. They paid up.

Another of Miss Marshall's tricks was the mixing of coffee. Coffee was sold as beans in large green and gold metal canisters, which stood, numbered in a gleaming row on the shelf behind us. As imported goods became in short supply, and the customer asked for a mixture of Kenya and Brazil coffee, she dipped her hand into No. 11 and No. 15, making a mixture for the customer, and grinding it in the shop machine for him. The satisfied customer went off with his mixture, not aware that all the canisters contained the same kind of coffee. We, the assistants, enjoyed the heavenly aroma of freshly ground coffee. Miss Marshall was not entirely oblivious of the fact that she was a slave driver, who paid no overtime for our daily long nights of work; but she compensated by making us a nice cup of tea at about ten o'clock in the evening and gave us a ration-free thickly buttered and freshly baked brown bread called Hovis, to sustain us through the late evenings.

Jonesie closed at 6:00 p.m. and went home to the hostel to join Lizzie there, and to wait for our return for supper. I cannot imagine now, how I had free time to devote to hobbies and make extra money, but I did. Maybe on Sundays, I collected empty jam jars and painted them with oil paints, making pretty little flower designs on them. I intended to give them away, but to my surprise people wanted to buy them. So, again I made some pocket money other than my weekly wage.

After one year with the delightful Miss Marshall, I became restive. I said to our mother, "We can't go on like this. I have to learn something, I have to improve myself. There is no time and no facility in Dorking to do this. I must go to London to find a home for all of us and to see if I can find a job and some opportunity to learn a skill." Mother let me go with trepidations. I had never been to the huge city of London. I had no idea where to start looking, but I thought that accommodation was my first assignment.

I took the Dorking train into London and on arrival at either Victoria or Waterloo station I bought a newspaper, looking for vacant accommodation in its advertisements. The area of Kilburn somehow caught my eye, and I went into the bowels of the earth to locate an underground train that would take me to Kilburn. Everything was very exciting for me. My eyes never stopped roaming and taking in all the different scenes and names through which the train was now passing, not to speak of my studying the passengers with whom I was riding. Would I ever be one of them, going to work by train and coming home tired, sitting behind a newspaper, as these people were doing? I rode on the Bakerloo line which came above ground after Swiss Cottage into West Hampstead. The next stop was Kilburn.

I got out of the train into the street and bought a map on which I looked up the street which was mentioned in one of the advertisements. As I wandered in the direction of that street, somebody called out from a first floor window: "Hilda, Hilda, what are you doing here?" I looked up and saw that it was a young woman called Thea who had been interned with me.

"Come upstairs, come upstairs," she was quite excited. "Come upstairs" she cried. In her little room she asked me again what was I doing in London? Well, we exchanged chit chat about what had happened to us since we were released from the Isle of Man, and she told me that she was secretary to the managing director of a company producing children's clothes.

"By the way," she said, "we need somebody in the company in the despatch department. Would you be interested?"

Without thinking I said: "Why not, anything goes at the moment."

"Okay," she said. "You can stay the night with me and tomorrow I will present you to Mr. Goldberg, our managing director." Tomorrow came. I went into East London with Thea, dressed in my heavy plush teddy bear coat and white woollen scarf around my head. Mr. Goldberg looked me up and down, asked what qualifications I had, and when I told him my history so far, he waived it off and said "It doesn't matter, we'll tell you what to do in the despatch department." It was many months later that Mrs. Nelson, a senior head of department told me that Mr. Goldberg had come out of his office after I had left and said: "I have just engaged a smashing blonde."

That day, he took me straight down to the department where he showed me rows and rows of baby dresses in different sizes and colours hanging on rails throughout the room. He now pointed to some order sheets for different customers. "Now you see, this one wants ten of size 16 colour lemon (yellow) and twelve size 18 colour blue, and ten size 20 colour pink. Now when you pack these little silk dresses between tissue paper into these cardboard boxes according to the orders, look at them very well and make sure that there are no mistakes in the manufacture of any of them."

"I will", I said. "But Mr. Goldberg, I do not really know what mistakes to look for. Could you allow me to spend one or two days in each department of production of these dresses so that I may know what mistakes can occur?" I can see him now, a handsome little man with green eyes and dark hair looking up at me, head on one side and then saying: "Yes okay. You can do that. Go and start in the cutting department." He took me there himself, and as I entered the floor with its long tables, whirring cutting machines and all the colours of the rainbow in silken materials strung up on the wall ready for cutting more baby dresses, I thought I had gone to heaven. He then introduced me to the head cutter, Mrs. Nelson, and told her that I would be with her for two days. He mentioned the background of our conversation. He then left us. Nelsie, as I later dared to call her, was very kind to me. I saw a chart of sizes 16, 18, 20, 22 hanging up in the centre of the large room. She explained to me that these were the lengths of the little dresses measured from the nape of the neck to the hemline according to the age of the child. Sixteen inches long would be a one year old child, 18 inches may be two, 20 inches three or even four years old and 22 mostly four plus.

I saw that the girls were ripping pieces of silk, tearing them according to lengths of the smocked front. I was surprised and asked why they were not cutting with scissors. She explained that the fronts of these dresses were to be smocked (which is an intricate way of embroidering a pattern onto the silken pleats of the front) and that if the material was not cut on the straight grain, the smocking would hang crooked. It was only by tearing the silk that one could be sure to get the straight grain. The rest of the little dresses like the sleeves, the collars, the plackets for the opening and the crossways for the binding of the sleeves were all cut in thick layers on the cutting table. I was enthralled. To be surrounded by colour and texture was my heart's desire, but I did not mind when I had to go up to the next floor the following two days to see how the dresses were smocked in one department and then stitched together in another. There was a great humming of sewing machines. There were thirty of them on the floor. The cut bundles were divided between girls making only collars or only sleeves, or only plackets or only stitching yokes onto the smoking. Another fascinating experience. Two days in that environment and I changed for the upper floor where there were machines now hemming the little dresses. Some were making button holes, and some were stitching on the buttons themselves. And then there was the pressing room where steam irons were flitting over the silk, putting the finishing touch to each little creation.

When I had been through all the floors I went back to report to Mr. Goldberg that I had seen it all. "Good" he said, "you can now go back to the cutting room and stay there. I will get some dunce to do the packing." I was dismissed with a wave of the hand and happily returned to the cutting department with all its silky texture and beguiling colours.

There was one little snag though. I told Mr. Goldberg that I would have to go back to Dorking to report to my mother and brother and also to look for accommodation in London so that they could come over and join me. Good naturedly, he gave me some days off to sort out my affairs. I had been staying with Thea but started to look for a flat that could hold us all. It was not difficult, because nobody wanted to stay in London. Everybody who could, left London for the security of the country. I found a large upstairs flat in Willesden Green. It had been blasted, which meant that a bomb had not made a direct hit but had landed near enough for the impact to shatter all the windows and bring down some of the plaster from the ceilings. The house agent told me this and pointed out that after the blast the flat had been redecorated.

I thought that it was ideal. It had a sitting room, a dining room, a large bedroom and a small bedroom, a long corridor which led to the kitchen, and from the kitchen a wooden staircase down to the garden which was part of the flat. There were apple trees in the garden which seemed a great bonus, even though they were sour cooking apples as it turned out. I also did not know at the time that the kitchen was built to the north of the house and was bitterly cold in winter. The rent was so reasonable that I took the flat without looking at any other, and not long after that my mother, my brother and mother's friend Lizzie, came to stay in London. Whatever happened to poor Miss Marshall, bereft of most of her staff I cannot now remember, but kind as she was, I have the feeling that she wished us well.

In another town near Dorking, in Leatherhead, also in Surrey, there lived a member of our family whom I have not mentioned before. She was my cousin Laura, daughter of my father's brother. She had left Germany before me, but had not been interned. We were the same age. As babies we had been pushed in a pram together by our mothers who had been close friends before they became sisters-in-law. Sadly, Laura had left her parents behind, and had no knowledge of whether she would ever see them again, or when. She and I had been very close too, and now, of course she shared our family life whenever she could. She was a Montessori teacher-in-training who had obtained a post as nanny to a family with children.

On her days off duty she hopped on a Green Line bus in Leatherhead, to arrive in Dorking an hour later, to spend time with us, mostly on Sunday. We hated parting with her when we moved to London and she stayed behind in Surrey.

Settled in London now, Johnny also felt that it was time for him to take a job and learn a skill. He was still interested in interior design, so he took up any employment that would give him practical experience towards this end. He took up welding and carpentry, and continued to earn good money by playing his accordion with well-known bands now, some of whom played in the B.B.C. He also won an accordion championship for Northwest London and nobody doubted his musical skills anymore. Lizzie and my mother had no occupation as yet but Lizzie being from Vienna had contact with the Austrian Centre. She went there to ask if they had any homework, anything she could make or do at home for payment. "If you want homework you have to bring some designs for us," said the organisers. "What kind of designs?" she asked. "Well", they said, "you know all jewellery is now off the production list because all metals are needed for the war effort. We can produce things in raffia or leather or bits of material made into attractive adornments."

She came home with this information, and my mind immediately went to work. I had passed by a shop which sold off-cuts of coloured leather. I had also realised that the fashion was very much based on men's uniforms, in other words, women wore jackets with lapels and what could be better suited to a lapel than a brooch on it? But the brooch could not be made of metal. Therefore what decoration could I invent that would take the place of a brooch?

With the pieces of coloured thin leather which I had bought, I now designed what were then called fobs which one pinned on the lapel to dangle. I can remember a bunch of three dice, and a Chinese face made of yellow leather with the pointed *kuli* hat in another colour and a black plait hanging down from under the hat. I also made a palm tree. I know I made five designs in all, and the Austrian Centre bought all of them at five pounds each. My luck seemed to be following me. I just could not believe that somebody would pay that much money for my few playful ideas.

What was to come was even better. My mother and Lizzie now got all the orders for these fobs. They were exclusive to them because they had brought the designs, and for almost two years after this they were kept busy, and were paid for their work, which they pursued tirelessly but in the comfort of our home. I can still see the string across our room where they hung the leather dice to dry. They were not easy to make because all the edges of the cubes had to be painted with rubber solution first, had to be dried before the edges could be fitted together. One side was left open to be stuffed with cotton wool and then that side too could be glued together. At first we did not know how to handle this rubber solution, we did not know that both sides had to be painted and dried before fitted together. It was a painful learning process. The other difficulty was in making the silver dots on the dice to be accurate and in the centre, one for one side two for the other, three for the third, four for the fourth, five for fifth, six for the winning side. Then there were three dice on leather strips hung from a safety pin which had to be fixed at the back so as not to be seen. I daresay mother heaved many a sigh. Lizzie was more patient, not as active a person as my mother. However, they were content to have employment that could be carried out at home.

At the Austrian Centre too Lizzie met a young man from Vienna who was asking where he could store his parents' furniture. They had sent it out with him, ahead of themselves, hoping to join him soon in England, but war had broken out, and they had not been able to leave Austria. Thinking of our big empty flat for which we had only just been able to buy second-hand beds, she offered to "store" his furniture for him free of charge, if he would allow us to use and take care of it. He agreed to this excellent deal, which pleased both sides.

Our flat was now elegantly furnished with beautiful rosewood pieces gracing our dining-room and sitting room. There was a deep settee which became my bed in one room and a comfortable divan on which Johnny slept in the other. A glass fronted book-case with pure silk curtains held our few books and Johnny's sheet music, while the classy dining-room table and chairs made our meals that much more enjoyable. We were really lucky.

In the meantime, I had progressed in the cutting department and had gone to evening classes after work to learn how to make dress patterns. These had to be mathematically calculated, and needed to be very accurate for each size, because the fit of the dress which would be made in hundreds, depended on the accurate pattern. Nelsie was about to retire and groomed me to take over from her as head of department when she saw that I was really keen and passionately interested in the production side of children's fashions.

There came the day when the boss, Mr. Goldberg, came into the cutting department and said he wanted to go into production for bigger children's dresses. We were four young girls in the department, and he now asked each one of us to take four pieces of cloth each from the stock room and to design children's clothes to our own imagination.

The production of fashions had been severely restricted because of the war effort. There were guidelines for the industry: only one and a half yards of cloth were allowed for ages 6-12 years for instance. No more than four buttons could be used on each dress. Hems on skirts could not be more than two inches, and trimmings of ribbons or lace edging were limited to one yard per dress. Children's wear was so far considered essential manufacture, so that we were still allowed to work in that industry, instead of being called up for war work.

The storekeeper, a man called Bill, issued to us the materials we asked for, whatever pattern and colour we wanted, and we set to work, busily imagining, drawing, cutting, and having our designs stitched together in the machine room. When they were all ready, hanging on a rail we asked Mr. Cowan to come and see. He checked through the sixteen dresses that were there in different sizes, styles and colours, flipping through the hangers and murmuring "hum hum, not bad" and then exclaiming: "oh, this is a winner", and he took one of them out. Then he flipped through again and came across one and said: "yes, yes, this is a winner too." We waited with bated breath until he picked out another one and said" "this is excellent." And yet another he held up and said: "that's a good one." Then he turned to us and asked:

"Who designed this one?"

"I did", I piped up.

"Oh! And who designed this one?"

I was embarrassed and said: "I did Mr. Goldberg."

"And who did this one?" He held another one up.

I said: "That is my design."

"And this one?"

And that too was mine. I was thoroughly embarrassed and feeling guilty almost that I had knocked out all the others who had tried. He muttered to himself looked at Nelsie and nodded, then he took the four samples away with him to show to the customers in his showroom.

I could feel the antipathy of my co-workers. What was in their minds was "We've been here for years. This one has only just come, who does she think she is?" In fact, one of them said not long afterwards "Why don't you go back where you came from?" And I heard mutterings of "bloody foreigner."

I kept myself to myself. I understood their envy, but could I help it that my designs were picked ou ? Of course, their anger exploded when Mrs. Nelson left because her husband had been *demobbed* (demobilized) from the army. I was now in charge but how to handle this hostile mob? I tried to be just as pally as before, but it took a long time before their resentment subsided. They must have been relieved when my call-up came.

The war was escalating to such an extent that Britain was desperate to have all hands on deck. It was now 1943. A law was issued that all able-bodied women must report for duty. I applied to join the women's territorial army, but I was refused, not only because I was a foreigner — the only job I could have been given was that of a cook in the army — but because I had varicose veins in my legs. Cooking would have meant a lot of standing, and my legs would soon have bothered me a great deal.

The next choice open to me was to be trained to make munitions. Mr. Goldberg was upset to see me go and made a special application to the Ministry saying that children's dresses should still be exempt from the war effort, but his application was turned down.

Between the time that the women's army refused me and the training for munitions had not yet begun, I worked as a dental nurse when my own dentist told me that his former nurse had left and he could get no replacement. I offered with alacrity to help him out. I now watched in fascination how he meted out to the patients on the chair the treatment that I had so often endured at his hands. He was a brilliant dentist from Vienna. I watched him drilling and filling, polishing and filing, taking impressions, giving advice, extracting teeth and putting patients to sleep with gas, laughing gas it was called. I knew from experience that laughing gas often caused vomiting afterwards and I stood, prepared to clean up the mess when the poor patients woke up from their trip into laughter land. We lived in hope that maybe medical services would be counted as contribution to the war effort, but it was not to be. After three months of assisting my dentist in my white overall, and experiencing the exclusiveness of Harley Street, I was again called up for the war effort.

The Place: Industrial Training Centre, Acton, London, May 1943. A vast ground-floor factory, perhaps 100 ft x 200 ft. partitioned along each side into cages by expanded metal. There were no solid walls between them. Each cage held 10 trainees who were being trained in different spheres of light-engineering for war-work.

We came from all walks of life. We had been recruited from "inessential" jobs to help the war effort, and we were asked to state our preference for which section of engineering. I was put down as a fitter. Not that I was fitter than anybody else, but I did not have a clue as to what all the other choices meant, instrument maker, welder, precision fitter, mechanic, machine-operator — what did they all mean?

Anyway, I was glad the decision was made for me and I was excited to become an overalled war worker in a cage with nine other boys and girls. We were taught filing and deburring, sawing, drilling and tapping metal. We had to read blueprints and construct weird shapes of iron plates to specified curves and angles and mathematically correct measurements. We embellished these plates with drill holes of varying sizes according to blueprint instructions. Some were left plain, others were tapped for screws to be threaded into.

I was fascinated. Not only did I like using my hands, I liked the smell of oil and metal, I liked the camaraderie among the students. I was uplifted by the feeling that I would contribute SOMETHING towards the war effort, but best of all I liked the variety of people with whom I now came into contact. I loved people, and still do. Particularly people from far away exotic countries. I was curious. I wanted to hear about life in other worlds. I wanted to learn, to compare, perhaps to adopt what was best in each of them. I was particularly drawn to Africans. I knew nothing about their continent. I was under the impression that everyone spoke French there, my favourite language. I liked its musical romantic sound better than German or even Spanish. So when I saw that we had several Africans in the Training Centre, I used to draw near at break-time to hear their conversation. But not a word could I understand.

One day, I took my courage in both hands and approached two of them. "Hello," I said, and sat down near their bench where they were munching their sandwiches and drinking mugs of the strong, sweet tea which the canteen provided. "I am Hilda. What's your name?"

One of them grinned broadly and uttered between his teeth a name which seemed to end in "...ello" and then I heard "from ...eria." Was it Algeria I had heard? The other smiled, lips pressed together and then pronounced some unintelligible sounds. It was not until much later that I knew he had a speech defect.

At this moment, though, I was disheartened and cast about in my mind for what to say next. "Parlez-vous Francais?" I asked hopefully. "Eh?" enquired the first.

"Do you speak French?" I repeated. He shook his head.

"Please write down your name for me," I encouraged him, fishing for the pencil in my overall breast pocket.

He wrote Bello. Aha, I had heard correctly.

"From?" "Nigeria," he wrote.

"Oh, that's interesting," I exclaimed when, to my relief the bell rang — for I had no idea where Nigeria was. The bell now called us back to work after the break and we parted with a smile and a wave of the hand.

At home that evening I rushed for my world atlas. The map of Africa. Ah, there it was. The big continent looked like the profile of a face to me. The top of the head: North Africa. The nose: Ethiopia. South Africa, the neck; and then I discovered to my delight that Nigeria was there, on the left, yes the West Coast, and there it nestled just at the back of the head — the occiput.

"British Colony," I read.
Language: English.
Religions: Tribal, Christian, Mohammedan.

Vegetation: Tropical rain forest in the south. Savannah
              in the north.
Produce: Rubber, palm oil, palm kernels, groundnuts,
              coconut fibre...

Armed with this information I felt better equipped to have another go at conversation with my dark-brown colleagues. Alas, it was hard work. Bello grinned so broadly all the time that his words were distorted. Akin — I now knew his name — spoke through his nose, without moving his lips. For all I knew he might have been speaking Swahili – or Chinese! I gave up and confined myself to waving, nodding greetings and exchanging sandwiches or biscuits with them.

I was in my fourth week of training, when a new batch of trainees arrived in the neighbouring cage. Among them I noticed another African. He stood tall in his dark blue dungarees, then leaned nonchalantly against a tool-cupboard while the instructor explained things to his group. Some days later, we were on an assignment, sawing, filing and hammering away at the work-benches which lined up outside the manager's office. "Music While You Work" was blaring from the radio loudspeakers. We, the girls, were singing along and there, in front of the manager's door, stood the dark newcomer.

"Hello Snowy," said a passing instructor. "You on the carpet already?"

"No," answered Snowy. "I've been called to broadcast to my folks in Nigeria."

I pricked my ears. Wow, this man spoke English! Loud and clear!

"Some of us came over here to study. But it's wartime. Our ship took three months to get here. We came in a convoy. The BBC wants us to tell our folks that we got through safely. They also want us to talk of our first impressions of Britain." His voice boomed above the clatter of the workshop. "They do, do they?" said the instructor. "And what are you going to tell them?"

The Nigerian beamed. "I am surprised to see the women over here. They are doing men's work. Mind you, I can do women's work. I can cook, I can wash and iron clothes, I can clean the house. The only thing I can't do is — have babies!" At this he laughed uproariously and we girls joined in. The instructor thumped him on the back. "Good luck, mate," and passed on.

I was fascinated. This man not only spoke good English, he had a sense of humour as well. He was uninhibited. He was sure of himself. My curiosity grew. I had my chance when we, the fitter trainees, assembled in the classroom for mathematics. I found myself sitting next to the Nigerian. We exchanged names. His was Tommy. "Not short for Thomas, you know" he explained. "It's Thompson. Thompson Ajemijereye. (T.A.). My friends just call me that. T.A."

We now fell into animated conversation until the instructor hushed us and the lesson began.

So Tommy bowled me over with his booming voice, his excellent English, his cheerful nature and lack of inhibition. He was also very frank, unbearably so at times, but I preferred to know where I stood with him rather than that he should keep me guessing as to the real meaning of his words or intentions. I introduced him to my mother and Lizzie and to my brother of course, all of whom liked him immensely. He was very courteous but no sycophant. He also was a practical man who offered to do some heavy chores for my mother in the house. The first time we invited him to visit us, a neighbour opposite us in the street phoned the police and reported that she had just seen a black man entering No. 2 St. Gabriels Road. I went downstairs when the door bell rang and saw two policemen standing outside.

"Sorry to disturb you Miss", they said "but we had information that a black man has just entered your house."

"Yes", I said, "He is our guest. We invited him."

"Oh, I see", said the policeman. "That is alright then, sorry to have bothered you." He saluted and went away.

This episode will explain how unusual it was in London in those days to see any African about. It also demonstrates how efficient the citizens were in alerting the security services if they noticed anything unusual. Tommy often said all through his life that the success of Scotland Yard depends on the co-operation of the citizens.

Tommy had told me that he was married and had two children and that he would ask his family to come and join him as soon as he was settled in England. However, his wife refused to come to England whereupon he asked her to send the children, a boy and a girl, so they might be educated in England. She refused that too. I did not understand any of this at the time. I did not understand the significance, because I did not know the customs and traditions of Nigeria. However, I bore in mind that Tommy was a married man and I was not going to break up anybody's marriage, even though I was becoming very fond of him.

Perhaps that is an understatement. I was falling in love with him. I felt curiously safe and protected with him and perhaps foolishly so, because he was not only six years older than I but he had seen much of life. He had been a married man, he had children, he had attended the famous Kings College in Lagos, he had been a manager in training for the UAC (United Africa Company), a customs officer and a freelance photographer.

I felt somehow related to him. It may have been a racial affinity because the Jewish race stems from Africa and the customs of the orthodox Jews and the Africans of today are in some way similar. Jewish men are circumcised as are African men. African laws of hygiene forbid their wives to come near them when they are menstruating. So too Jewish wives have to stay away from their husbands during that time, and after they have finished menstruating they have to immerse themselves in a ritual bath to be properly cleansed. There was an affinity between us which brought us closer together, and now, after fifty years plus I realise that perhaps, sub-consciously I threw my lot in with Tommy since the sign of Hitler's days in Germany which said "Jews and Negroes not wanted here" had been indelibly inscribed on my memory.

Tommy seemed so worldly-wise to me. I looked up to him and admired his burning ambition to become a lawyer and to return to

Nigeria and help his people. He was not sponsored by anybody and had to work very hard to earn enough for his living, his family and his junior brother who was studying medicine in Nigeria. He sent home money to all of them. At times he volunteered for night work because it brought better pay and enabled him to study in the day time. I think it was these qualities plus his elegance and haughty bearing which made me fall for him, it was not just romantic love. I felt yes, this is the man for me", even if I cannot marry him. So, when he showed openly that platonic friendship was not for him, I decided quite coolly that I would agree to be his girlfriend.

The very first time I visited him in his small student's den, I climbed the stairs of his boarding-house in fear and excitement. My heart beat so wildly as I clutched the wooden banisters, that I had to drag myself up step by carpeted step for fear of falling. My legs were shaking. I looked around me furtively at every noise. So strictly had I been brought up that I was terrified I might meet on these stairs someone I knew, who would tell my mother. I felt wicked and deceitful where my mother was concerned, but at the same time deliciously daring and grown-up to be visiting a man in his room for the very first time.

At last I reached the door which had Tommy's number on it. I knocked timidly. Immediately the door burst open I looked into his big smile and his voice boomed "welcome." The room wasn't small, it was tiny. Minuscule. It harboured a narrow single bed, one chair and a wash-basin. This I did not know until later because it was covered by a wooden board and served as a table. On its white cloth lay an array of chocolate bars which he offered me. My eyes popped when I saw them, for I had long since finished my ration coupons for chocolate for that month, and I was touched that Tommy was sacrificing his to buy chocolate for me.

And then, "Try these sandwiches which I prepared for you," he said, reaching his long arm out of the window and retrieving from the outside window-sill a plate of triple-deckers. "I kept them cool out there," said he. The perfect host. The sandwiches were delicious. Strange, — but delicious. Exotic.

"What did you put in them?" I asked.

"Well, there's a layer of onion," (it was obvious), "a layer of ham, and a layer of marmalade."...

You might say, the mind boggles, but in those days it didn't, if you know what I mean. The expression was then not known. However, I enjoyed every mouthful of Tommy's creative concoction and who's to say that the way to only a man's heart is through the stomach?

Later I learned to enjoy his fantastic stews made from scrag, that is the neck of lamb. Scrag was the cheapest cut which meant you got the most quantity of meat (and bone) for the two shillings meat coupon you were allowed per week.

Another of my favourites was a fresh pink salmon dish. Tommy used to go to the fishmonger. There, after queuing patiently for an hour or so among the women customers, (he swears he was the only male member of the Housewife's League), when his turn to be served came he would ask the fishmonger for a salmon-head for the cat, knowing full well that (a) it was a lie, we had no cat, and (b) the kind man would give him the head with a good three inches of the fish body attached to it. Perhaps it wasn't quite a lie. I was born under Leo and the lion is a big cat, isn't he? Anyway, Tommy turned out to be a prudent shopper, a super cook and resourceful housekeeper. He was well-known and popular, be it at Sainsbury's, at the greengrocer's or — as I have said, at the fishmonger's.

It was very difficult for me to keep my involvement and my excitement at having become a woman, a secret from my mother. She had so carefully and so devotedly brought me up to preserve myself for marriage that I knew it would be a blow to her to know that I had given myself to a man who was not only an African but who was married, and promised no future for me. The lying began, the excuses for nightly absences, and when one day Tommy gave me six precious fresh eggs which were a rarity during the war years, my mother now asked me: "Why should he do all this for you?"

I could no longer look her in the eye and tell another lie. I blurted out: "because he regards me as his wife." My mother burst into tears, and I well understood her grief. She liked Tommy very much. She had nothing whatsoever against his race. She as well as I, regarded all human beings as being the same, but the fact that I seemed to be destroying my future burdened her. I still see us sitting on the edge of the bath as I was preparing to go to bed, and I did not know what to do to comfort her. Luckily it seemed to have been Lizzie who helped me out, or rather who herself did not hold the same strict views as my mother who had been brought up in Northern Germany. The Viennese were a more light-hearted people. Romance was part of their daily lives. And she may have told my mother that at nearly twenty-two she and I had done well for me to be still a virgin.

Anyway, my mother was no less friendly to Tommy after that and he did everything to prove to her that he regarded me as his precious girlfriend whom he would protect at all times.

Tommy did protect me. Often he said to me, when we were seen out in the street together and people gave me looks which I did not even notice, or when we travelled in the underground together and I was oblivious of the stares people gave me: You have a strong heart. You are a wonderful girl. When people see a white girl and a black man together, they think either he is a prince, or the girl is a prostitute." Well, he was a prince, but he never made use of it, and I did not even know it then.

A subtle change came in the minds of people with the advent of the Labour Party winning the election in 1945. Mr. Clement Attlee became Prime Minister. About that time Peggy, the daughter of Sir Stafford Cripps, a labour minister and respected member of Parliament, married a Mr. Joe Appiah of the then Gold Coast. There had been much publicity in the *Daily Mirror* about this union.

One day as I was standing in the crowded underground train with Tommy holding his arm across my shoulders to support me, I spotted a little man sitting by the window behind his newspaper. As he turned the pages I watched him closely once or twice and then nudged Tommy, whispering "Is that not Attlee?" The man now felt my eyes upon him, looked at me and looked at Tommy, folded his newspaper and got up making his way towards us in the swaying and shaking train. He looked at me questioningly. "Peggy?" he asked. I smiled and said: "I'm sorry I am not, but you are our Prime Minister, are you not? We admire you greatly."

"Thank you" he said, doffed his hat and made his way towards the exit, so that he could step out quickly when the train stopped. It struck Tommy as truly democratic that a Prime Minister should travel in an underground train with the crowds. No limousine for him, no outriders, no sirens.

Fate was very kind to me, she not only gave me my first great love, but in the very same year I met a woman called Marlene. She too was a Jewish refugee from Germany, and she became my guru, my mentor, from whom I learned much about life, and in whom I could confide, just when I desperately needed to.

A young girl's first real love brings a tremendous turning-point in her life. It is difficult to suddenly handle the doubt, the guilt, the passion and fear, yes, fear. I could not verbalize all these feelings or even distinguish them.

I could not discuss them with my mother, because she was emotionally involved with me, and I could not break her heart, even if mine was in constant turmoil.

Marlene was very different from my mother who was a down-to-earth Taurus. Immensely sensible, practical, intelligent and brought up strictly. She was never dull though, always cheerful and active, with wholesome common-sense and great wit.

Marlene was born under Virgo whose critical faculties had made her an art critic in Germany. She was an artist herself, and she had lived in Freudian circles where everybody's behaviour and utterances were analysed and discussed endlessly. She herself had been psycho-analysed, and I think that after such an experience the person is never the same again. Too much introspection seems to destroy all natural actions and reactions. But, I did not know all this then; in fact, I knew nothing of the abstract.

Marlene lived in a bed-sitter in Swiss Cottage where I visited her, without fail, once a week. I found that she was a lonely woman, whose only son by her German husband was prevented from joining her. She was also extremely impractical, unable to hold down a job, if she found employment at all. I do not even remember how she earned her living. She was always in need. Too proud to ask for unemployment benefit. I know that she suffered and did my best to help her out when I could.

She was such a good human being who carried the suffering of all the world on her shoulders. So empathetic was she that any misfortune which befell another, would plummet down to the depths of her soul. She took me to her bosom like a daughter. With her I could open up and spill all my worries, and those that I was too shy as yet, to talk about, she would skilfully extract from me and offer her wise explanations.

I learned a lot from her regarding the psychology of men and women. She opened my eyes also to art and taught my brother John to paint in oils. His very first painting, a portrait of a little girl, is still with me in my house now, fifty-five years later.

Into Marlene's willing ears I poured all my love and admiration for Tommy, all my hopes and fears for our future, and always she would regard me with her keenly penetrating looks and sometimes ask: "Are you sure you can cope with all this?". The "all this" she was referring to was an agreement between Tommy and me.

In the same frank manner in which he had informed me that he was married with two children, he said casually one day, "you know, we Nigerians always have a girl-friend in the corner somewhere. These girls come and go. They don't know what love is. They come for the money, they attach themselves to important men for their protection, and they try to have children for them to have some claim on the men. But they only get the crumbs that fall from the wife's table."

For a long time I pondered over this statement, looking at it from all sides as best I could, piqued by Marlene's contribution that she could not possibly enter into such an agreement. She would not be able to endure the knowledge that her beloved man's hands whose touch electrified her, could caress another woman's body and then come back to her. No, no, — she could not, would not share her man.

Maybe in defiance of her, there rose in me my strong (and ignorant) idealism, my "noble" Leo nature. Yes, I could, and I would make the superhuman effort to make my man happy. Afterall, I was marrying into a totally foreign background, and I felt I needed to make small compromises where I could. The way in which Tommy had described a girl in the corner and "the crumbs from the wife's table" I felt it was a compromise I could cope with.

There came to my mind the saying "If you love something, let it go, if it comes back, it is yours. If it does not, it never was." If Tommy needed some freedom, I would give it to him. I further argued that, if I was to marry into a foreign background where polygamy was not a part of living memory, but was still practiced today in the rural areas (as I was told) I must be prepared to make some concession, however painful. I thought I would be able to spare some crumbs from my table. Little did I know that theory is one thing — practice another.

Where religion was concerned, there was no friction between Tommy and me. Tommy often remarked that it was strange that he who had been a choirboy in the Anglican Church in his youth, should be an agnostic now. He did not bother with religion. Later in life he said he believed in destiny. I on the other hand, was comfortable with my Jewish way of life. I did not need organised religion; I carried the Jewish tenets in my heart. They were part of me. I did believe in the one God, and I prayed to Him in my own way at any time. My family belonged to the liberal or reform branch of Judaism. Before we left Germany my parents had asked the chief rabbi of Hamburg to come to our house in the suburb twice a week to give us religious instruction. He did prepare my brother for his Barmizvah when he was thirteen years old. I was then fifteen but both of us had very little bonding with Hebrew characters of writing or with the prayers. We could recite one or two of them by heart, without understanding their meaning. For me, the Jewish way of life consists basically of observing the Ten Commandments and retaining a democratic and compassionate heart.

Had I been born into an orthodox Jewish family my marriage later to Tommy would have caused intense grief to them. For marrying outside my religion, I would have had to be ostracized to the extent of being declared dead, and the family would have sat shivah (deep mourning) for seven days. They would have sat on the floor or on low stools, grieving over the loss of their daughter, and I would never have been allowed to return to them.

Tommy had been living in a very tiny room. He had now moved to an equally tiny one in West Hampstead. He was only two underground stations away from us in Willesden Green, but it meant taking a train. It was not just around the corner from me. Adjoining his tiny room there was a built-on kitchen almost like a balcony with a gas cooker and a sink. He had only a bed to sleep on but nowhere to keep his books.

One day on my way home from work, I passed by a bombed site. This meant a bomb had made a direct hit on a multi-storey building and there was nothing left but a huge pile of rubble and twisted girders. Among the rubble I spied a solid wood door all in one piece. I went to test its weight and thought I could manage to carry it home. I tucked it under my arm with some difficulty and lugged it down into the tube. It was an encumbrance inside the train where people stood, tightly wedged like sardines in each compartment. My door was not popular with them. It had corners, and I had to be careful to keep these out of peoples eyes. At Willesden Green I hauled it up the stairs from the train's platform. I then carried it home which was ten minutes walk. My mother was appalled when she saw what I had brought. "What are you going to do with this?" she asked. "I want to make a bookshelf for Tommy" was my reply, and as soon as I had taken off my coat I got out my brother's saw and began to divide the door into five pieces, leaving some narrow strips for the crossbars at the back of the bookshelf. It took me several evenings to saw and plane the edges of the shelves.

I worked with joy in my heart, anticipating the surprise on Tommy's face when I presented him with the finished job. I had to curb my impatience, because after sawing, planing and nailing the thing together, it still had to be painted. I chose dark brown wood-like paint and let it dry overnight. The struggle began again when I carried the now finished piece back into the underground train, and down two stops to Tommy's station. Again a haul up the stairs from the platform into the street and then across two streets before I got to his house. The effort had been well worth it. Tommy was not only pleased but astounded that I could have performed such a feat. He now could take his precious books off the floor and make his room into a respectable student's den.

Not many days after this the air raid sirens wailed again which meant that enemy planes were coming. While the sirens were still sounding there were crashing noises in our vicinity, and we were really frightened. When the all clear sounded, I looked out to see if anything had happened nearby. I saw fires blazing, turning the sky red, in the direction of Kilburn and West Hampstead. I now was terrified that something might have happened to Tommy. I had to get to him by all means. I got to the underground station and found that no trains were running. No buses were running either. I had to backtrack from the station to the direction of Kilburn and West Hampstead. I had to reach Tommy on foot. There was no other way. I ran, I walked, I stumbled and ran again with pounding heart not only from exertion but from anxiety. After one hour I reached the corner of his street with trepidation, but saw to my relief that his house was still standing. I tried to get my breath before I climbed the stairs and knocked on his door.

"Oh, I am glad you have come," he said. "See what happened to me." He then told me that he was resting, but when the sirens went he was curious enough to look out of the window by the side of his bed and saw a bomb hurtling directly towards him, or so it seemed. In a flash he put a pillow over his head but when the crash came nearby he was flung out of bed onto the floor. Luckily, he thereby missed the glass that shattered from the window onto his bed. When he opened the door to his little kitchen it was there no more. It had been clean blasted away. The shock had been so great that he suddenly found a patch of white in his otherwise black hair. We sat together in dumb silence, imagining what might have happened to him.

As his accommodation was now no longer habitable, I talked it over with my mother and asked if Tommy could move into our flat. She agreed, and never regretted her generosity, because Tommy was such a fantastic helper in the house. He was a first class cook and an experienced shopper. He washed and ironed his own clothes, he scrubbed the long corridor for her, — the only thing my mother had against him was his argumentative nature. Of course, he was training to be a lawyer and she suspected that she was his guinea-pig on whom he practiced his skills. She said she did not have the stamina to withstand his arguments, even though she found him very interesting.

We were both working in different factories now but neither knew what part the other was playing in the war effort. We were simply not told, because of the great secrecy that had to be maintained in all war efforts. 'The walls have ears', posters said. "Careless talk costs lives" was another poster and we certainly did not want to put anybody at risk by divulging secrets of the manufacture of war items in which we played a part. My own work place was very far away from home. I had to travel one and a half hours by train and bus to reach it. After a ten-hour day at the work bench and another one and a half hours journey home, one can imagine how exhausted I was in those days.

Tommy was soon assigned to night work, during which he serviced and inspected fighter plane engines when they came back from battle. He loved this work. It gave him a sense of purpose and very good earnings.

Tommy had arrived in England in 1943. We were now in the year 1944, and as each worker was entitled to one week's holiday in a year we decided to take ours at the same time with my brother John. We rented a caravan in a farmer's field outside London. This meant a fully-fitted living accommodation with a tiny kitchen, a tiny toilet, sleeping accommodation and a table at which to eat and write or read. This caravan could be pulled by a car, but this one was stationary in a field in Surrey and was let during the summer to visitors. We had a lovely time in the country for those few days, but one day, as I was coming from the nearest house where I had bought eggs from the farmer, a rumbling noise in the sky made me look up. Johnny was with me while Tommy was in the caravan preparing lunch. Suddenly, Johnny grabbed my arm and said "I think it's a bomb," and pushed me down into a ditch where he also took cover. Even in a moment of danger I had some compunction about lying down in the ditch. What if I crushed the precious eggs? No sooner had the thought occurred to me when a loud bang indicated that indeed a bomb had fallen somewhere not too far from us.

That was the first of the Doodle Bugs. These were unmanned planes directed from Germany over to England and so timed that they would explode over London. Surrey is a county adjoining London, so this first one fell short of its target. Later the route on which these Doodle Bugs would come was called Doodle Bug Lane. Barrages of huge balloons were soon manufactured and so positioned in the air, anchored to the ground, that they would intercept the Doodle Bugs on their merciless journeys. Sometimes they did.

Worse was to come. The Doodle Bugs were called V1 missiles by the Germans (V for victory, number one victory). They rumbled in the sky like a motorcycle approaching, but when the engine cut out one knew they would soon drop. All of us sat in nervous expectation not knowing whether the noise we heard was a real motorcycle or a V1 and hurried for our shelters if the engine cut out above us or seemed to be above us. The shelters were Morrison shelters which were large cages made of strong steel and positioned on the ground floor under the window so that any shattering glass would fall on the shelter rather than on the people. We, the people, were sleeping under that great table, my mother, my brother, Lizzie and myself. We did not have rest for nights or days. We were always on edge, not knowing when these engines would come to our vicinity. Later the V2 bombs were far more destructive and dangerous than the V1 but we preferred them. They did not make any warning noise, no warning engine noise, no cut noise. They fell suddenly out of the clear sky onto unsuspecting victims below. If I say we preferred them it was because we did not feel that nervous tension which the V1 bombs had caused. We had become fatalistic, saying to ourselves "Well when my number is up, I will get it."

The British had not only their wonderful humour but a sense of acceptance in the worst conditions. Their philosophy was "The stiff upper lip" and the universal answer, when one asked somebody "How are you?" was "Mustn't grumble". In other words they did not complain. They were great in adversity.

The bombs, expected or unexpected, caused many fires. It became necessary for the population to be on guard and to watch for nightly attacks. In the early days of the war we had all been issued with gas masks in case of a poison gas attack from the Germans. Air raid wardens were installed often on the roofs of houses, so that they could send alarm if necessary to the defence authorities. The gas masks were issued free to these air raid wardens. Soon a ditty was composed:

> "Under the spreading chestnut tree,"
> Mr Chamberlain said to me,
> "If you want to get your gas mask free,
> Join the local A.R.P."

There was also a Home Guard of which Tommy became a member in army uniform. The Home Guard was called out sometimes in cases where German parachutists tried to land in England, and the British soldiers were not around. They were fighting abroad on all fronts. The Home Guard was composed of men too old for the army or non-nationals who were not compelled to join the forces.

When the V2 bombs began to fall, it was clear that a Morrison shelter would not be strong enough to withstand such onslaught. Thousands of Londoners now decided that the only safe place would be the underground train stations which were really in the bowels of the earth. In Willesden Green, we had to travel to Kilburn to West Hampstead, to Swiss Cottage, where the train went underground. On those two stations, it was above ground and there was no protection on those platforms for us. So, night after night we all packed our bedding, our precious belongings, a little food and went by train as far as Oxford Circus which was two stops after Swiss Cottage because all the platforms at Swiss Cottage and Great Portland Street were already crowded with humanity.

It was in Oxford Circus we found space on the platform on which to unroll our bed-mats and go to sleep at midnight. The last train left at midnight and the first train in the morning came at five o'clock when we had to vacate the platform. We had five precious hours of sound sleep, but as soon as we emerged from the underground station the air raid sirens would go again and air attacks would begin anew.

Tired, dirty and bleary-eyed we would stumble out of the underground station and make it to our home to wash, get dressed, eat something and get ready to go to work, back into town. My mother always said she had no imagination, and that was a very good thing for her. Johnny and I both brimmed with imagination and foresaw all kinds of horrible events which never happened, thank Heavens. Nevertheless, I think my mother was terribly brave to see us go to work everyday in dangerous London and wait ten or more hours whether we would return or whether a V2 had got us.

Our suffering came to an end in May 8, 1945 when victory in Europe was declared. It was an unbelievable relief. Really, we could not believe that Britain had won this terrible war against all odds in the beginning. What a nation! What a powerful, courageous leader we had had in Churchill. His rousing speeches, made without his teeth, yet with his ever present cigar and two fingers making the V for victory sign, had kept everybody going, and had indeed helped to win the war. What remained now was the war between America and Japan. The war of Pearl Habour which was ended with the dropping of the lethal atom bomb on Hiroshima and Nagasaki, but that was in August.

Now, in 1945 we all celebrated the end of anxiety, the end of loss of life. Tommy and I went to Piccadilly Circus in the heart of London, just to be among the celebrating crowd. People were dancing around the famous statue of Eros in the middle of the large square. There was good excuse for getting drunk, for waving flags, blowing whistles, setting off fireworks, embracing and kissing openly. Very soon though, we had seen enough and went home in the quiet knowledge that we would be able to sleep through the night. Johnny of course was busy playing in a dance band somewhere as he was on all high holidays and special days. He had been so shy and wary of the opposite sex that he always felt it was safer to stick to his instrument and to his beloved music.

His chance for romance came one foggy, foggy day in November. When I say foggy, if you have not lived in England, you can have no perception of how thick and yellow lay the sulphuric fog over the city of London on a November night. On such a night when darkness fell at about four in the evening we stood in the entrance to the underground station wondering whether we dared step out onto the road and make it to our house which was about seven minutes walk away. We could not see the kerbs in the street, we tried to hold on to the fences of houses we passed, not to lose our bearing. We counted the side roads as we crossed them and then imagined that we were near our own crossing on the opposite side. That was when we now had to cross the main road to St. Gabriel's Road where we lived. Fortunately, our house No. 2 was the first house on the left after the church at the corner.

Traffic had come to a stand-still because even the headlights of the cars could not penetrate the fog. Our mother stood in the window with lights on but we did not see them until we got really close up. Virtually, you could not see your own hand before your eyes in such weather. All sounds were muffled by the dense smog, (which is a combination of smoke and fog.)

It was on such an evening that Johnny plucked up courage to speak to a girl he had been watching for weeks, as she came home on the same train as he and got out at Willesden Green Station. This night as she stood hesitatingly at the exit of the underground station he ventured to speak to her.

"Hello," he said. "Where do you live? Can I help you to find your house?" She lived in a street not far from ours and he offered to escort her to the two turnings past ours. She was his little damsel in distress. Edith was little indeed. He towered above her, much as my father must have towered over our mother. They say that men often marry the type of woman similar to that of their mother. Certainly Johnny had made that choice not only in her size, but she too was born under the sign of Taurus and had great similarity with our mother born under the same sign. From this meeting evolved a long-standing friendship, then romance, and finally marriage.

Soon after VE-day, when hostilities in Europe had ended, my mother received a notice from the Red Cross to say: "We regret to inform you that your husband Leo Gerson died in a concentration camp in the year 1942."

This of course cast a great shadow over the celebrations. I am sure that my mother never stopped grieving over her parents nor over her sister although she never found out what had happened to them, where and how they had died. It was years later that we pieced together bits of information from a cousin who had survived the concentration camp and was living in Berlin. My father had lost courage when it came to using his faked French passport. My mother had been the courageous one who led all of us. Without her it seemed he was lost, until Hitler marched into France and foiled his plan. He had hesitated for too long before making a move out of Germany. He was then picked up with other Jewish victims and sent to a death camp.

Our mother always kept grief and worries to herself so as not to burden John and me with them, so that we had no real idea of the depth of her sorrow. For the moment, I am sure, she was glad that her children at least were safe and alive.

Chapter II

PEACE, CAREER AND MARRIAGE

The return to normal in Britain after the war took a very long time. It was a gradual process, but the relief of knowing that hostilities were over made us all feel light-hearted and content to continue in our jobs until we were told to let go. These were eventful years. As soon as the war ended I applied for British citizenship. I had been in the country exactly five years from 1939 to 1944. I could not wait to belong where I was.

A year later, when the Labour government offered free legal aid, Tommy sued for divorce, for which his wife had given him the cue. He was told that his was the very first case they were taking on in the Legal Aid Department. It took five years to come through.

As soon as possible Mr. Goldberg made an application for me to return to his company. This time it was granted. I now shed my factory clothing, my factory hairstyle, maybe even my factory manners which I had adopted so as not to be too different from the crowd of my co-workers who would have thought my speech "la-di-da". I had picked up a good deal of cockney expressions. I found them amusing and very colourful. I had also learned to smoke because the boredom of standing at a work bench for ten hours a day, could be relieved somewhat by sitting in the factory toilet on the floor, leaning against the wall and having a few puffs. I did not really enjoy the smoking nor did I inhale, but it seemed the thing to do!

The return to the children's clothing factory was a joy to me. Many of the former employees had left, and there was a new atmosphere in the company. No doubt, the bosses too were uplifted by the feeling that there would be no more bombing, and they also now directed their thinking towards expanding the production of babies and small children's dresses. This gave me greater scope to design for teenagers. What stood me in good stead here was the fact that my own teenage years were not so far behind me. I remembered vividly my discontent during my pre-teen and early teen years, when all the clothes available in Germany were either too childish for me, or too grown up. There was nothing in between.

With great zest I turned my attention to the sizing especially for early teenage girls. I had to convince my bosses that they were not dainty, slim little people. They were chubby, not to say fat, young people who yearned to be smartly dressed but did not want to look old. Nor did their mothers want them to. I suggested exploring several girls' schools where we would take measurements of the children of different ages and base our sizing and designing on those findings. My bosses thought it a good idea, so I was given the time and a car and driver to visit several schools. When I say my bosses, I am referring to Mr. Goldberg, the senior and also to a much junior young man who had inherited his share of the business from his mother who had owned it before her death. He was a very humane and natural young man, free of all airs and graces; he had been refused by the army because of a health problem of which, unfortunately, he died a few years later. He and I discussed and found we had many ideas in common. Young Colin and Mr. Goldberg had many a quarrel over this new venture into teenage dresses, but when Mr. Goldberg saw the delight with which his customers bought large quantities of the new range of styles, he had to concede that it had not been such a bad idea after all.

From the first successes of the early teen dresses I advanced slowly into designing for the older teenagers imagining them to be up to the age of 18 and 19. That too was very successful. We did not understand the secret behind our success in this range, until I ventured also into designing teenage evening dresses. Little by little reports came to us from all the chain stores and shops we sold to, that women were buying the teenage evening dresses for themselves. That was the explanation! Women's dresses were still rationed, whereas children's dresses were somehow limited in their design but not rationed. So we had inadvertently hit upon a market which was there to be exploited.

I so enjoyed my work basing my designs always on what I would have worn a few years ago, age 18 or 19. Mr. Goldberg now thought it was right for me to be given my own office, so that I could design undisturbed. He gave me a lovely large room with loudspeaker, telephone and the requisite long cutting table. The table had to be at least four yards long and one and a half yards wide so that I could open out the material to its full size before marking the patterns onto it with chalk.

The loudspeaker was part of a tannoi system over which I could be summoned to go to the Managing Director's office, or to bring certain model dresses to the showroom, or to answer questions that Mr. Goldberg might have had regarding production. Much as I enjoyed hearing my name everyday: "Will Miss Gerson come to Mr. Goldberg's office, or Miss Gerson please attend to such and such a customer in the showroom", it grew to be a curse. It did not allow me to concentrate on what I was doing, and the novelty of it soon wore off. The telephone too was a nuisance, because now manufacturers of buttons, of laces, of belts used to ring up with offers or requests for an appointment to discuss the possibility of using their products for my designs. I was also consulted about the buying of fabrics. Sometimes even, if young Colin or I had an idea for a dress and we felt strongly enough that it would be a winner, we would order a fabric to be made to our specification, sometimes for hundreds if not thousands of yards in different colours. It was most exciting to be in on the ground floor so to say.

Life was always hectic, because for every season spring and summer or autumn and winter a whole range of new designs had to be composed. As every fashion designer will tell you, they have to design for spring and summer in the cold winter and for autumn and winter in the hot summer. It is not always easy to project oneself into the future and FEEL the season for which one is designing.

Apart from that, bosses have the irritating habit of thinking of new ideas at the last minute and rushing the poor designer, the cutters, the machinists, and the finishers to produce a creation that MUST go into the range. These brainwaves usually hit them a day or two before the final fashion show. I lived on my nerves, but almost like a last rehearsal for a stage show, which pumps adrenaline through one's body, one can perform what is expected of one. I loved my work. When I got home everyday raving about it, Tommy always said: "I am so glad you are happy in your work, otherwise I would feel guilty to let you go out to earn money."

Lately, I seemed to have risen in Mr. Goldberg's esteem, for he invited me out to two elegant social occasions in Prestige Hotels in London. One was the "Junior Age" ball organised by the trade magazine for which I was writing a monthly article. The other was "Ladies Night" of Mr. Goldberg's Lodge. Both times we were in a party of twenty guests, and both times I had to wear the same shimmering evening dress which I had made myself. It was intricately cut, and the first time his appreciative glance took in my appearance he asked: "Where did you get this dress?" "I made it myself." His eyebrows shot up and he nodded.

At both events he sat me on his right side. This did not mean anything to me at the time, but when I look at the photographs now — having lived a lifetime — I see that he must have had plans for me.

The crunch came one day, when I had forgotten my glasses at home. Without them I could not see the fractions of inches which were so important in pattern cutting. I telephoned Tommy and asked if he could bring them to my office. He did. He stayed just long enough to meet my colleagues, then hurried back home.

A few days after this Mr. Goldberg's called me into his office.

"You know," he said, "you are spoiling your future. Many men have shown interest in you and asked me to introduce them to you."

"Who are they?" I wanted to know.

"Ha, — that would be telling," he said.

"Anyway, thank you Mr. Goldberg. If you are referring to my African friend who brought my glasses the other day, — I am going to marry him."

His mouth dropped open slightly, then he swallowed and warned: "Think well before you do."

"I have done so," I said and left the office.

Time went past very quickly. In 1947 a letter came from the American Embassy telling my mother that our affidavit had been processed, and our application for immigration into the USA was approved.

It had taken nine years, from 1938 to 1947, for this goal to be reached. My mother was happy to go, although she loved England. But she said that America offered better opportunities and a better standard of living, and for the sake of her children she would go. Johnny was in agreement with her, but I had no desire to leave Tommy and start another new life in America. My mother understood, but it was a sorrow to her that she would have to leave me behind, as my future with Tommy still was so uncertain, even though he had said on many occasions that, come what may, we would go to Nigeria together.

Mother and Johnny left for the United States in 1947 on a cargo ship called the Chinese Prince. I had comforted her by saying that I would start saving money and travel to visit her as soon as she was settled. Luckily, by now she had relations in the United States who helped her to find an apartment and a job as soon as she got there. She became circulation manager in a high-brow magazine, and Johnny did everything he could to become an interior designer. In the meantime though, he joined the American Army at Fort Dix. He was musical instructor to the military band of his unit where he played the Xylophone and Triangle as well as his accordion.

Tommy and I now had the flat to ourselves. Not only was it too big for us, but we missed the salaries that used to support us, and so we took in a paying lodger. He was a Yoruba law student, who now occupied the small room in which Tommy had stayed. During these years after the war more and more Nigerians were coming over to work and study in England. So we had a steady stream of visitors from Tommy's home, and he was the ever generous host who cooked for everybody and made room for any and everybody that needed to stay with us for a few days or even weeks.

Food was still rationed in 1947, which was such a wise move by the government. Everybody continued to have his share, nobody went hungry, there were no bread queues, though occasionally there were queues for special items which were just beginning to come into the country again. There is a joke of a woman joining a queue in the West End asking the person in front of her — "What are they queuing for?" The answer was "Hoffmann's Tales". "Oh, — never mind my husband eats anything these days." (She took Tales to mean tails.)

Tommy no longer serviced aeroplane engines. That job had come to an end with the end of the war, and he got different work. It was a worker's market. Britain was still short of manpower, so it was easy to get a job at any time, to leave it and get another. Tommy had by now enrolled in Gray's Inn. It had taken him a long time not only to work and save three hundred and fifty pounds that it cost to enroll, but he also had to learn Latin which was a requirement for enrolment in those days. Not only that, he had in fact had to pass matriculation with Latin, because in Kings College, Lagos, he had been directed into the practical stream in his last year there, because he did not imagine that he would ever have the chance of going overseas for further studies.

However, everybody is the architect of his own fortune, and here he was now, in England, without the necessary requirements to enroll in the Inns of Court for the study of law.

I had done Latin in school as an optional subject, so I suggested I would go with him to study Latin in evening classes, to encourage him. This joint effort was very successful. Tommy passed the Latin and also passed the other subjects for matriculation and enrolled in Gray's Inn in the year 1946.

That was a mighty step forward. He was now looking for night work again, and there a friend of his, Mr. Omotosho, encouraged him to join the company he was working for. He did casting of plaster of paris lamp bases. They were later painted a bronze colour and looked impressively antique. I have still in my possession such a lamp. To cast the plaster of paris in two parts and then to join the moulds together with strong rubber bands, required the kind of strength which our Nigerians had plenty. Again, the pay was good and the day was there for Tommy to do his studies, while I went to work.

Tommy's friend Omotosho whom I knew only as Omot came to our house almost daily. I still see him in our kitchen watching Tommy cook while he had a basket of the sour apples from our garden in front of him and munched them one after the other while they chatted. Sadly, this young brilliant Omotosho who collected degrees one after the other while in England, died in a motor car crash only two or three years after returning home to Ibadan, marrying, and having a baby son. It was the tragic and senseless death of a brilliant scholar.

The year was 1950, it was now three years since I had seen my mother. Alas, I had not been able to save enough money to go and visit her. In the meantime though, Mr. Goldberg had been to America and met my mother. She must have regretted the fact that she had not seen me for three years, and now, believe it or not, the kind man offered to pay my passage to the USA if I would bring back some sample dresses which could be copied in our business. I was overjoyed at this generosity, even though I would contribute something to the business by bringing the samples.

I booked a passage on the French Liner "Ile De France", thus adding the French flavour of cooking and speaking the language to the enjoyment of my trip. What a thrilling and generous arrangement this was! How lucky I was.

Our reunion with mother and brother was so happy, and I was impressed to see how comfortable my mother was in her little apartment, which had one bedroom, one sitting room with a curtained-off kitchenette, plus a bathroom of course. There was a buzzing fridge, but it did not disturb me when I slept on the divan in the sitting room. All was pleasantly furnished and cozy. After hours and days of chatting my brother took me out into New York. I saw the dizzying heights of the Rockefeller Centre and the Empire State building. When I tried to look up at it from the street, I bent backwards so much that my little pink hat fell off my head.

The city was a confusing maze of criss-crossing streets. My brother explained patiently which were the avenues from south to north and how the side streets would cross them from west to east. The trams and taxis whizzed by at life-threatening speed, but worse was the underground, the subway. The first thing I noticed were the many half smoked cigarette stubs littering the entrance to the subway station. In England we were still in post-war mode, and this waste of cigarettes brought to my mind the "Waste Not Want Not" slogan by which we lived. Later, my brother explained that smoking was forbidden in the underground station and trains, so the passengers needed a few hasty puffs before entering that dreaded zone.

On the day I entered such a subway by myself, I stood waiting for the incoming train to unload its passengers, before we the new crowd got in. As I was standing, politely waiting, somebody pushed me roughly in my back shouting "Waddaya standin' there waitin' for? Geddin you dope." That was the rough and tumble of New York.

When Johnny took me through 42nd Street and Broadway I could not believe my eyes when I looked at the shop windows, whatever goods they displayed. I had to stop every few minutes to look at especially earrings, costume jewellery of course. Here were the big designs I had craved for so long, and which were unobtainable in England. After patiently stopping with me every few minutes Johnny observed wryly: "You seem to be earring-orientated." Indeed, I was.

Broadway led into Times Square where a huge billboard, advertising Camel cigarettes stayed in my mind because it blew out regular curling smoke from the mouth of the advertiser.

A few times I went with my mother to her office job. Mr. Levitas, the editor of "The New Leader" and mother's boss, took a liking to me, gave me little jobs to do so that I could earn a few dollars pocket money. At lunch time he would send to the nearest delicatessen (Italian of course) and order pastrami on rye for mother and me. This delicacy was a mighty slice of juicy boiled beef on rye bread, topped with a pickled cucumber and a blob of horseradish sauce.

Now I had to follow up several introductions which Mr. Cowan had given me to different manufacturers of children's and teenage dresses. My mandate was to buy one of each of those that I thought would fit in with the style of his own manufacture.

In between sightseeing and fashion-seeing there were numerous coffee parties at which all our relations and my mother's friends wanted to see me. It was a happy time. One of our distant cousins, a young man of about my own age asked permission to take me out one evening to see the night life of New York.

Why he took me to a transvestite club, I shall never know. True enough it was a lavishly decorated establishment where one had to drink alcohol and view all the glamorous show girls who were actually men. My escort may have expected enthusiasm on my part, but I was simply confused, not knowing whether these men dressed up for the show only. They were convincing 'females' indeed.

This young cousin had a car in which he took me home but I had not anticipated that kissing and necking were to be part of the evening. It was quite an effort to escape his advances in the confines of a car. He got me home safely but disgruntled, when he dropped me at our house, and I did not see him again for the rest of my stay.

A much more pleasant outing was a visit to "Birdland". Johnny, passionate musician that he was, took me there to hear the most famous jazz and blues played. It held in a cellar, thick with blue cigarette smoke. It was dimly lit, but Johnny stood, in awe of such famous players as Dizzie Gillespie Duke Ellington and others whose names I have now forgotten, fifty years later; but the rhythm and the intensity of all the inspired players who improvised without sheet music to read from, got to me and created a strong emotional response in me.

All too soon I had to start packing my things and the samples I had acquired, to say goodbye again and to board the ship for my return voyage. I was sad to leave my family behind but full of happy anticipation of seeing Tommy again. A few days into the voyage I was called into the Captain's office to take a phone call. It was Mr. Goldberg making this transatlantic call to tell me that if the customs asked me about the many dresses I had with me, I should say they were all my personal property. He then wished me bon voyage and happy landing.

The landing was not so happy because ever since that call I had had serious misgivings about deceiving the customs. It occurred to me that the dresses were all different sizes and had manufacturers' labels attached to them. I began to worry that I could not tell a convincing lie if I was really questioned about the goods. It worried me so much, that I could not enjoy the last few days of my trip. On landing, true enough, customs opened all my cases and asked: "Are these all your personal belongings?" The lie stuck in my throat. I blurted out "Some of them are samples for me to work with".

"Oh I see" said the customs man. "We have to have a look at them," and together with another officer they began taking stock of all that I had brought and assessing its value. One can imagine that Mr. Goldberg was very angry, when he was presented with a bill for duty to be paid, and until he paid it he could not collect the goods. I was extremely sorry that I had let him down when he had been so generous to me, and I could just not explain to him why I, a whole 29 years old, could not have told that lie.

CORONATION 1953

One of Tommy's close friends was Stephen Awokoya who later became the eminent professor of Education. And then there was Tommy's close cousin Professor Oritsejolomi Thomas, the first great surgeon F.R.C.S. at University College Hospital, Ibadan. He, with his wife and two children, often stayed at our flat, except for one spring in 1953 when they had rented a house in the country and invited us to watch on television the coronation of the young Queen Elizabeth. That was a great experience.

GRAYA of Gray's Inn, Tommy's Inn, celebrated the young Queen's accession to the throne with a grand ball, which we attended. It was a magic event on a warm spring night. The grounds of the Inn were all lit up. We walked over the soft grass to the huge pink and white striped canopies where long tables were laid with gleaming silver dishes and sparkling crystal glasses into which champagne flowed. The food was heaped all along the buffet. People served themselves, and stood around the grounds eating and in animated conversation. I remember best the dessert of fresh strawberries and cream, but Tommy dragged me away to join the dancing.

If it had not been for the twinkling lights of the chandeliers, the long ballroom might have been awe-inspiring. In heavy gilt frames, stern faces in wigs and robes hung all along the dark panelled walls. They spoke of famous Lords Chancellor and Masters. It was history at every step as we whirled around the room under these paintings to the rhythm of the live band.

Tommy was wearing tails and white tie. I had made a simple, straight long gown from a remnant of heavy gold coloured satin. I had draped a scarf of white crepe across the front neck. The long ends of the scarf were slung over the shoulders and hung down to the floor at the back. They moved as we danced, and maybe caught the eye of not Sir Elwyn Jones, — the Coroner of Swansea at the time, but of his wife, an artist and author. They beckoned us to join them at their table at the edge of the ballroom. After introducing ourselves, we learnt that the wife's pseudonym was Pearl Binder. She showed great interest in finding out more about us. Lively intelligence exuded from this petite, charming lady whilst Sir Elwyn was courteous and urbane in a kindly manner. Saying after a while "We must not keep you young people from the dance floor, please come and visit us at our home in the near future." We exchanged addresses and continued with the pleasure of the evening.

We did visit the Elwyn-Joneses in their large but simply furnished house. A fire was burning in the grate. Sir Elwyn tended it himself, stoking the coal and placing a bottle of red wine in front of the grate, so that the wine would attain room temperature to improve its flavour. He was relaxed and friendly. He and Tommy soon began to talk law, while Polly (as she called herself) was keenly interested in our mixed marriage, in Tommy's country and my feelings about our future there. I spoke with my usual enthusiasm, which, it seemed, made her wish she could come with us to Nigeria. She gave me a copy of a book she had written and illustrated lavishly. We kept in touch for many years. At one point, after I had settled in Nigeria, I sent her some artifacts of simple everyday things, such as native combs, eye-makeup (Kohl), a home-made child's toy, a calabash spoon among others. She wrote back thanking me and saying that I was a "natural anthropologist."

We had the occasional outing to a party or a dance, so that we did not miss a television. I liked to see a good film at the cinema now and then, but I had to go alone. Tommy did not enjoy films. He did not want to watch action, he wanted to be in/on it himself. On the rare occasions, in our early years, when I persuaded him to come with me, he promptly fell asleep in his seat, and I was deprived of the thrill of holding hands.

Not only was a television a luxury we could not afford but it would have distracted both of us from our occupations. Tommy had to concentrate on his studies, and I had taken up sewing for private customers in the evenings, after coming home from work. I did not like sewing, I had no patience with it, but we needed the money, and I enjoyed designing for different women. To get their custom I would place a small advertisement in the shape of a hand written card in the window of our news agent near Willesden Green station. I liked the designing and cutting of individual dresses, I liked the machine sewing to an extent because it was quick; but the finishing on the inside of the dresses left much to be desired. However, the customers were always pleased with the effect of the finished garments.

Tommy had brought with him a few raffia mats from Ikot Ekpene. Their bright colours and patterns fired my imagination. I asked if I could have some of them. To his question "What will you do with them?" I replied "Wait and see".

I had ideas but first needed to solve the technique of handling the mats. The raffia was straight and stiff and frayed easily when cut. When stitched, the seams could not be turned, but every evening when I came home from work, I went straight to my sewing machine to experiment. Finally, I got it. The cut edges would have to be covered with bias binding and then stitched together. Yes, that was it! I busily cut and stitched every evening, lengthening my machine stitches, so that short ones would not split each raffia "thread".

There took shape in front of Tommy's eyes a collection of raffia shoulder bags, book-covers, ration-book holders, tea-cosies, napkin rings and belts, all edged in different colours. He shook his head in wonder. "Why haven't my people thought of making something out of these mats? They've been selling them just as they are," — upon which I answered philosophically, "You know, people never value their own products. Anything from another country is always preferable. The prophet is not acclaimed in his own country, — don't you know?"

At my request, Tommy sent to Nigeria an order for more raffia mats to be brought by, anyone coming over, — and they did come. I could now assemble a good stock of my different articles, and added to them also items made of leather, including mother's and Lizzie's fobs. I then made a small exhibition (I called it a Bazaar) in our flat, inviting friends and associates to come, look, and buy. None of them stayed away. Everybody was hungry for something new, something different. I made £40 in that one afternoon, not counting the pineapple punch we offered all comers.

I also made all my own dresses because, constrained as I was by not being stock size; and by my own taste which was never the public taste, I was forced to create my own dresses. I always liked simple shapes with perhaps one dramatic detail, like a stand-up collar or slit pockets from which could unexpectedly emerge a coloured silk handkerchief to match the colour of my earrings and necklace.

Yes, on the point of fashion I must say that I did not come into my own until my mother left for the USA. She had always told me to dress discreetly. Right from home I was usually seen in navy blue with a white touch or mid blue to match my eyes. She had my ears pierced at birth, but never allowed me to wear earrings. They were common she thought. Now that I was free of her influence I blossomed into all the colours that were the real me. As a girl born under the sign of Leo I was drawn to the colours of yellow, orange, red, and vivid purple. I was free also to wear big earrings and matching big necklaces to dress up an otherwise sober dress. I was not the type to wear frills and lace and pretty pretty flounces, and when I saw them on so many English teenagers, I felt they needed to be taught some dress sense.

I asked Mr. Goldberg whether I could be allowed to take out some dresses from our teenage range to visit youth clubs after work and teach fashion sense. I explained to him that I would be doing a kind of social work, and at the same time would advertise his company of Remy et Cie. I also promised him to get publicity for such demonstrations which would be good to alert the public to the needs of teenagers and young women and again which would give his company publicity. He agreed to this suggestion provided I had the dresses invoiced out by the production manager and would check them back with him the following day.

So, there started another exciting episode in my career. I was a novice of course where publicity was concerned, but I managed to learn which editor to approach in which newspaper and to make appointments with various girls clubs and link up the editors with the clubs so that when I went there to give my demonstration the journalist for the respective paper would be there also. On one occasion we were even filmed by the Pathe Newsreel. Apart from the dresses, I always took with me some chalk and large sheets of paper, so that I could sketch designs on either a blackboard if it was available or on paper if it was not. The girls were always delighted with the demonstration, and enjoyed trying on the dresses I had brought with me from the company. Their endless questions always were "Miss, what would suit me? I have no figure." or "I never know what suits my complexion", or "my bust is too big. I can never find anything to fit me". Apart from the dresses I had taken with me I always advised that they should have simple shapes and dress them up according to the occasion with either scarves or beads or belts; or I would take with me bunches of artificial flowers or cherries and demonstrate to the girls that all these should be used in moderation. One thing at a time to get the desired effect.

I always returned home very tired but happy and satisfied that I had enlivened an evening for the simple young girls of the Eastend of London. The girls were also happy that they met a real live designer who had a special interest in their age group and who could incorporate their own ideas in future designs. That the club premises were usually bare and badly lit did not bother any of us.

One evening the club leader, a young man looked in on our performance and later came to talk to me. "I am glad you are giving us a lift by this colourful talk of yours. I try to bring variety into the club. We also have a boys' section, and next year I am going to take all of them on a holiday to Spain. We are beginning to save up for it now". At the mention of Spain I pricked my ears and asked immediately "Can I join you?" I had taken up the study of Spanish many years ago when I was still in Germany age 15.

A young friend of ours was hoping to emigrate to Argentina and for this he needed Spanish. He had bought himself a book on the Spanish language and showed it to me. I encouraged him to read a passage from the book but by instinct I knew or thought that he was not pronouncing correctly. I took the book from him and studied the instructions for pronunciation. True enough, he had not interpreted the instructions correctly and I began to explain the sounds to him according to the book. "Oh, why don't you join me? I think I shall make better progress if we study this together." Yes, I did join him, and while I was teaching him from the book, I picked up the Spanish myself, but I had never put my knowledge to the test. This now was my opportunity. The club leader after a few minutes thought agreed to take me on board. We were going all the way by train to Sitges on the coast of Spain. There was plenty of time to save up for the trip and for me to further my study of Spanish.

In 1949, I had been called before my solicitor to swear the Oath of Allegiance to His Majesty the King of Britain (England). It was unbelievable, it was like a dream that now I was somebody with a country. Now I was somebody entitled to a national passport which told the world where I belonged. I now was a British citizen.

Tommy had gone on a trip to France in 1948. Friends of ours invited him but I could not go with him because I did not have a passport. Now a year later, I was able to travel. My first trip outside England on my very own British passport! Tommy did not like to travel. He called himself a couch potato who enjoyed staying at home. This was the salient difference in our astrological make-up. I, the Leo, was a fire sign and Tommy, the Cancerian, was a water sign. Ah well, nothing is ever perfect in life, and so I often allowed his water to quench my fire. But basically, we were attuned to each other. He, the teacher and I, the pupil.

At the appointed time, I joined the bunch of youngsters and their leader on their trip to Spain. After the Channel crossing into France, we went right through that country, across the border into Spain. There the journey stopped at Barcelona. We then piled into a rickety bus for the two hour trip to Sitges, on the sea front of the Mediterranean. It was but a village, with a few comfortable hotels. We were accommodated in one of them. I enjoyed myself from the word "go" drinking in the sight, smell and sounds; but most of the youngsters of the youth club complained about the food, the late meals and the "putrid tea".

Years later, when I had become familiar with Nigeria, I realized that Spain, for me, was the halfway house between Europe and Africa. The sun, the colours, the rhythm, the exuberance and the passions had all prepared me for the continent which was to be my home for the rest of my life.

After my return I offered to write a monthly column for the Trade magazine called "Junior Age". I made the proposal to the editor of this magazine who knew the company well because we advertised in the magazine. She told me how many words I would have to write every month and asked for my photograph to head the column called "As I See It" by Hilda Gerson. I did not have a clue what to write about nor how to assemble an article of so many words but a dear friend of mine called Jean Jacoby helped me with the first few editions.

I had met Jean through my job. One day a tall middle-aged gentleman had called on me in my design office. He was a lace manufacturer who wondered if I could incorporate his products into my designs. He really was a gentleman, well spoken, cultured, with impeccable manners.

I could not use his laces. They were too expensive and too sophisticated for young dresses — but there was some rapport between us and we continued chatting. He asked what my plans were, would I stay in children's fashions all my life? "Oh no," I smiled. "I am going to be married and will go to Nigeria with my husband." "Nigeria?" He was surprised. "Yes, my future husband is a Nigerian."

"Oh," he exclaimed excitedly, "you must meet my daughter, my Jeannie. She is going to Nigeria to teach. She is an English graduate". So, this chat with charming Mr. Jacoby, started my life-long friendship with Jean Jacoby, author of "Abimbolu", a recommended reader for primary schools in Nigeria; and later as Jean Evans (her married name), she wrote "Punaku Treasure" and her autobiography "Not bad for a Foreigner". Both, she and her father had an irrepressible sense of humour which went straight to my heart.

So then, Jean helped me with the construction of my first few articles. After a difficult beginning the regular feature became part of my monthly assignments, and of course I was paid for it.

From the age of fifteen I had suffered from a calcified big toe joint. It was extremely painful to walk on as the toe could not bend, and I could never wear high heels. Tommy often said: "You are amazing. You dance on this painful toe, but you never complain" to which I answered, "I have to walk on it everyday, and dancing is a lot more fun!"

When we consulted Prof. Thomas on one of his visits, he recommended surgery to be done while we were still in England.

In early 1952, Tommy was granted the Decree Absolute on his divorce, and he insisted that we should get married immediately. I was booked to have the surgery done in February that year and asked that we should wait until my foot had healed. It was done in Hammersmith Hospital, London, — a long ride for Tommy to visit me everyday for three weeks. He did come, but always late, always delayed by cooking special dishes for me, though the hospital diet of three meals a day was more than adequate. I would have preferred to have more of the one hour's visiting time with him, but understood that he was showing me his love with food and caring.

From Mr. Goldberg and Colin there arrived a big basket of flowers one week, and a basket of luscious fruits the next, wishing me speedy recovery. This took longer than anticipated, because even though I was discharged after three weeks, my foot was still very swollen and painful to put down. I could not yet get into my shoes and now knew it would take weeks for me to get back to normal. I was worried about my long absence from work and knew that the spring production would be delayed. I telephoned Colin and asked if he would like me to do some pattern cutting at home before I could manage bus and train to get back to the factory. He jumped at the offer and in a couple of hours he brought all the equipment I would need! The first pattern of each style, the cardboard, the heavy scissors, cello-tape, punch and hooks and the instruction sheets for me to write on.

I worked from home for another few weeks, (attending physiotherapy sessions in-between working), and the bottleneck in the production of the Spring deliveries was solved.

When I got back to the factory however, great changes had been made in my absence. My bosses brought a couple, a lady designer and her husband from America, where this couple had had their own business in children's dresses. They went into partnership with Mr. Goldberg and, as the American fussy styling was so different from mine, they decided there was no room for two different designers. It came as a bit of a shock to have this sudden change of direction thrust upon me, but I got another job immediately at twice the salary that I had been getting. I now earned twenty pounds a week which was very good money then. The new company was not very inspiring, mainly large women's dresses, almost like house dresses or kitchen overalls, and I did not work with the same enthusiasm as I had done at Remy et Cie. But now that mattered less, for we were on the last lap of our long journey towards reaching Nigeria. Tommy had too many distractions from his studies, because he was always doing the house work, which he seemed to prefer to studying. He struggled to pass his exams, which is a surprising fact when one looks back on his brilliant career as a lawyer. He spoke excellent English too, but in the beginning I had been baffled by his pronunciation. The first time we arranged a meeting in town somewhere, he left me waiting for almost half an hour. When he arrived finally he apologized and said he did not see the boss. "Why did you have to see the boss?"

And he answered: "To come here of course".

"Why do you have to have permission from your boss to meet me"? I asked.

"But to carry me here the boss..." and then he mentioned the number of the bus.

"Oh, you mean bus". I now called it bus.

"Yes, that's what I said, isn't it"? he asked.

"Eh, sorry, the way you pronounced it, it sounded like boss."

"What is the difference?" he wanted to know.

"The word bus does not have an o sound in it" said I.

"Oh, I see". We walked on in silence. He, deep in thought.

Misunderstandings continued to occur, which irritated Tommy. Each time I pointed out that they were due to his pronunciation, and so he finally said "Look, anytime I mispronounce a word, please correct me." I was only too glad to do this and happy that he would not be offended. His vocabulary was so wide, that it was a pity to have it marred by his accent. He was an excellent pupil, but in his efforts to break with the accustomed pronunciation and replace it with the new, there was a period during which he almost stammered, trying to decide which was the correct way to call a word before he uttered it. It took, maybe, two years for him to be word perfect.

After the war work, and after the casting job which he had taken up, he worked for a firm of engineers, who hired out heavy machinery. All negotiations with customers were done by telephone. On occasion the customers would meet the person they had negotiated with on the phone and would be taken aback to see that the voice on the telephone belonged to an African. I think this was the greatest testimonial to the successful efforts Tommy had made, and his clearly articulated speech and booming voice were part of his success as a lawyer too. In fact, one of his lecturers at the Inns of Court had told him: "You will do well in court, because the Judges will be able to hear you." Tommy himself was so happy with his progress in speaking that he began to correct and mimic his fellow country men's speech at any opportunity. To those who would argue "English is not my language, why should I speak it like an Englishman," he would answer: "You'll be the loser, if you don't. You will also make mistakes in spelling because the sounds you think, you hear are not the words that you connect them with. Do you know the difference between park and pack? Do you know the difference between reverse and revise, or cult and colt, or liver and lever, or live and leave? If you do not pronounce correctly you will not be understood correctly."

His criticism was accepted by his countrymen as was his outspokenness about people and events. His legendary frankness often hurt me more on behalf of the people he addressed, than it hurt the people themselves. They seemed to accept his superiority and arrogance that made him a leader. I often cringed inside me because I did not like arrogance in anybody. Maybe because of our situation in Germany I had been brought up to stand back and not draw attention to myself. There could have been no greater contrast between Tommy's attitude and mine. Later, if we went to any function, he would make straight for the front seats, even when they were reserved. If I nudged him and asked "did you not see the notice?" He would say "If I don't sit on these seats who should?" But that was many years ahead.

We got married on July 5, 1952 at the Registry of Willesden. We had invited our close friends and whatever relations Tommy had in England at that time. He, the busy host and excellent caterer always, had prepared mountains of sandwiches with different fillings and was still wiping his hands on the kitchen towel when the taxi drew up to take us to our ceremony.

Everything went very well, but the Nigerian contingent complained that there was no jollof rice. "How can you get married without cooking jollof rice?" they complained. I was so happy I did not care what we ate or drank. Our flat was full of happy noisy people and I had a future at last. I had made my own wedding outfit, which of course was not in white, but a pale blue dress with a black silk coat that had the same pale blue lining as the dress. The coat had short elbow length sleeves and I wore pale blue long gloves to match the dress. I also wore the fantastic hat which Tommy had brought from Paris and my mother had sent me diamante earrings which covered the whole ear. Just my cup of tea. After the ceremony, one of Tommy's guests from Sapele, a beautiful fair skinned Nigerian who wore a small hat with a short veil, hugged me to "kiss the bride" and my earring got caught in her veil and pulled off my ear amid great laughter. Apart from that, there was no hitch. There was no honeymoon either, as we could not afford the time off from our jobs, nor the money to travel. But I could see a kind of happy satisfaction in Tommy that he had made me secure — and he had secured me!

Again, three years had passed since I last saw my mother and brother. This time, my mother sent me the air fare to come for a visit. My first transatlantic flight! This time, I was a married woman. This time, my brother was married to Edith, and together they were going to night school, both to study interior design after closing from work. Their course took seven years to complete and both of them came out with a degree.

My mother had been right about the USA. The salaries were higher and so was the living standard or she could never have saved enough to pay for my ticket. So the opportunities were greater too, for those who knew how to grab them. My brother was still dedicated to his music too and had kept in touch with "Birdland", so the news got around that his sister was in town, now married to her African husband and preparing to go to Nigeria with him. This interested the Afro-American community, so that the sister of Duke Ellington, a famous jazz clarinettist, asked me for an interview on the black radio station at which she was a presenter. Exciting! It was a forum for promoting my husband – our mixed marriage, – and Nigeria.

On this visit I was a more mature tourist. I no longer craved big earrings and big hats. I now had plenty of them. I could concentrate on the finer points of art, and the art of living! My family was well settled and content to a point. Deep down the three of them never lost their yearning for England, for the more subtle way of life, the gentler interaction between people. Of course, New York was particularly brash, as capitals often are. Everything was on a huge scale, and people who stood at street corners, chatting, invariably discussed the dollar. The mighty dollar.

Eventually, Johnny and Edith designed and built their own house in the woodlands of Guilford, Connecticut, where the pace was infinitely slower, the people friendly and neighbourly, and the incredible breathtaking fall (autumn) colouring of the leaves of the trees something to look forward to every year. I think their brilliant hues of golden yellow, of bright red and copper colour, with greens and browns in between, must be world famous now that the world has become so much smaller, so much more accessible to travellers.

Now, I enjoyed the Museum of Modern Art, the Guggenheim Museum, and the global arts and crafts section of the United Nations Building, with its myriad of national flags fluttering in front of it. My return flight offered an unexpected interlude. We had to land at Newfoundland to refuel, and the passengers were encouraged to disembark from the plane to avail themselves of the airport facilities for relaxation. It was early November, and knowing the cold winds of New York, I had come in my home-made roomy and stylish coat which I had lined completely with fur. I had also put strips of fur around my ankle-boots, but neither could withstand the icy blast that hit me as I stepped out of the plane.

For a moment I stood stunned at the top of the steps which led down to the ground. I was afraid to breathe, lest icicles should form inside my nose. The wind was painful. It whipped my legs above the boots and lashed my face bringing tears to my eyes. It bit my ears and I nearly turned back into the shelter of the plane, but then the landscape held my eyes.

I was looking out at a fairy-land of white glittering snow everywhere. The vastness of the scenery took my breath away. No houses in sight, only the low airport building, its roof laden with snow, the white faintly blue in the moonlight. The sky twinkled with stars so bright and so many, as I have never seen before or since. Descending the steps I held on fast to the railing so as not to be blown away, but lower down, the wind was not so fierce. I crunched my way through the thick pure snow, now inhaling deeply the cold clear air. It was intoxicating. So was the stillness, the calm, the peace of pure untrodden snow for miles around. In the airport lounge I sat by myself at a round table, writing to my mother immediately, to share with her this unique experience.

What was not so unique was the unbidden company of a flight officer who sat down at my table, asking what I was writing. "A letter to my husband," I said pointedly. Insensitive to my marital status, he offered to show me around the station, emphasizing the luxury of their bedrooms and well appointed bathrooms, all for the use of the flight staff. Instead of slapping him, I said, "Maybe later.

Let me finish this letter." As he left the table and made his way to the bar, I hurriedly packed up my things and returned to the plane, grateful for the fresh air again, as I stepped out from the overheated airport lounge, my coffee unfinished.

After I had returned from my second visit to New York to see my mother and brother and other relations, I promised my mother we would now make a concerted effort to reach our final goal of going to live in Nigeria. The following year, 1954, my mother came to see us in London. I had prearranged a Tour-holiday to San Remo in Italy. Since my childhood she and I had never had a holiday together, and she and I were both inveterate travellers. This was in the late summer of 1954. I came back sun-tanned and full of vitality and happiness so that it was almost a natural consequence that I became pregnant. We had waited so long, deliberately postponing having a child, because we could not yet afford to give up our jobs or even one of them. But now it had happened, and we were very happy.

When I became too big to stand behind the cutting table and bend over it, I left the kitchen dress company and took a part-time job in the small office of a button manufacturer. I kept his books. It was a one-man business, and he was also a refugee from Germany. Now I had a sit down job which was easier but as the time grew near for the baby to be born, my boss, hinted that he would not like the baby to be delivered in his office. I passed the job on to a friend of mine who later told me that the boss had regretted letting me go and said: "Hilda is like wine. The older it gets the better it is." It was early March 1955 when I had gone to work at this little office. There was thick snow on the ground when I got out from Oxford Circus and hurried to catch a bus. I fell on the slippery ground, nine months pregnant, but thank Heavens it did not harm me or the baby.

He was born, yes it was a he, a boy, on 24th March, 1955 in the Middlesex Hospital, Mortimer Street, London. We were overjoyed and proud parents, and I think this gave Tommy the final spurt to pass his exams and make for home. We discussed our financial situation and he decided that since I was able to get a better salary than he, I should continue to work and he would look after the baby. This suited me fine. I had this darling sunny lovable bundle to look forward to when I came home from work, and Tommy was a doting father and husband, looking after us with great care. He made my breakfast before I went out to work and made sandwiches for me to take; and while I was away, he bathed, fed and clothed our little boy whom we called Monubarami (Itsekiri meaning I have faith in myself). Of course I would not be deprived entirely of looking after my baby, and I bathed and fed him and played with him when I came from work. In the night, if he cried, Tommy would pick him up and have him sitting on his lap while he was reading law. When he went shopping, Tommy would sit Monu in a basket on his bicycle and ride to and from the shops with him. There was always a meal waiting when I got home, and what I appreciated even more, was the tropical warmth which he created in our flat with kerosine stoves.

I had never seen one of those things before, and our gas fires or electric heater had never provided enough warmth for me to be comfortable. I welcomed this new way of heating, even though I did not like the smell of kerosine. Also I did not know how to handle the wicks or how to clean them so that they would not smoke. But Tommy was in charge. I did not have to worry. One miserable cold night he left the stove on in the kitchen to dry baby's nappies which he had washed and hung on a line. In the morning he found the nappies black with soot from the smoking stove. He did not complain. This is something I admired about him. He took adversity calmly. He simply took the nappies down and washed them again, and of course, he trimmed the wick of the stove.

My mother took another holiday from her job and came to see her grandson. He was a really adorable baby, who spoke very early. At one year old he had quite a vocabulary. He was certainly the pride and joy of our household. As 1956 approached, Tommy sat and passed his final exams and was called to the Bar. He had waited and striven for this goal for so long, that he had to adjust to the idea that now we would be going home. He had been away fourteen years and used to say: "When I reach Nigeria, I shall kiss the ground, when I step off the boat." The reality was a little different, — but I am pre-empting myself.

The anxiety of looking for exam results, when they were due, was such that Tommy and his colleagues would travel to the big railway station of Waterloo at five o'clock in the morning to see the train arrive with newspapers of that day when the results were expected. As the train drove into the platform the guard would throw out bundles of newspapers and the desperate students would pounce and buy one copy for maybe six of them to read the list of passes. Very often, there had been disappointments like outright failure or resit of a certain subject. Now the joyful occasion had come. Tommy had passed his final Bar exams.

This was the moment of truth. There was nothing to keep us in England now. But with nostalgia we both looked back on the intervening years. We had learnt a lot and Tommy had enriched his experience, widened his horizon by being addicted to the radio, not only to news and political broadcasts, but also to cricket results which were his great passion. Sometimes I would come home from work and hear the radio blaring through the open windows or if he was in the garden picking apples he would take the radio with him so as not to miss any sports results. If I reminded him carefully that the neighbours would not like his noise he said: "I am paying rent here, why should I not listen to the radio when and where I want to?" He was belligerent on such occasions, but luckily our neighbours downstairs and to the side of the house did not complain. Maybe they were in awe of him.

We had had social life as well, starting from the early years in WASU, West African Students Union, under the able leadership of Mr. and Mrs. Solanke. That is where international students met, debated, and danced. Tommy was an excellent dancer. He and I loved dancing. We were well matched in height, and both of us loved this pastime. Not that we had much time to pass, but occasionally there would be good reason for an outing. One such reason was the visit of Zik to London. Tommy had told me much about him and his newspaper *The West African Pilot*, and I was now interested in meeting this prominent man.

We were a threesome, Zik, Tommy and I. Efforts to secure a partner for him failed, but we went dancing all the same, to the Hammersmith Palais de Danse. I remember the crowded floor and on the ceiling the huge revolving crystal ball which poured specks of rainbow lights from its prisms over the jitterbugging couples. Tommy and Zik took it in turns to dance with me. It was a tiring but enjoyable and interesting evening, though the men's conversation between dances went right above my head. I knew that Zik with his writing in *The West African Pilot* had alerted his countrymen to the idea of freedom. Freedom from their colonial masters, and Zik was revered by his people. More detailed discussions about politics in Nigeria were double Dutch to me. The throwing about of famous names and political parties meant nothing to me, — I yawned inwardly.

It was always the same. When we had Nigerians visiting, the heated discussions revolved around politics. Every one of them became an armchair politician who knew best how to rule his country. Apart from their individual career goals, this was the topic that drew everyone. The other topic was food: everybody longed for their home-cooking; but in the nineteen forties and fifties shops in England did not sell Nigerian ingredients or vegetables as they do now.

Tommy made pseudo-Nigerian dishes, very rich and tasty with whatever he could get. These were eaten with a thick lump of semolina cooked with water. On the lucky occasions when someone would come from home and bring real *gari* (cassava root grated and dried) there was rejoicing that the thick "soups" could be eaten with genuine *eba*. Most times though, one turned to good old "semo" as a substitute. On one occasion we had some guests for rice and tinned fish. When Tommy reminded them to go easy on the pilchards, as they were bought on ration points, — one guest wanted water to drink and asked, "Is water on points too?"

One frequent visitor was T.O.S. Benson, Tommy's erstwhile colleague. They were in the Customs together at Port Harcourt, before both came to England, to study law. One day, while my mother was visiting us, T.O.S. mentioned his brother Bobby who was a popular musician but lacked enough capital to set up his own band. He needed the sum of two hundred pounds for the percussion set and microphone; and asked if my mother could help towards this with a repayable loan. She did. All the two hundred pounds, and Bobby paid them back promptly within the stipulated time. It was a success story, for Bobby's Hotel and Night Club on Ikorodu Road, Lagos, later, was the proverbial oak tree that had grown from an acorn.

On another occasion we had arranged to go and hear Awolowo speak in London. It must have been shortly before our departure for Nigeria, because I had just had my TAB innoculation against yellow fever and typhoid. My injected arm was terribly painful. It was hot and swollen. I could hardly lift it to get dressed to go out. I was late meeting Tommy in town. He was very angry that I had made him miss the beginning of Awolowo's talk. He was so angry that he did not speak to me for one week.

At one time in the early years he had asked me, "what must I not do in order to drive you away from me?" "You must never raise your hand to me" I replied.

I felt most strongly that no woman should be beaten by her man. Any man who could not control his anger in any other way, did not have my respect. Well, Tommy never did raise his hand to me, but retreated into an icy silence to subdue his anger, and I was miserable for the time it took for him to defrost.

Within our social life we met many people. My relationship with Tommy became a catalyst for the young intelligentsia of my personal circle and of course, Tommy's Nigerian circle was always present.

Through my relations in France I befriended the family Lewin whose sons and daughter were my age group. Their father had been a keen promoter of Esperanto, which was to be the world language, so that all nations could easily communicate with each other. We know now that this utopia has not been reached, but old Mr. Lewin was a brilliant man, and he and his wife warm-hearted and interesting people. Philip their son took a great liking to Tommy and at one of his get-togethers introduced to him a young man, who wanted to know about conditions in Nigeria. He had taken up a post at the University of Ibadan to teach phonetics as an extra-mural subject. It was his first time of going to Nigeria.

He was an intense young man from whom exuded a burning intelligence, but his English had a German accent and intonation, and I wondered how this would affect his teaching of phonetics. Apparently though, his accent did not hinder his climb to fame – for this young man was Ulli Beier.

Ulli loved and dedicated himself to Nigeria. He was a success with his students. He learned to speak the difficult tonal language of the Yorubas. He translated Yoruba literature into English and even understood the language of the Yoruba drummers. He preceded us to Nigeria, but later, Tommy and I kept in touch with him through all the years he spent in Nigeria, lately at Ife University; before he left the country to settle in New Guinea.

On one of Ulli's leaves from Nigeria, we met again at Philip Lewin's party. This time my French cousin Georgie was there too. He was the youngest of my three cousins; Pierre, the senior and a medical doctor; Titi the girl, an interpreter for English, German and Russian; and charismatic Georgie, the budding film director. He was a real charmer, but unaware of the effect he had on the opposite sex. He was just naturally interested in people in a gentle and affectionate manner. The party was animated as usual, only Ulli seemed quiet, almost melancholy. When we all parted, Georgie said, "If any of you ever get to Paris, come and look me up, Philip has my address."

Since I now had my passport, and Georgie's address as of right, I decided to take Georgie up on his invitation that very summer, for my one week's holiday. As I stood on the front step of II, Rue St., Maur in the Latin quarter of Paris, ringing Georgie's bell, I heard many voices and laughter in his house. When the door opened and he saw me, he gave me a bear hug. "Come in, come in," he said warmly. "I have other visitors from London, but you shall have the divan to sleep on." What privilege! The other eleven people, mostly girls, were sleeping on the table, under the table, on chairs or on the floor. Each one of them had thought that Georgie's invitation had been for HER alone, and all were disappointed when he now presented his very chic girlfriend Lola, whom he later married and with whom he lived happily ever after.

Ulli Beier was there again, still quiet and morose. So I asked whether we could go for a walk, maybe he would show me MONET's water lilies in the Jardin des Tuileries. He was an art lover, I knew, and he readily agreed. We sat on benches in the centre of the room, where all around the walls, at eye level when one sat down, MONET had painted his beautiful Water Lilies. So true to life, so natural in their pastel colours, their petals all at different stages, some budding, others half open, or fully blooming, while some were drooping, past their prime. One could almost see them swaying in the breeze, could almost hear the water rippling.

We sat still for a long time, drinking in the cool, peaceful scene. I felt Ulli relax a little, and when we came out into the sunshine I thanked him for leading me to this unique little pavilion, the "Jeux des Paumes". We walked on across the Place de la Concorde, then stopped, leaning across the balustrade of a bridge over the Seine. Looking into the muddy waters and watching the tourist boats go up and down the river, Ulli told me about his first impressions of Nigeria. He liked his work, he had good relations with his students, but underneath I felt he was a lonely man.

For the first time he spoke of his Jewish father left behind in Germany. He had been Director of the Classical State Theatre in Berlin. His removal overnight from this great post had been very painful to him, but he knew that Hitler could do worse. For the time being he was concerned only for his son Ulli and urged him to leave Germany fast. Now I understood the artistic side of Ulli and continued to ponder over it, after we had parted and I had returned to Georgie's house.

That night Ulli did not come home. He came for a meal the next day, but did not come again for the night. However, he was much more cheerful, exchanged jokes with us, told stories and seemed like a different person. The third night he stayed out again. There was only one conclusion: "Cherchez la femme." Yes, Ulli had met a wonderful girl. An artist, half Swiss half Austrian. They had clicked immediately. They found so much to talk about. They were on the same wavelength. Ulli was happy for the first time. He had met his alter ego.

He had met Susanne Wenger! In Nigeria this name carries weight. Susanne is the great artist who came with Ulli Beier. Together with Ulli they explored Nigerian art and culture, Nigerian folklore and traditions for years, until Susanne so immersed herself in the rebuilding of ancient shrines that she eventually became a priestess and gave up her marriage to Ulli.

Chapter III

ARRIVAL AND EARLY LIFE IN NIGERIA

Finally the great day of our departure came. It had been a giant task to move out of our large flat and out of the attic the piles of things we had accumulated over the past ten years. Tommy had been deliberately buying at auctions goods which he felt would be useful to take home to Nigeria. We counted among these blessings sacks of lace materials and edgings, sacks of elastic satin pieces from a defunct swimwear factory, large pieces of hotel catering equipment which neither of us knew how to use, a canteen of cutlery, large black office files, two sewing machines and, of course, books upon books upon books.

I never questioned his judgement. Afterall, he knew his country and I did not. He had also told me on several occasions when we had held different views, "allow me to know my people better". We booked first-class passages on board the Elder Dempster steam ship "Apapa" which would leave from Tilbury Docks around the middle of December 1956. He spent weeks gathering together trunks and cases of all shapes and sizes and wisely bought professional packers' steel-banding equipment so that no case could burst open. None did.

I was of little help at this time as I had just come out of hospital after an operation on my legs. I could hardly look after our little 21-month-old son. Fortunately he was a sunny, placid child who sat in his highchair supervising the chaos and banging his spoon on his table when he wanted attention. The only thing I could help with were the keys to all the different locks and padlocks. I numbered and recorded them. No mean feat, considering we had one hundred and twenty-nine pieces of luggage all told. Tommy worked day and night with the inexhaustible energy which was so typical of him — and so daunting to me.

At last all the cases had gone in advance to Tilbury docks, to be stowed in the hold of the M.V. "Apapa". We now only had our personal belongings to take — yet when we finally closed the door of our flat behind us, there were still stacks of books and records to be collected by a kind friend who would forward them to us at a later date. Among these "leftovers" was a tin-trunk full of newspapers and cuttings, including the full issue of the Coronation of Queen Elizabeth II in 1953.

I had struggled to get Monu into his quilted snow-suit — it was December 1956 — and I'd got one foot and baby into the taxi when Tommy ran back. He'd forgotten something. He came out again triumphantly waving a flexible-neck desk-lamp — which I still use to this day, 44 years later.

With this desk-lamp in hand we boarded train and ship and our first-class voyage of 12 days began. It was Heaven. I see Tommy now, slumping down on the bottom bunk in our cabin, leaning his head against the wall, eyes closed, legs stretched, a blissful smile on his face.

After all the strain of fourteen years living and striving in a foreign country — after the pressure of final exams – the exultation of being called to the Bar and shaking hands with the Queen, the stress of getting together enough money for fares and living, of seeing me into and out of hospital, of meanwhile looking after our baby, and then the ordeal of packing — after all these, he had finally reached his goal. He was going home!

The twelve days on board were utter luxury of leisure and pleasure. Different social events lured us out of our cabin every evening. We could enjoy ourselves in the safe knowledge that there were baby-watchers in the corridors. Should any baby wake and cry they would notify the parents.

Xmas Eve, Xmas and Boxing Day were grandly organised. Tommy was a natty dresser and elegant dancer. When he came out of our cabin in tails and white tie, the stewards (Europeans at that time), flitted down the corridors from pantry to pantry whispering to each other: "He's wearing tails! Who is he?" In evening dress and long white gloves I brought up the rear.

Only one thing marred Tommy's complete satisfaction that night. He found that he had packed his black shoes in a tin trunk in the hold of the ship and no amount of pleading with purser or captain could get them to open the hold for him. "Not until the next port, sir. I am sorry", was the persistent and firm reply. So, brown shoes it had to be, and to this day he has not forgotten the embarrassment which this blemish to his attire had caused him.

Be that as it may, he danced superbly, as always. We tangoed, waltzed and fox-trotted across the polished boards to applause from watching passengers and crew. And no, he didn't learn ballroom dancing in England. He had taught himself from a book by Victor Sylvester long before he had had any notion of ever going abroad. Slow-slow, quick-quick-slow — or, as the cartoonists would have it after a heavy blizzard in England, Victor Sylvester stepping out of his house looking around and saying, "Snow-snow, thick, thick snow."

The voyage had taken twelve days with one stop at Takoradi, Ghana. From the time we started cruising down the West African coast the weather had become hotter and more humid, so that by the time we reached Lagos I was already conditioned to it.

The hustle and bustle of the disembarkation and the getting ready of our little Monubarami momentarily made us forget that now was the moment. We had really come home. Tommy's dream and goal had been fulfilled. As we went down the gang plank the idea of kissing the ground of Nigeria on arrival was more difficult than he had expected. No sooner had we come off the ship than we were surrounded by a tight group of relations and friends to welcome him and us. There was no room on the ground to be kissed. There was his mother, of course, dear Madam Obinu, his sister Mewe, his children, Ching-Ching the daughter and Freedom, the son. There was his close cousin and best friend G.B.A. Egbe. There were also his sister Mewe's daughters Tunde and Lily and hordes of other relatives that I did not yet know.

It had been arranged that we would stay at Cousin Gray's house but before we went there, we were taken to the Catering Rest House for a meal. There, in front of it, was a group of Hausa traders displaying their artifacts. I was instantly attracted to their display and stood feasting my eyes with the artistic and varied hand made objects that I saw until Tommy dragged me away, saying "come on now. There is plenty of time for that later." But that was the beginning of my passionate interest in African crafts.

After the meal we were taken to Cousin Gray's house. It was now late December, and it had been arranged that we would stay with Cousin Gray over the new year, before proceeding to Warri. Gray was a permanent secretary in the government. His accommodation was a lofty house in the old colonial style in Obalende. It was a happy home-coming. We were very comfortable in the big house but I had not got used to other inhabitants in the shape of insects.

I am not normally a squeamish person, but when I opened the bathroom door and something green fluttered into my face I let out a yell. Tommy was instantly nonplussed with me: "It's only a praying mantis" he said. "Don't be so fussy." Considering that I had never seen a praying mantis before nor did I know what it was or what it could do, I thought I was entitled to some understanding on his part.

The next experience was caused by my wiping little Monu's mouth after he had eaten a jam sandwich. We were in a hurry to go out visiting, so I threw the sponge with which I had wiped off the jam into the bathroom sink before we left. On our return in the evening, I wanted to get him ready for bed. I picked up the sponge from the sink and instantly swarms of tiny sugar ants crawled from it over my hand and up my arm. I let out another yell, hoping Tommy would not hear it, and then dipped the sponge into water to wash off the ants from it and from my arm. "Well, old girl," I said to myself, "this is Africa and you must expect the unfamiliar."

Little Monu, our sunny adaptable child was now nearly two years old. Everybody made a fuss of him, and was amused by his antics. "Alaro" they called him, as he picked up the drinks stools and carried them on his head as he had already seen people in the streets carrying head loads. When I announced that I would like to go for a walk to find my bearing, as was my habit, to see for myself my new surroundings and possibly visit a market nearby, there was horror in everybody's exclamation. "No, you cannot go out alone. Ching-Ching and Lily will go with you." "Why" I asked. "Why can I not go out alone?" "Ah, you do not yet know this country, we want you to be safe."

I should have been touched by their concern, but I was such an independent person that it irked me not to be able to go when and where I wanted. I then reminded myself that I had married into a foreign background, and would have to toe the line. The two girls proved to be delightful company, even though I had difficulty in understanding their English. I had not yet got used to the accent, nor to the strange expressions, which had to be analysed and translated in my mind before I understood their meaning. On our way to the market we bought what Ching-Ching called cherries. Bunches of twigs with velvety black flat round fruits attached to them. Very different from the cherries I knew, but sweet and tasty. Part of the excitement of travelling lies in experiencing different sights and sounds, smells and tastes, and many of my memories are connected with the taste of food. That is how I remember my very first strange fruit in Nigeria.

Tommy made arrangements for our loads to be taken on a motor launch to Warri by waterways. For the trip to his home town, another relation, the kindly Mr. Asaboro, the rubber and timber magnate of Sapele, sent his long American car to Lagos to take us to Warri. It was an arduous journey on narrow roads which had lost most of their tarred edges so that traffic going both ways was fighting for the middle of the roads. There were no highways, no expressways, no dual carriage ways in those days. To me it was all very exciting and interesting.

The fatigue of the journey was soon forgotten when we finally got to Sapele. There, we waited for the ferry to take us and the car across the Ethiope River unto the other side from where we would continue to Warri. Already, at the ferry, a group of relations and well-wishers greeted us but that was nothing, compared with the joyful reception we had on the outskirts of Warri.

Before I left, my friends and family were full of doubts for my happiness. How would a white woman be received by her husband's family? In what way would their old customs interfere in our lives? What would be the position of children from mixed marriages? To begin with, I must say that I was very lucky. I had known my husband during all the fourteen years he had spent in England, working and studying. Ours was not a whirlwind courtship, and he had taken very great pains to prepare me for our life in Africa. Even if I was to find theory one thing and practice another; he certainly had given me a sound footing on which to build my relationship with his family, which was most important. He had taught me a little Itsekiri, the language of his tribe; but I knew that most of his old, illiterate relatives would speak a little broken English, and the educated ones would speak English as the Lingua Franca of Nigeria.

When a Nigerian family hears that their son is bringing home a white wife, they have doubts, of course. Will she fit in? Will they understand each other? Will she not be lonely? But there is no colour prejudice as such. It is rather as if an Englishman were bringing home a French wife. In fact, so far, there is still some prestige attached to having a white wife, and the children of mixed marriages are held in esteem as much for their achievements as for the lightness of their skin. Oh yes, I was very warmly received.

I shall never forget the day we arrived at the little village of Ugbuangwe, the old seat of my husband's forefathers. We had driven three hundred miles inland from Lagos, the capital, where our ship had docked. As we approached the old place, three canon shots were fired to announce our arrival, and hundreds of relatives who had been waiting for us, surged forward from the rubber trees that flanked the road.

Like bright balloons they burst upon us, shouting, chanting, clapping their hands, stamping their bare feet. Brilliant were their loin cloths. The women's gold jewellery gleamed in the sun, and their dazzling silk head-ties bobbed up and down in the crowd like huge butterflies. Tied on their mothers' backs, babies' heads lolled with the rhythm of dancing.

Teeth glistened white in beaming faces. Brown hands fluttered in through the open car windows, searching for ours, gripping us — pulling us. And all the while the Itsekiri greeting *Doh! Doh!* vibrated in our ears. "He has come! The Lawyer has come! Welcome! *Doh! Ayami doh!*"

It was a great day for my husband's people as it was for us. He had been away fourteen years! A long, long time. They had almost given up hope that he would return. Yet here he was. A full fledged barrister — a great pride to his mother, and an asset to the whole family.

"*Otomi, aghan waren. Aghan waren, doh!*" "My children, you have come, you have come at last! My husband's mother, a small graceful old woman gave him and me a bear-hug, and then she snatched our two-year-old from us, placed him on her hip and danced round and around with him, chanting happily. "One went away and three came back. I have cause to rejoice," my husband translated for me.

We were surrounded by scores of relatives. Aunts, uncles, nephews, nieces and cousins galore. What a large family they were. My husband's grandfather had had fifty wives, each with numerous children. His grandfather's father had been a prince, and it was to his shrine that we were now taken to give thanks to the great ancestor, before we should proceed to our official reception at the house that had been rented for us in the nearby town of Warri. Two old uncles took my arms affectionately and led me out of the throng towards the shrine. They chattered amiably in their broken English, telling me of how great a family I had married into, and each explaining to me whose sons they were and what was their exact relationship with my husband.

"My brother's wife gave birth to him," said one. "My brother is dead, but his son is my son too." "And you," said the other, "you are my wife. You are wife to all your husband's family now." He had a twinkle in his eye and looked a grand old rascal. He was magnificent in his native robes. A double row of wire-strung coral beads marked him as a chief. His grey hair and moustache gave him an air of distinction, and the traditional ostrich feather nodded gaily on his straw boater.

I was not perturbed by his remarks. I knew that it was the custom for all my husband's family to call me "*Ayami!*" my wife, whereas I would call all of them "*Okomi!*" my husband, and I answered him, "*Okomi, doh!*" I greet you, my husband." He gave a shout of laughter. He was delighted that I had understood and even knew a few words of their language. He squeezed my arm, and I felt warm and protected and already part of the family.

Only a few elders were admitted to the shrine. I was the only woman. We sat in the bare cemented room, and it was an odd feeling to know that under its floor was buried Prince Yowunren, my husband's great-grandfather. The old uncle presided over a table which was covered with a white cloth. In a flat white dish he crumbled a piece of chalk over a kolanut, chanting earnestly the while, thanking the great ancestor for having protected their son and for bringing him home safely. At times he touched the floor with his fingertips, then touched his chest, then pointed upwards to the sky in thanks. He bit off a piece of kolanut, and passed the rest to the company for each to take a bite. I took a small one. It was very bitter and its texture reminded me of raw chestnuts.

And then the cork of a gin bottle popped. Uncle Merogun filled his glass, but before he put it to his lips, he dashed some gin from it to the ground three times. This was the ancestor's share. He downed the rest himself and again passed it round for everyone to take a sip. Then my husband and I were asked to kneel down to receive the ancestor's blessing for our future.

I knew that my husband had laid aside the old beliefs long ago, and the ceremony meant nothing to him. Yet, from the way he was holding my hand, I knew that he was as strangely moved as I. He was touched, no doubt, by childhood memories and by the fact that he had been away for such a long time that he could never again be the same person to his family. They seemed dear and very pathetic to him, but he knew that many a clash of opinions lay ahead.

The first one happened as soon as we had emerged from the cool of the shrine into the blazing sunshine. Before the waiting crowd could close in upon us again, my husband's mother and eldest sister stepped forward and led him aside into one of the tiny red mud-houses that made up the village. I saw my husband duck as he entered. He looked strange in his immaculate worsted lounge suit among all the gaily robed men. My thoughts followed him fondly. I quite understood that his mother and sister should want a few moments' privacy with him. But he almost immediately came out again, looking angry and determined. The two women followed, gesticulating and exclaiming to one another.

When he had fought his way back to me he said, "These women call themselves Christians and go to church every Sunday. Yet they had prepared a charmed drink for me. God knows how much they paid the native doctor for his recipe and ingredients. I know my mother means well," he continued, "she can ill afford the expense, but she hopes this drink will help me to success and protect me from evil. Of course, she was appalled when I refused to take it. I had to make it quite clear, once and for all, that I do not believe in her medicine, and I have forbidden her or anyone else to come near us with such nonsense."

I protested mildly in defence of the poor old woman, but my husband turned on me savagely. "Now that we are here, let me repeat to you what I have often told you before: allow me to know my own people, and to deal with them as I think fit." He almost hissed the words, and I could see by his agitation that, if in the conflict between the old and the new, the new was to conquer, there could be no happy medium. There would have to be a drastic break, and the sooner he started putting his foot down, the better it was.

There have been more clashes of course, but the elders of the family have learned to accept my husband's new ways of life and no longer try to force theirs on him. My husband's firmness in such matters is mixed with sufficient respect for them, to enable us to enjoy their native ceremonies as onlookers.

We left the little thatched houses nestling between palms and banana trees, and the procession of our slow moving car accompanied by drummers and dancers, threaded its way noisily into the town of Warri, up to the house that was to be our new home.

The days that followed were a kaleidoscope of faces, voices and of feasting for me. My mother-in-law cooked for us and for the many guests who continued to arrive from outlying villages and towns to welcome us. She and Mewe, my husband's eldest sister, had closed their tobacco stall at the market for a week of rejoicing, and they now directed their children and grand-children to relieve me of any kind of work, including that of looking after our two-year-old Monubarami. He had taken all the changes calmly, but he now definitely objected to being carried on anyone's back, and his cousins had to be content with hanging around him while he played about my feet.

Everyday my mother-in-law took glowing tales to my husband, of how much all those who had met me, had liked me. "You have chosen well, my son," she said. "She is beautiful. She is not one of those thin sticks of coral that some white women are. Her nose is not too long, and we like her thick legs, her long straight hair. She tries to eat our food and speak our language. And she is always smiling. We don't know why, but it is good. You say she likes to work and earn money. She will be a good wife. You have done well."

They were glad too that I had arrived with at least one child. Although this was a poor effort compared with the average Nigerian woman, I was at least spared the merciless contempt that falls on those who have the misfortune of being barren, and there was always hope that I would bear more.

When the first onslaught of relatives had died down a little, gold edged invitation cards began to arrive. Mauve, pink or blue, — they turned up in our post box, requesting the pleasure of our company at this dinner or that luncheon, and summoning us to the judge's cocktail-party, where we were to meet the other barristers, my husband's colleagues.

Our first obligatory visit after arrival in Warri was to the Olu of Warri, the traditional ruler of the Itsekiris, and then to the Resident, the British representative of his government. There, one only had to sign the visitors' book, stating name, address, date of arrival and status/profession. An invitation to call would then follow.

To me, the visit to the palace of the Olu was quite awe-inspiring. Tommy had taught me to bend my right knee, greet him with my right fist and say the customary greeting of "Ogiamien". He, of course, did the same, and the Olu His Highness, Erejuwa II was gracious and genial. Great dignity emanated from him. He sat on a throne, a large carved chair with red velvet seat and back. He wore his traditional crown, which was more like a cap woven of small, red coral beads, with strings of coral dangling down by the side of his ears. The customary sword-bearers stood behind him and one young boy was fanning him.

Much of the conversation between him and Tommy was conducted in Itsekiri after His Highness had first asked me, *"Wogbi Itsekiri?"* and I had answered *"Kekere"*. (Do you hear Itsekiri? a little) He smiled and looked at Tommy with a little nod. *"Osengwa-o"*, (beautiful) was a word I heard often and understood, but I gave no sign of it this time. His Highness now spoke in English, offering Tommy, this great representative of the Itsekiri people, a chieftaincy.

Tommy refused eloquently and politely, saying: "Your Highness, you know I am a Prince, descended from Prince Yowunren, I cannot accept the title of Chief which is lower than that of a Prince." The Olu did not seem offended, but now offered a chieftaincy to me. Tommy responded in the same vein, thanking the Olu for the honour, but repeating that, as the wife of a Prince, I had become a Princess and could not accept the honour of a chieftaincy for the same reason. We then accepted a glass of wine from the ruler and Tommy assured him that if he ever needed his assistance, he would be too glad to serve him.

The look of the palace had surprised me a little. Having come from Europe with visions of Buckingham Palace, of Versailles, of

Schonbrunn, of even modest Kensington Palace, there was this contrast to what I expected. Later I understood how many slaves it must have taken to build, a century ago, a walled compound, palace and outhouses without any machinery, all by hand. How rich the owner must have been to possess that many slaves!

Not long after we had signed the Resident's book we received an invitation to a dinner-party at the Residency. "Black tie" it said, and we took great care over putting on our finery of evening dress, before taking off in someone's borrowed car, we had not even got the Beetle yet.

The Residency was not more than five minutes drive from Khalil Road, which was the last road before the Government Residential Area (G.R.A.). On arrival, a well-uniformed steward stood at the entrance and asked for our invitation card. Tommy looked dumbfounded for a moment, felt his pockets and then said: "sorry, I left it at home." The steward was sorry too. No admission without the card.

The proud Tommy turned on his heels: "come on, Pooppie, let's go." We drove back home, not to get the card, but to stay home. Tommy had not yet got to the stage of "don't you know who I am?" — but refused to go and bring the card, like a schoolboy who had forgotten his exercise book.

We had hardly got home and up our stairs, when a driver rushed into our compound, on his lips profuse apologies from the Resident and his wife. The steward had not realised who we were (how could he?) and would we please come back with their driver and car, who would also take us home after the dinner. Smug and mollified, Tommy led the way down the stairs again (without card) and we arrived in style at the Residency.

The lovely open and airy house stood in beautifully groomed gardens which led down to the river. But now we entered as cocktails were passed around before dinner. Wherever Tommy entered, tall, slim, impeccably dressed, his straight and regal bearing made people look up. Heads turned. The Resident and his wife again apologized for their steward's mistake and led us around the guests who had arrived before us. Of course, practically everybody knew Tommy. There were loud friendly greetings, embraces and backslapping, while I stood, glass in hand, as a decorative appendage, waiting to be introduced to Tommy's friends and colleagues, before I was ushered over to where the ladies stood in a group.

In the 1950s mixed marriages were not yet common in Nigeria, and it seemed that both, the men and the women were ill at ease with me. The women were not so emancipated as they are now. Maybe they were a little nervous about not "hearing my English". They were beautiful and expensively dressed in their native attire, but conversation was not flowing.

"How the children?"

"How market?"

"How your *hosband*?" were the three topics.

Fortunately my "trade" made a bridge between them and me. I divulged that I was a fashion designer and sparked off instant curiosity.

"*Hein*? You are a seamstress?"

Not quite the same, I tried to explain, but was interrupted with:

"You make for people?"

"Later," I said. "I have not started yet."

"You make that dress?" they pointed to the long green satin evening dress I was wearing.

"Yes, I did, but I like your native dress much better. I hope somebody will show me how to tie such lovely headties too."

"Now they clamoured, "I will show you."

"I will give you my own."

"Will you wear headtie?" And a bond was forged.

Where the men were concerned, it took me time to realize that it was just not done for a man to be seen talking to another man's wife. So, when we met, the man would greet me, ask "how are the children?" and walk past me in a hurry. There was no easy exchange of even a short conversation, no "free speech" between the sexes as there is now, in the late nineties.

In fact, I have been privileged in my own life-time, to see the men of Nigeria make such tremendous progress, as I had not thought possible in only forty years. I now delight to see them educated, professional women, smartly dressed, confident drivers, confident people, yet still diplomatic with their men-folk. Caring mothers too! Sophistication has not destroyed this most important assignment for woman.

I struggled with my own kind of emancipation in Nigeria. I had so much to learn, not only in the way of dress but of social behaviour, of tact and diplomacy, and of being deferential to one's husband. The social greetings, for one thing, seemed to me very laborious. I appreciated their charm and timelessness, everybody had time to enquire after one's health, one's business, one's children, did I hear from my mother and brother, and although this might have been perfunctory, it was charmingly time consuming. I had to drop my brief European ways when one said "hello" at any time instead of "Good morning", "Good afternoon" and "Good evening". And the quaint idea was that morning was morning until noon — 12 o'clock, logically anything after 12 o'clock would be afternoon, but in Nigeria it was strictly confined between 12 and 4 o'clock because after 4 o'clock one said "good evening" until in the evening to my mind when it got dark, "one said good night." To this day I have not really absorbed this time distinction. To me, "good morning" is before lunch, "good afternoon" after lunch and evening begins at dusk, I would say.

Itsekiri table manners were such that anyone ate with his hands, and most people preferred that native way, they said the food tasted better; so after eating with one's fingers one would lick the fingers loudly so as not to be mistaken for a thief who had secretly dipped his hand into the pot. One never ate with one's left hand. One did not even pick up a biscuit or a piece of bread with one's left hand, because that hand was unclean. It was used to wipe one's self after going to the toilet. Tommy soon freed me from such prejudices by saying; "Hilda uses her right hand." This made everybody laugh but I was exonerated. Again up to this day, I consciously think of the company I am in and adjust myself by not offering food with my left hand.

The business of kneeling to senior relatives and influential people was modified by me into a curtsy. To make Monu kneel down for any relation was a tough job. He was so self-conscious, he just would not obey, and Tommy did not particularly insist. As a result some senior aunty would insist that he should kneel. *"Dakun. Dakun"*, and she would point to his knees and to the ground. I am afraid I was often accused of not training my child properly, because he would simply refuse. Whatever Itsekiri words he learned came from me now, because his father became too busy to bother with teaching us anymore.

In the choice of native dress, dear cousin Aggie (Mrs. Esiri) came to the rescue. She helped me to choose *'wrappas'* (wrappers) which were worn in two layers by the Itsekiri women. There was a long wrapper from the waist to the ground first, and then a shorter one on top of the long one gathered tightly around the waist and tucked into it somehow. This was very tricky for me because the top layer kept falling off. The first layer, Tommy told me was wrapped around the waist while the woman was standing with her feet wide apart to give enough room for walking later. After that the top layer was secured around the waist by, preferably, a lover's necktie. It could of course, be the husband's necktie!

Always, there was a dainty frilly blouse worn over the bottom layer and then secured by the top wrapper. I found all this not only cumbersome for an active day, but hot around the legs. First of all I modified the bottom skirt by wrapping it and then stitching it down with an elastic band running through the top around the waist. I did not need a lover's necktie. The top layer I somehow managed because even if that fell off, there was still the bottom layer to protect one.

Of course the women were so used to it falling off or at least getting loose, that they continued to secure the top wrapper with one deft movement of the left hand which tucked it under and around the waist again. Added to this precarious way of dressing was the slippery silky headtie which just would not sit on sleek European hair. It was comfortable on thick curly hair but shifted from angle to angle on straight smooth hair. I devised a short cap for myself which sat tightly on my head, then I wound the headtie around that. A workable solution, but rather hot. However, I enjoyed wearing headties. To me it was a way of identifying with Nigeria, more than the wrapper could do. Eventually I even made the bottom wrapper into a skirt with zip and waist band, but the total appearance was still that of native dress.

I learned how the women of the Yoruba tribe dressed with only one wrapper but a petty-coat was obligatory, in case the wrapper came loose. But I found the Yoruba cloth easier to tie in later years, because it was thick hand-woven cloth that stayed in place.

The choice of native material was not so easy. There were thousands of the most wonderful and varied colourful patterns, but all of them were geared to the African market. All of them, or most of them, suited the dark brown skin. There again it was a question of tribe, because the Itsekiri liked bright red and orange whereas the Yorubas wore mostly blue or blue-gray tones. It was fascinating, when we travelled and passed a Yoruba market, there would be this sea of blue clad humanity busily buying and selling their wares. In Warri now, although I liked red and orange I did not like wearing it all the time. I liked green but the greens were the olive green kind which did not suit me, nor did the browns, the beige or the gray evoke any enthusiasm in me. They were not enough contrast with my skin and made me look dull.

In all fashion I have always expounded my theory that it is a matter of addition and subtraction. If the person is colourful that is, dark eyes, dark hair, maybe dark skin subdued tones are very becoming. But if it is a fair-skinned and possibly blue-eyed person who has little of her own colour, colour has to be added to make enough contrast with the skin.

I never liked the pastel shades of light pink, light blue, lemon yellow, and the pretty summer dresses, which many expatriates wore. They looked so odd, so insipid, in the vibrant tropical setting. Also, the short skirts, with anaemic looking legs protruding from under them, did not look attractive to my mind.

Talking of short skirts, I had one altercation with my dear mother-in-law, Granny Obinu. She was shocked beyond belief when she saw me in shorts. And long shorts they were, going to the middle of my thigh while I was cleaning the house. She remonstrated vividly that I should take them off, and when I did not seem to understand, she called Sister Mewe to explain that I must not show so much of my legs.

It was a little surprising to me, because had I not played tennis with Tommy in England in these shorts? Well, I must have reflected on "When in Rome do as the Romans do" and obliged Granny Obinu by changing into a skirt — but this was the only criticism I ever had from any of the family.

Everyday, presents continued to arrive at our house. People of the town, as well as relatives and friends, sent chickens, fish and yams, pineapples and bananas, and precious eggs. One present came in the form of free advice from a witch doctor. He visited us, and after a large glass of gin, drew my husband aside confidentially and said, "buy a new white handkerchief. Wash it yourself in soap and do not rinse it. Put it on the grass in the sun to dry. Do not allow your wife or any woman to touch it. Fold it six times. Always carry it in your left pocket, and if you wipe your face with it three times every morning before you enter the law-courts, you will win all your cases, and success will be yours."

This prescription might have normally cost a bottle of gin and six yards of cloth, but it was given free and I was touched by so much generosity. My husband put a little damper on my enthusiasm. "You know," he said, "these presents are tokens of friendliness. But they are also investments. After a while, everybody will expect you and me to do something for them." That was true enough. Requests for favours came rolling in.

I found that, as a white woman, I was thought not only to be omnipotent, but rich as well. I was asked to advise on housekeeping and often house-building and furnishing. I was expected to contribute to scholarships, or buy books for this or that relative. Some brought me watches and cameras to mend, but most often, medical aid was needed.

"Missus," said Uncle Omadukpe to me, "my wife, she refuse to take my pickin to hospital to have needle. I beat her three times, but she refuse. Make you talk to her now." I talked to her as best I could, and showed her the vaccination mark on my own little boy's arm. The following day she allowed me to accompany her to the hospital to have her child vaccinated.

Roli, our niece, wanted to wean her baby. How could she stop the flow of her milk? she asked me. Little Richard had a cough, did I have any medicine? Alero had cut her toe on a stone. Could I put a bandage on? Sissy wanted some needles and thread. Cousin Amos asked me to "beg" Lawyer to take him on as a clerk. Asifo wanted to send me his nine-year-old daughter to live with me, to be trained and to serve me. But most frequent of all were the requests for me to do some sewing. The news that I had been a fashion designer in London, had preceded my arrival, and the women had eagerly looked forward to having in their family a "real seamstress" to make them gowns and fine blouses with which to dazzle their rivals in church on Sunday mornings.

I learned to refer every single request to my husband who alone could sort out the deserving cases. Altogether, I soon realised that I had stepped into a world where the husband is law. That was, and still is, the most difficult thing for me to accept. I had always looked to my husband as the captain of our team. I loved him for his strong personality and his leadership qualities. But while we lived in England, we had been a team, and there never was any doubt about my equality. Now, in Africa, he subconsciously reverted to the attitude of his forefathers and expected his orders to be carried out without questions, and his opinions to be accepted without challenge.

In some directions, my husband's authority was of great help to me. With much courage he kept his family from interfering in our affairs. All requests and complaints were brought to him first, often without my knowledge, and his decisions were accepted as final. The women respected him as a man, and the men, because he was more educated than they, and so I was spared some of the endless squabbles that go on in Nigerian families.

There were to be other receptions of different kinds. They were more official, all very enjoyable, all eye openers to me. The first one was arranged in Warri at an open hotel garden belonging to Mrs. Nkune. My problem was always to find a toilet where I could have privacy.

As we arrived at this hotel garden one of Tommy's relations, Mrs Agnes Esiri (nee Ogbe) came forward, embraced and kissed me, which so touched me that I felt instantly at home with her. So I whispered to her whether she could lead me to the hotel toilet, but she took me by the hand and led me and my little boy towards her car and said "you cannot use that one. Come, I will take you to my house." Little did I know that it would take ten minutes to drive to her house in Cemetery Road, to walk up two flights of stairs because her doctor husband had a medical practice on the ground floor, — and then to drive back to the reception. I thanked my stars that I had not left it too late before I was granted relief.

Back at the reception there was the high table, which was a novelty to me, and the subsequent many speeches by different members of the family extolled the good fortune that they had to receive back into their midst their son who had been away for a long fourteen years, yet he had returned as a qualified lawyer. My husband also spoke to thank all comers and the organisers of the function and permitted me to say a few words as I had asked him to do. He had taught me many Itsekiri words and sentences while we were in England. I was happy to use them now to say simply "*Aghan doh, Enedokpe gidigbo*" and sat down among laughter and applause, and I was relieved when Tommy later said I had done very well. I had not made a fool of myself.

It was a good beginning. I had simply said "I greet you all and we thank you very much." Later I learned many simple sentences so that I could greet Tommy's mother and sister and other visiting relations by asking "How are you? Please sit down. What do you want to drink? Cold water?" Or if they stayed at our house I might ask "Are you tired? Do you want to sleep?" And in the morning I would say "Good morning, you have got up. What do you want to eat?" Other conversation revolved around "I want to go to the market" or "I want to go home." Or "I want to sleep." Then the complicated questions and answer of "How are you"? if I was asked, I would answer "My body is good", but the ubiquitous word of *"doh"* covered most occasions.

My mother-in-law was a slight, gentle, lovable woman, who spoke little English. I was soon ill with malaria not once, not twice, but very frequently, and she would sit by my bed side for hours saying *"Doh, doh, doh."* Then after a pause she would start again saying *"Doh, doh* my pickin," which I found very touching and reassuring. Tommy's children Ching Ching and Freedom and his sister's daughter Lily had all followed us to Warri and were now staying with us. They were delightful young people who took charge of little Monu immediately so that I had no worries about him. Writing from England Tommy had asked his cousin Chief Athur Prest, to find a house for us as near to the government reservation as possible. He had rented No. 4 Khalil Road to which we climbed up on an outside staircase. It was nice and airy to be upstairs but the accommodation was one huge room. Tommy said it was like the hold of a ship and had to be partitioned to make a semblance of rooms from it.

When we arrived there was no furniture except one large double bed with mosquito net which stood in the middle of the vast room. We had brought four folding chairs with us from England and these served us for some time. When our loads arrived from the motor launch there was beehive activity. While the porters carried one hundred and twenty-nine pieces of crates and luggage on their heads, on their backs, up outside the open staircase, all were dumped in the big room and arrived safely, except one case which dropped from the bearer's head when he wanted to put it down. When the cases were neatly piled side by side, and Tommy decided to open one or the other, his mother sat in front of them daring anybody to come near and help himself. When the partitions were erected we had two bedrooms, one office and in the middle of the big room we ate and played. Outside on the verandah, through which one entered the house there was a kitchen one end and a shower and toilet at the other end. The cemented shower had been fashioned by careless bricklayers, who had dropped blobs of cement here and there and left them to harden into sharp stones. It was like a fakir's endurance test, to walk across them with bare feet to have one's shower.

The youngsters did all the sweeping and dusting, such as it was, and the two girls went to market to shop and cook for us. I still remember that two shillings worth of *nama* (beef) was enough to feed the whole family. We lived out of trunks and boxes until a carpenter made a wardrobe and chest of drawers, a table and other furniture for us. The big bed had a mosquito net which I rather liked, it felt cozy to be underneath it. The young people slept on mats on the floor. As soon as my sewing machines arrived, requests for blouses to be made by me began to arrive. At first I had to refuse them, saying that I was not settled yet.

Tommy now went to court. We had no car but as we were near the reservation, perhaps fifteen minutes walk from the High Court, he walked on foot, and I see him now, immaculately dressed in 'black over trou' (trouserine) with his bowler hat and his blue bag containing wig and gown slung over his shoulder. His relations remonstrated with him, offering to lend him money to buy a car. He refused, saying that he did not want to go into debt. Very often he was given a lift on his way to the court, by colleagues who owned their cars. Eventually, he succumbed to the pleadings of his family, and bought a Volkswagen Beetle for three hundred and eighty pounds.

I enjoyed going to the market myself, but Monu hated it. He did not like the crowds around him, nor the heat and the flies, nor the lengthy arguments which arose over prices. I held him by the hand of course but he dragged behind me and hampered my progress. The next time I went out by myself on my bicycle. Even though the market was not far from us, it was easier on my feet to ride rather than walk. One day I came home into Khalil Road, my bicycle negotiating a narrow strip of tar between two potholes, but my bicycle and I fell down near our house. I got up quickly dusted myself off, as if nothing had happened, and hoped nobody had seen me. But from all the surrounding stores at the bottom of our house people rushed out to help me saying *"Doh, doh,* did you wound yourself?" asking concerned questions. I smiled brightly, thanked them and limped home.

When Tommy heard that I had fallen off my bicycle he forbade me ever to use it again. "A lawyer's wife should not be seen falling off her bicycle" was his angry statement. So, I was deprived of my own means of transport, until five years later I had my own little car. It was a Fiat 600 which barely accommodated my long legs, but I felt exhilarating freedom when I learned to drive it. Tommy never wanted me to learn to drive. As a lawyer he said "I don't want to have to defend you if you have an accident" and later, as a magistrate it was "I don't want to have to try you."

Upon my pleadings though, he tried to teach me on a strip of quiet road between Warri and Effurun, which was all bush in those days. Each side of the road lay virgin land with not a house in sight. His efforts to teach me to drive ended disastrously. "If you don't remember to clutch when you change gear, — I leave you standing in the road. Here and now! Get out of the car," he shouted. He was so irate that I had to decide whether to continue driving, or save my marriage. The latter won.

It was but a ten minutes walk into the Government Reservation to what was then called the European Club where I took Monu to play in the sand and to watch canoes and ships and motor launches go by. The club house was on the edge of a river in beautiful surroundings. It was mostly used by the European officials and the highlights of the club's functions was the monthly curry lunch on Sunday. We had become members as soon as we arrived, so I was among the women who would take it in turn to cook something for the curry lunch. It could be either palm oil chop or curry and rice with side dishes. The ladies were given instructions as to what to cook and for how many people and we got our money for ingredients refunded after the lunch. It was always a nice outing but Tommy did not seem to enjoy anything.

He was always angry. He was always irritated coming home from court and deriding conditions there. "You people," he would say addressing his friends or relations, "you people have told me that Nigeria has made much progress in my absence. Come and see the dirty court in which I am supposed to sit in my gown. I had to call the court clerk and make him sweep the cobwebs from the corners of the room and dust the benches, so that my gown would not be dirty." He had much criticism for any and everything that occurred in the beginnings of our life in Nigeria. So much for kissing the ground. He was like a bear with a sore head. At one point he said to me "I can't stand it, I can't. I am going back to England, where things are orderly and people are reliable and prompt". I reasoned with him saying "Tommy your people need you to make things better. You cannot turn your back on your country. Help to make improvements where you can and accept conditions as they are for now. A growing country needs time."

He said in later years that if it had not been for Hilda he would have left Nigeria and stayed in Britain. In the beginning, as a "new wig", cases were slow to come in, until Tommy took up one or two appointments to act for the Crown Counsel. Both were murder cases. Once people had felt his presence in court and heard his voice, they began to consult him. They came at all hours, and as his office (chambers) was in our house, often our little Monu, then three years old, would stand at the wooden gate, which we had made for his safety at the top of the outside stairs, and call down to the clients, "My Daddy has gone to court." Some came late in the night, when I was in bed, ready for sleep.

The plywood partitions had now been erected and painted, but they did not reach the ceiling.

There was a good two feet gap at the top, and through this gap I could hear the voices of Tommy and his clients. Not that I understood the conversation, which was conducted in either the vernacular or in broken English (pidgin English) most times, but often I heard the unmistakable sound of coins clinking as the fees were counted out in shilling pieces.

Another sound that kept me from sleep at night was that of the night watchmen stamping their sticks on the ground at intervals, to keep themselves awake. There was also an outdoor cinema at the back of our house where the popular Indian films portrayed galloping horses, clashing swords, screaming women, — and the shouts of the participating audience kept me awake. But at least, I knew that this disturbance would stop at midnight.

Noise was the most difficult aspect to adapt to in my new environment. Loud voices in most homes. Loud music. Loud radio, not to talk of the noise of hooting traffic and music in all shops. Everyone was connected to "Re-diffusion". The one local station which supplied everybody's wireless box with their one programme all day. Street markets at every corner gave the whole town an air of perpetual fun-fairs with their brightly dressed, shouting women vendors and customers alike.

I actually enjoyed them for a while, so long as I could then retreat to my own, relatively quiet home. Sometimes, in a shop, I would ask the owner to turn down his radio music, or I would not be able to buy anything. I simply could not concentrate on choice of fabrics or other goods with music blaring in my ear. The shopkeepers always obliged, but must have thought that these oyinbos (white people) were strange creatures.

My other painful sensitivity was towards quarrels and physical violence. It was such a contrast to the controlled lives of the English (British) who would never like to intrude, nor would they have liked to let their neighbours know of any discord in their homes. Here in Warri, the shouts of quarrels, the loud cries of a child or a wife being beaten — the wailing of mourners when a death had occurred and the subsequent solemn drumming always produced anxiety which held my heart in a vice. The youngsters in our household also raised their voices and abused each other at times, but I always quelled the uproar as soon as possible. Myself, I never knew how to quarrel, — to this day I cannot raise my voice. I burst into tears instead, which renders me powerless.

I was a poor match for Tommy's endless tirades over small matters. The decibels of his powerful voice alone laid a shutter over my tired brain which had only one desire: that the harangue should stop. Never mind, if I should lose the argument. What did it matter, anyway, that I had forgotten to buy Maggi sauce, or that one of the children had allowed the bottom of the rice to burn in the pot? On one occasion, I poured salt from the container into my hand to season the soup I was cooking. I had poured too much, and as it could not be returned through the spout into the container, I brushed it off my hand into the sink. Tommy saw me and shouted "Look at you! You are wasting my money! Have you no sense? You should know how much salt you need for the soup, ..." on and on he went.

Even in our fourteen years in England, I had always been amazed at his overreaction to, in my mind, small incidents or mishaps. Vowed, as I had, to make this man happy, to support him in his goals and cushion him from hurt, I at first put his rantings down to the difficulty of adjusting to life in Europe — then to the stress of war, — later to anxiety about exams, some of which he had to resit, and finally to financial problems; although he never voiced any of these. For that matter, our finances were not that desperate. We both earned good salaries, and despite his obligations to his family overseas, he managed, over the years, to assemble an impressive collection of law-books and an equally impressive wardrobe — suits for every occasion.

Now in Nigeria, at home at last, I attributed his irrational behaviour to his disappointment and frustration with his own people and his country. At all times, I tried to soothe him and to undo his knot of anger, subduing my own resentment, making excuses for him and letting my love prevail. It was no easy task when his irritation turned upon his children, Ching Ching and Freedom and his niece Lily. He beat them mercilessly for any small misdemeanour which I could not cover up. If I intervened and begged for mercy for them he shouted: "If you interfere, I'll beat them all the harder."

The lashes of his cane and the cries of the children beat into my psyche, and on one occasion I fainted. I fell to the floor unconscious, until Tommy picked me up and laid me on our bed. When I woke up I saw his anxious face bent over me, but as soon as he knew I was all right, he said, "I have told you before, when I was a little boy, my uncle gave me six lashes of the cane every morning, to make me a good boy for the rest of the day." Tommy was brought up by his father's sister, Mama Rosa of Forcados, because his own mother, Obinu, could not manage to keep him after his father, Edema Brick Ogbe, a marine engineer, had left her.

As he spoke, I burst into tears as much for the sake of his children who had just been beaten, as for the injustice done to my Tommy when he was a little boy. My brother and I had never experienced anything more than a smack, given in a moment of honest anger by our mother, and well deserved it always was. Systematic caning was a different matter.

I remember only two of the offences poor Freedom had committed. One occurred when we were developing and printing photographs, and he accidentally dropped the timing clock in the darkroom and broke it. The other was the loss of the key to our post office box. It was his job to ride on our bicycle to the post office to check for mail. The key to the box always hung on a string around his neck, and really, neither he nor we could understand how he lost it. For this crime he was not only caned but was put in solitary confinement for one week. Nobody was allowed to speak to him, though he was fed. He was not allowed reading or writing matter, and I thought it was hard punishment for this lively intelligent boy.

The three youngsters were really lovely, good people, but they had grown up in Nigeria and could not be expected to turn overnight into something like British children. I felt that this was what irritated Tommy who, it seemed, wanted instant success from them. Freedom was enrolled in Hussey College, Warri. Ching Ching and Lily had finished their schooling, but still I tried to teach them, at least, more English. Their quaint expressions had to be translated, such as "Auntie, my laps are peppering me" Lily, a buxom girl, could not make me understand. So I said "Show me." It turned out that the insides of her chubby thighs had rubbed each other sore.

Freedom asked me, "Mummy, why is it that when I stumble, it hurts me to my heart?" The explanation as I saw it was: "When you stumble you get a little shock, and that shock feels like pain in your heart." Ching Ching observed me, bent over the sewing machine and then, pointing to my green eye make-up asked, "Mummy, do you paint your eyelashes, or is this how God made you?" They were endearing young people.

Ching Ching now helped me with the hand-sewing. I had yielded to pressure and was making blouses to order. I had not had any experience with such insistent customers though, who wanted a new blouse made overnight. I was still plagued by malaria on-off-on-off and one Easter-time I was so weak and dizzy that I told a lady I was very sorry but her blouse would not be ready in time as I was sick. No, no, she would not have it. I could sit down at the sewing machine, could I not? She sat with me, urging me on, while I could hardly see for headache and dizziness, sweat rising on the tops of my arms, running down the crooks of my elbows and out of my hair, until all the ruching on the blouse and all the lace frills were in place. Exhausted, I fell on the bed, not even caring whether the woman who had gone off with her blouse, had paid her five shillings or not.

That day I vowed not to make anything to order any more. Instead I made dozens of blouses in different styles, sizes and colours, strung them on a line across our "sitting-room" and let those who wanted ready-made come and buy. I did make one wedding-dress though for the bride of Barrister Ovie-Whiskey. She was a dainty lady, and I wanted to make something extra special for her. I designed a crinoline, a voluminous skirt that would show off her tiny waist. In true crinoline fashion it had whalebone hoops stitched all around the under-skirt; to make the dress look very full. She really looked like a fairy tale princess in it, but, in my ignorance of local churches, I had not taken the width of the aisle into account. It was narrow; very narrow; and as the bride was led up to the altar, her skirt was compressed by the pews which she passed and her skirt ballooned out back and front like a ship in full sail. Happily, it sprang back into its hooped round shape once it and the bride reached the altar. From what I heard afterwards, it had been a sensation, but I refused further orders for wedding dresses or any other kind.

I made men's leisure shirts instead. Unusual materials from Chellaram's, unusual styles from my head. Russian-type collars, Chinese-type openings on the shoulders, stripes placed at angles to each other, and pockets that sat in unusual places on the shirts. The elastic swim wear satin pieces from auctions now came in handy to be made in glowing colours into swimming pants for men. Again, I was ignorant of the fact that most educated Nigerians in those days did not swim. All the same, at the rate those pants were selling, I realized later, they must have graced many a bedroom scene.

I was writing happy letters to my mother and brother. I loved Nigeria, I took small inconveniences in my stride. After all, I had chosen to leave Western comforts behind. There was no reason why I should now complain about anything. We had an airy upstairs flat — no fan as yet until Tommy bought a second-hand table fan from a destitute cousin. Air conditioning was not yet thought of and could not have worked in our flat anyway, because we did not have glazed windows, but wooden louvres. They concealed the interior of the house but generously let in fresh air, insects and rain. Oh yes, rain was a frequent visitor in Warri which lay in the low delta region of South-west Nigeria.

Often there was a fine spray of rain through the shutters and through the mosquito net of our big bed. I comforted myself with the thought that it was good for my skin. It was being moisturized. When the fierce sun came out, of course he created a damp, humid atmosphere, which made us long for cold drinks. We did not yet have a fridge, but a kind Lebanese neighbour supplied us with ice cubes everyday. There was no cold store in Warri either. We made the weekly car trip into Sapele, thirty miles away, to buy butter, cheese and other European necessities if we could afford them. We bought them at Kingsway Stores, of the U.A.C. (United Africa Company). Sapele was a thriving town in the Nineteen fifties, because it not only lay by the Ethiope River which had busy water transport, but it had Nigeria's only Plywood factory — the A.T. & P. (African Timber and Plywood). We were able to visit it on one of our trips, and even little Monu enjoyed seeing the vast machinery on which mighty tree-trunks turned round and around to be "peeled" into thin layers of what came to be known as plywood.

A visit to Kingsway Stores always meant a cold drink, — but what I missed was ice cream. The thought suddenly struck me. What? In this hot country, no ice cream for hundreds of miles around! Bitten by this "bug", I wrote to my mother, telling her that here was a business opportunity going to waste. Could she help me to buy professional ice cream-making equipment? My dear mother, as impulsive and adventurous as I, set to work immediately from the USA. She wisely consulted British manufacturers, because
(a) the freight from Britain to Nigeria would be cheaper than from the USA and
(b) the current of AC220/240 would be compatible with Nigeria, rather than the USA current of 110 which would need a transformer.

Catalogues and quotations started flying between her and Britain, until in 1958 mother came to Warri to stay with us, bringing with her a long, gleaming chromium ice cream-making machine and all accessories for it.

What excitement; first of all, to be reunited with her in our new home, secondly for our Monu to hug and welcome his Granny, and thirdly for her to have accomplished this feat, this marvelous Italian-looking machine! She had also brought the British ice cream powder, the paper cups printed with my name "Hilly's Ice Cream" and the chemicals which would make up the *brine* with which the machine was to be filled so that it plus electricity would freeze the product and keep it frozen.

The first mix was Vanilla flavour, the second was Chocolate, and of course they were mixed in separate batches and stored in separate "sleeves" of the machine, in paper cups. I hired two boys to go out on bicycles, for which I had the carpenter make two boxes insulated with crumpled newspaper, and the welder had made the necessary metal frames to hold the boxes. The bicycles had to be licenced, so I got from the Sanitation Department a licence to sell the ice cream. I had invited the Sanitary Inspector to come and see the surroundings where the ice cream was produced and showed him that I boiled and filtered the water for the mixture. We had placed the eight feet long machine in a room under the outside stairs which led up to our flat. There it stood, in all its shining glory, complete with three chromium lids to close each "sleeve". They were lifted by their big black knobs. The Sanitary Inspector walked away happily with a few sample cups of creamy mixture.

I need not have bothered actually, because in Warri, the seat of Tommy's family, at that time practically every official was a member of his large family. His father's side the Itsekiris, — his mother's side the Urhobos. We could have asked any favour from anybody, but I was used to doing things properly and started off on the right foot. The bicycle boys were pleased and felt safe because they had a Hawker's Licence each. Hilly's Ice Cream, sweet and smooth on the tongue and cooling in the throat soon claimed addicts, but first all relations and friends had to be given free samples for their large families, so that profit was delayed for a while. When I began to distribute to Kingsway Stores, Sapele and to Chellaram's Warri, my efforts began to look more like a business.

The bicycles went out into the town where there were crowds. They sold at markets, at schools, after church on Sundays and at football matches. They would come back to the house for a refill if they had sold out, or in the evening to return unsold cups to be kept frozen.

My mother meanwhile enjoyed witnessing the success of my idea and her co-operation. More than that she enjoyed her grandson Monu, who was then three years old. He loved being read to, and she would sit for hours, reading to him from colourful storybooks she had brought. He often sat on her lap, sucking his thumb and listening very attentively, so much so that, when she re-read some stories, leaving out a passage or two, as she was getting tired, he would notice it and demand that the text should be read as he remembered it.

The family put on a special reception for her at the Warri Town Hall, where the small in stature Chief Ovu addressed the crowd saying "We have had important visitors before. We have had Chiefs and Judges, Government Officials, Professors and Clergy, Politicians, District Officers and Residents, — but never have we had a mother-in-law visit us from far away America." He then continued a rousing welcome speech. Gifts for my mother also came to the house. She was so touched, in fact, overwhelmed. Chickens, eggs, different relations brought fruits and drinks, just for her!

She did become a little nervous though when our rascally handsome big Uncle Merogun brought her a beautiful fish and asked to take her out for a canoe ride. My mother, then sixty-six years old, clutched my hand and whispered "Don't allow it. Don't allow it!" So I made her excuses saying she was afraid of water, as she could not swim, but thanked him very much for the offer.

While she was with us, I developed a very stiff neck and pains in my wrists. One day, out shopping near us, one of Tommy's acquaintances, the chemist Ben Lawson, passed me, stopped and greeted me and then asked, — lifting up my hand, — "Why is your wrist swollen?" "Oh," I shrugged it and him off, "it's probably a bit of rheumatism, maybe caused by the cold when I dip my hand into the ice-cream machine."

Then he looked at my left wrist and asked: "Do you put that one also in the machine? It too is swollen." He shook his head but said no more, and I went home. A few days later there were swellings under my feet. Not painful, but it felt as if I was walking on a small cushion under each foot.

The crunch came when we drove out to Ughelli Government College to watch a cricket match at the weekend. Halfway through the game I developed a blinding headache such as I had never had before nor since. I plucked up all my courage to tell Tommy that he must take me home. Instantly irritated, because he was enjoying the social side of the game among old acquaintances, he frowned and said I should take some Aspirin. But then he looked at me! "Why is your eye so red?" I did not know, but my mother too looked at me, instantly alarmed. "Your whole eyeball is blood red. Tommy, you must take us home."

He did not defy this request from his mother-in-law. As we rattled our way back to Warri in our VW Beetle, I told him that Ben Lawson thought that I had something wrong with me, so that on arrival in Warri we looked for Ben. Not easy to find him on a Sunday, Tommy dropped Mum, Monu and me at our house and went in search of Ben, with whom he returned an hour later. Ben Lawson was not a doctor, but a sharply intelligent chemist whose diagnosis proved correct.

"I think Hilda has Filaria or Loaloa. It comes from a bite of a brown mosquito which lives in rubber trees. It bites and deposits its eggs under the skin of its victim. When the worms hatch from the eggs they course through the body of the patient causing swellings, and in this case a worm must have crossed Hilda's eyeball causing the redness and violent headache." During further discussions Ben advised that, if at all possible, I should be sent to England for treatment.

This would have been a monumental problem if it had not been for my mother. She offered there and then to pay for our passages and, within a week she had booked our cabins on another Elder Dempster ship, the M.V. "Calabar", so that I could visit the Tropical Diseases Hospital in London. The year was nineteen hundred and fifty-nine; and this unexpected trip was a godsend in more ways than one.

Although I was happy in Nigeria, Tommy's relatives were all very kind to me, and I had advanced from *"Ayami"* (my wife) to *"Egheyo"* (favourite wife in the family), Tommy had become more and more of an enigma to me! He was always angry, dissatisfied, critical, — so that my mother asked me, "Do you ever laugh?"

"No, — what about?" I answered.

It was true, all laughter had died out of me.

I constantly wondered if and where I was at fault.

He liked my mother and her presence among us. He used to tell people "I love my wife, why should I not love her mother? In England, this Mrs. Gerson baked me the first birthday cake I ever had in my life." He was glad too that she kept me company so that he could go out every night without compunction. Gone were the days when, in England we had sat in companionable silence, listening to the radio, or he studying and I sewing, — making occasional cups of tea for each other. Gone were our affectionate jokes such as, when I asked him "Do you love me?" He answered "I do not know love, I know only duty." I then changed my tune to "Do you duty me?" and he burst out laughing. "I don't know where you get these ideas from..."

Another time, in the kitchen, I crumpled up some papers, receipts I think. I lifted my hand to throw them into the open dustbin, when he shouted "Don't throw them away" but I had already launched them and said "sorry, I could not arrest their flight." He then shook his head. "Where do you get these expressions from?" — to which I had no answer. I did not think they were anything special. I just liked words — and I liked variety, in everything: food, clothes, books, furnishings, people,... except when it came to love. I had a solid one-track mind. Once my heart was anchored in one person, it could admit no other. Tommy showed me his love in practical and caring ways. Apart from bringing me food into the hospital — when I came home from it, he would have put fresh sheets and pillow-cases on my bed and flowers in a vase beside it. His pet-name for me was Pooppie. It stemmed from the French "poupee" (doll) and he called me his own version for the rest of my life.

The freedom I had granted him, he took discreetly. He had found a simple, "nice" girl who lived by herself in a small house a few miles away from us. He visited her twice a week on his bicycle in the night, when I had gone to sleep, but he would tell me beforehand "I am going out," and would be back in a couple of hours. The pain that this caused me, was assuaged by his repeated praise of me for being so tolerant and making no scenes. I always greeted him with a smile in the morning, so glad to have him back. I did love him so much that I could prove the depth of my feelings only by making this sacrifice. Besides, I thought that this association would end when we left for Nigeria, — though that was then still years away.

Tommy had also said on occasions that he could never live with a black woman again. He felt safe and at ease with me and knew he could believe every word I uttered. What had brought about this change in him now that we had reached his cherished goal of qualifying and returning to his country? Apart from his criticisms of conditions in Nigeria, — was I to blame? Did he feel responsibility for me too much of a burden? I was no financial drain on him, because I always made my own money to supply my personal needs, and my mother was a great help too.

So, was it perhaps too much trouble to consider me with every move he made? Was it too much trouble to consider me as a person? Had I been demoted to being "only" a woman after all, in his own setting, where women at that time, with few exceptions, were still second-class citizens? Was this where his conflicts lay?

On the other hand, he pointed out to me, full of pride one day, "Look! That lady is the first woman driver in Warri. She is Mrs. Obiogun, daughter of Canon Lucas in Lagos. She is a graduate." There were not many women graduates in Nigeria in those days, and certainly not many women drivers when there were few cars around anyway. If Tommy showed this much pride in the achievement of a woman, maybe I was wrong in my assumptions.

One of the many nights when Tommy had gone out, I was worried for him and went to his mother, Granny Obinu who, with his sister Mewe stayed in a room below our flat. I was crying, but the two women were comforting me. "Do not vex. You have a good husband. He gives you money for food, he does not beat you, he takes you out to parties. Do not worry. Do not complain." I could see that if those were their criteria, I really could not expect their understanding. Tommy went out socializing, he told me. He needed to get into circulation, and who better could make contacts for him than his cousin Chief Arthur Prest? But why did these introductions need all night? I wondered.

"Well, sometimes we get into a game of cards, and that goes on for a long time. Come and see for yourself." I did accompany him one night, leaving the sleeping Monu in the care of a nanny whom we had employed when the three teenagers left. I entered a cigarette-smoke filled room with him in Arthur's house. Some male companions sat around a table under a naked light bulb, playing cards. Much raucous laughter was going on, playing-cards were shuffled, beer and spirits poured down thirsty throats and various girls were hanging about in the background, ready to serve.

"Well chaps," Tommy said heartily, "Poopie wanted to see what we were up to, so here she is to satisfy her curiosity." The men could hardly be bothered to look up from the playing cards they held. They grunted some greetings, attempted to raise their bottoms from their chairs, but held fast to their cards, watching also the piles of money on the table.

I was nauseated. Was this where my husband wasted his time? A gamblers' den? I asked to be taken home again and Tommy said to them, "See you later, folks." On the way he told me that he needed to make some quicker money than the cases could bring, and when he had made enough, he would stop. I trotted out the time-worn arguments of "easy come, easy go," and that his professional skills would eventually earn him more money and a better reputation than gambling ever could. All fell on deaf ears. "I tell you, when I have got enough, I'll get out."

He continued, night after night, coming home in the mornings, bleary-eyed, bloodshot from hours in the smoky atmosphere. He was invariably late for court, forgot the dates of his cases, forgot appointments with clients, and, needless to say, his temper did not improve.

One day he gave me a packet of money, saying "Hold on to this. Lock it away. Do not give me any even if I ask you. I don't want to play Poker any more. My trouble is that I am too much of a gentleman. When I have made winnings I feel sorry for those who have lost, so instead of leaving the table I give them another chance and of course lose all that I have won. I am not going to do it any more. Hold on to that money." I was too glad to oblige and went to sleep. At three o'clock in the morning his Beetle roared into our street, Tommy stormed up the outside staircase, let himself into the house and shook me awake. "Give me that money. All of it. I must win back what I have lost." I could not believe what I was hearing. Was this the same man who, only hours ago had asked me to hold on to his money? I stalled, I argued, I reminded him of his former instructions, but he got more and more insistent. "It is my money, isn't it? Give it to me."

I was defeated, and in that moment I saw no future for us. How could I live with a gambler all my life? How could we ever make progress if all his earnings were to be lost on the card table? Not only that. What reputation would he acquire and pass on to our child? I had to leave this man. But how? How was I to cut him out of my heart and where would I start all over again?

At this very moment my filaria came to my aid. Here now, God was providing me with an exit, at least time to think things over and make up my mind. I did not voice any of my plans to Tommy, — so that when he took us to Lagos and we boarded the "Calabar" he had no idea that I might not come back.

In the Tropical Diseases Hospital at St. Pancras, London, I was admitted immediately. Yes, I did have filaria. The doctors were almost excited to confirm my condition, because they did not often see such a case. I was put on the drug Banocide, large doses at first diminishing daily during one week. The doctors told me to watch my skin and if I noticed a worm crawling under it, to ring the bell for the nurse immediately, so that she would call the doctors.

I did observe a thin worm under the skin of my upper arm. I stared at it in fascination. To be sure that I was not imagining things, I marked both ends of it with biro and rang the bell. Sure enough, it did wriggle past the ink marks, but before anybody answered my call, it disappeared out of sight, into some deeper lying tissues, presumably. The doctors were disappointed, but after one week, a bloodtest showed that I was clear of the infestation, and all symptoms had disappeared. No more pain, no more swellings. I was as good as new.

A friend in Switzerland had heard of my health problem and now invited Monu and me to stay with her and her parents in their big house in Geneva to recuperate. My mother wanted to go back to the USA to see my brother anyway, so this was another godsend solution. I would have time to think and distance myself from the poker problem. In the meantime I made myself useful, making dresses for our friend and her mother, despite their protests. I had been ill, I should rest, just lie in the garden and do nothing. Me? Do nothing? That would only make me ill again. I set to work, enjoying the making of lovely fluffy creations for our lean-looking friend. Both she and her mother were teachers and wore rather sober clothes. It thrilled me to glamourise them a little.

I also wrote a talk for Woman's Hour on BBC. The producer accepted it and on my return to London later I read it on the air, earning the princely sum of eight guineas. The subject was a description of my arrival in Nigeria with my husband. While I was writing it I became so homesick for the life I had left behind that I got more than ever confused, wondering how I could have the strength to give it all up.

Just then a letter came from Tommy saying, nay, swearing, that he had given up poker, and when was I coming home? The Good Lord had intervened again just at the right time. I told my hosts with whom I had stayed two months, that it was time for me to return to Nigeria. Monu, four years old, had had a lovely time playing with the water hose in the big garden, going to the zoo several times with our friend, being taken to the big Lake of Geneva (Lac Leman) to see the mighty fountain that sprang from the edge of it so high that it could be seen from miles away. We also went on a boat trip on the lake which started from the Swiss side and crossed over to the French side which looked very different indeed. We had also been taken to see the Chateaul de Chillon, the old stone castle on another edge of the lake. Inside the dank and dim castle the greatest attraction was the toilet. It was a big hole in a stone seat, from where the excreta would plop straight into the lake below. We could even see the lake water rippling at the bottom of the shaft that led down from the toilet seat.

Monu had often played on the swings in a playground near our friend's house. Children had always surrounded him, curious about his foreign appearance, wanting to touch his skin and his hair. "Mummy, what does teetapell mean?" he asked me, and I realized that he must have been asked dozens of times "Comment tu t'appelles?" (What is your name?)

Monu left Geneva with great regret. He had also enjoyed the sweet plums from our friend's garden and the ripe red cherries which he could hang over his ears like earrings, but I lured him away with the promise of yet another voyage and a swim in the ship's swimming pool, whose water heated by the sun was as hot as a hot bath — but it was wet and it buoyed you up. I was very grateful to our friends who had given me this respite, although I had not told them of what went on in my mind.

On the return voyage we stopped at Madeira of the Canary Islands, where the ship stopped but did not anchor, so that small boats came up alongside it offering us passengers local handicrafts and sweet foods and wine. I could of course not resist the handicrafts, especially the baskets whose cloth sides were embroidered with bright colourful wool flowers. I bought several, which had to be hauled up the ship side on a rope and hook. I am not ashamed to say that I copied this type of basket for many years later in Nigeria, replacing the woollen flowers with bright, locally woven cloth.

After Madeira, I became impatient to meet Tommy and time seemed to drag. Eventually Lagos came into sight, and yes, there he was waving joyfully his white Panama hat in greeting. After hugging us his first words were, "No more poker for me. Nope. I've been so stupid, wasting good money." Happy and hopeful, I still adopted a "Wait and see" stance, but hoped that I would never have to contemplate such a drastic decision again.

Bearing in mind the narrow rough roads from Lagos to Warri plus waiting time for the ferry at Sapele, one had to allow at least ten hours for the trip, driving in a Beetle.

This time Tommy decided we would stay overnight at Ibadan with his friend Omot. The latter was very pleased to see us, and we were happy to meet his wife and baby son. We left again in the early morning after a good breakfast, and the rest of the trip was certainly much easier than it would have been, had we done it in one stretch.

I bubbled as we drove into dear familiar Warri, even though I wondered what was so strange about the few beautiful storey buildings that were pointed out to me, every time we passed them. Suddenly I knew. They had no gardens! They were built straight on to the edge of the road. No front gardens, no garden gate, no hedge, no flowers. Why had it taken me so long to realize this?

When I mentioned it now to Tommy, he said: "Our people grow food — yams, cassava. You can't eat flowers." Too true, but now, fifty years later, major cities in Nigeria have many beautiful houses with well tended gardens, hedges, lawns, flowering shrubs and fabulous black and gold iron gates. The need for security has been turned into an art form. Tommy himself was to become a devoted gardener, but now, on return from Lagos/Ibadan, I was quite happy to enter our cemented backyard again. At the approach of our noisy Beetle, Granny Obinu, sister Mewe and her daughter Tunde ran out of their downstairs room and gave us a joyful welcome. The gentle Tunde with her beautiful smile, had baby daughter Alero tied on her back, while sister Mewe danced around with baby son Richard who could hardly walk yet.

It was a happy homecoming and it was so nice to have everybody bustling around, helpful hands emptying the car, carrying up luggage and foodstuffs we had bought on the way like yams and pineapples, pawpaws and plantains. Monu felt instantly at home again when he saw Eda, his nanny who had been with us since before my mother came.

I had hinted before that the teenagers had left. They had been with us about eighteen months and Freedom left after his solitary confinement, for which I could hardly blame him. He wrote to his mother and asked her to take him away. Then Ching-Ching too, apparently did not want to stay without Freedom. And Lily too left, all of them giving me excuses that I did not understand but saying that they wanted to go back to school. Later, much later, infact, I am still hearing stories of it now that they are all grown up. Much later I heard that Freedom continued his education in Hussey College where he was the best in the school although his father did not pay his fees. But apparently, the rest of the family clubbed together in order to keep him there and give him a good education.

The children had been promised by their father that they would be sent to England to be educated. As time went on however, they saw that they were little more than househelps. Apart from Freedom who went to school, the girls really made no progress other than learning English from me. I had not been aware of this promise, or I would have understood their disappointment and their sudden departure.

At that time we employed a young girl called Victoria whom Monu called 'Toya' and a houseboy called Ufot. Those who know Nigeria would understand that the name comes from the Calabar region. Victoria was untrained but a bright girl and nice with Monu but things kept missing. One day I was looking for Monu's comb and asked, "Victoria, where is Monu's comb?"

"I have not seen it," she replied.

"Then look for it," I said

After a while I asked her, "Where is Monu's comb?"

She said, "I am finding it."

"Ah, good you have found it", said I.

"No Madam, I didn't see it."

It was then that I learnt that to find something means to look for it, to this day. Another time, the kitchen knife was missing. Again Victoria was asked. It was a slim knife with a brown handle. Had she seen the knife and she said no she had not. But eventually she said, "Oh Madam I don see am. Look now." And there it stuck in the drain of the kitchen sink with the pointed side up. I dare say it had been concealed there in order to be appropriated afterwards. However, Toya and Monu got on well together.

I got into a problem with Tommy over Ufot. He was a nice and very clean boy who swept and dusted, scrubbed and polished the house better than the children had done before. So when I saw him eating his lunch with his fingers I thought he could improve his habits and gave him a spoon. Then my husband turned upon me and said, "You see, this is where you spoil these people. They are not used to eating with spoons. Leave them as they are. And when you give them instructions, don't say 'please', or 'If you don't mind', or 'Can you help me to carry this or that?'. Just order them. Give them short commands, otherwise you confuse them."

This was very hard for me. I had the attitude "There but for the grace of God go I". I felt obliged to help anybody in whatever small way I could, to climb up the ladder of his life. I felt that every small progress could lead to another progress and so on until the person had some self-worth, especially when such a person deserved encouragement. When one is brought up to be polite and caring to people, it is difficult to stop and suddenly change one's tune, selecting who deserves consideration and who does not.

In Khalil Road, we lived in one of a row of seven houses, which in England would be called semi-detached. Our backyards all ran into each other, but each house had its own staircase climbing up on its outside. In the yard adjoining ours there lived a very nice Itsekiri woman, the sister of Lawyer Kubeinje. She had a little trade going making puff-puffs every morning. They were little balls like doughnuts mixed from a yeast dough which was prepared with flour, palmwine and a little sugar. It was the fermented palmwine that caused the dough to rise. When it had risen, Eda, the name of the lady, used to pick handfuls, roll them into balls and fry them in hot oil, where they "puffed" up until they were golden brown.

We were on good terms with Eda who liked Monu and who also had living with her a nephew of approximately Monu's age, so that the two sometimes played together. Tommy now had the bright idea that Eda would be a much more suitable person to look after Monu than the young Victoria. He reckoned that her puff-puff trade could not bring her as much money in a month as a regular salary would do. Eda agreed to that suggestion and became a member of our household. She was a real lady, quiet and dignified, maybe forty years of age, unmarried, but always discreetly and elegantly dressed in her native clothes when she went to the Baptist Church on Sundays. She was gentle and helped wherever she could, even in the ice cream business.

Now I was back from overseas, and it did not take me long to slide back into the old groove. I enjoyed all the activities I had had before, and of course we went to thank Ben Lawson for providing the answer to my health problem. He also helped me with another matter. As I had mentioned before, Tommy did not want me to go to the government hospital for treatment because a relation of his was treating me free of charge, and he thought this relation would be offended if I sought another opinion. Consequently, when my regular attacks of malaria started up again I became very weak, so weak that again it was Ben Lawson who insisted that I should go for a blood test. I was afraid. I could not do this secretly, and Tommy would not agree to my going to the hospital. So Ben brought blood testing equipment to our house while Tommy was in court. He pricked my finger and dropped the blood onto a blotting paper where he could judge the colour of the blood against a chart he had brought with him. Even I was surprised that my blood was not red. It was orange colour.

"You see," said Ben, "You are very anaemic. No wonder you black out at times and you feel so weak. You must go to see the Scottish doctor at the hospital." With this evidence now on the blotting paper, he confronted Tommy and said: "If you do not want your wife to die you had better allow her to attend the hospital."

On my visit there I met the Scottish doctor who was well and truly drunk. He stood over me, swaying on his feet and with his slurred speech and Scottish accent, asked me what was the matter. My history of recurring malaria came out. He asked what was I given for the malaria and I told him it was paludrine prophylactic and paludrine cure. "Rubbish," he said. "Go on to nivaquine." He then prescribed the way in which I should take a course of nivaquine, and I never needed to go back to him again. The nivaquine did the trick. I was saved by the bell so to say. I had lost a terrible amount of weight. My neck stood like a lamp post under my head and all my dresses were hanging on me, but now I recovered very quickly because Ben also prescribed a blood tonic. Even now after fifty years I feel I have much to thank him for.

I had described before that all our houses in the street had cemented backyards. This was a sensible precaution against snakes. Also, the heavy rains in Warri would have made it impossible to cross the yard in anything other than gum boots. But beyond the cement there was land, free land, and as all Nigerians at that time were farmers at heart, Granny Obinu could not resist the temptation of planting something beyond the border of the cement, whether it was tomatoes or okro or cassava I cannot now remember. What I do remember is that one day she came running out of her plot of bush holding her head and shouting what I could not understand. The neighbours immediately rallied round, examined her head and poured palm oil onto it. Palm oil is the rich orange golden oil culled from the palm fruits that grow in heavy clusters at the top of a fruit-bearing palm. This oil is used for cooking in every dish and is rich in vitamins and no doubt responsible for the beautiful, smooth and gleaming skin of most Nigerians.

This time I wanted to know what had happened to Granny Obinu. It seemed that she had disturbed a colony of bees in the plot behind our house and the bees had attacked her. Her head was full of stings they left behind, and now that the palm oil had been dabbed on her head they were too slippery to be pulled out. The neighbours came to me to ask if I could do anything. I sat the poor granny down and surveyed the damage which was horrifying. In fact, I do not think any white person could have survived such a vicious attack. Her head was like a pin cushion even her ears, her neck, all full of the bees' barbs. All I could think of was a pair of tweezers with which to pull out the barbs one by one. The poor Granny Obinu was magnificently patient. She made no fuss at all, she just sat quietly as I pulled out sting after sting from her short curly hair, from her ears and back of the neck. People said it was my first heroic act in the family but I think it was the granny who was the heroine in her stoic acceptance of such misfortune.

Granny Obinu not only planted things behind the cemented yard, she also reared chickens. She was opposed to the idea of my wanting fresh eggs. "Oh no, no, no. Each egg would produce a chicken and a chicken would be food for the table."

So, it was very difficult in those days to get fresh eggs for breakfast or for cooking. Everybody thought the same as Granny Obinu. The eggs were future chickens and should not be eaten. Bread was also a novelty in those days. When we had first arrived in Warri we were told excitedly "Oh there's one man making bread now. He is becoming very rich."

The bread was too soft for my liking and too sweet. It had no substance. People used to eat practically one loaf in order to feel that they had something in their stomach. So I tried making my own bread, but I was not used to it and it came out hard and often too flat to make any good slices for sandwiches. Well, somehow we managed. Even in Kingsway Sapele, there was no better bread. It seemed that most Europeans were making their own.

Tommy seemed very pleased to have us back, but after a while he fell back into his mood swings which I could not explain. At times life was quite lonely for me because I had no one to talk to who would be on my own wave length. There was one other girl married to a Nigerian professional but she seemed reluctant to entertain any social contact with me. I met her at the club and introduced myself. She was very young, a simple Englishgirl with four children. I had only my one little boy and she did not bring her children to the club. She spent her time at the bar sitting among the men. Later, when television was created in Ibadan her husband told her he would send her to England for training so that she could become a television star. She was a very pretty girl and jumped at the idea.

While arrangements were being made for this event her little girl of two, a pretty child with blonde curls and blue eyes fell ill, but her mother-in-law, who lived with the couple, did not allow the mother to take the child to the hospital. She swore by native medicine, but the child got no better. In despair, the young mother finally borrowed a bicycle, tied the child on her back and rode the twenty miles it took to reach the American Baptist Hospital in Eku. There the child got adequate treatment and improved. When arrangements had been completed that the young woman should go to England for the promised training, she left her children behind in the knowledge that she would soon return to Nigeria but she never came back. The young woman's three sons survived but her blue-eyed baby girl died in her absence.

We had the luck of having new neighbours in the street who were compatible with our family. Mrs Barbara Nnoka and her twin children Cathy and Barrett became close friends, the mother with me and my mother and the children with Monu. Barbara taught in Urhobo College, but being American she had to train herself to correct her American accent so that the students would understand her better. Her greatest effort was in calling water instead of *'wora'*. She was a highly intelligent person, and a Quaker, who was married to a nephew of Zik. Cathy and Barrett were a year younger than Monu but since they lived in the row of houses in Khalil Road it was not dangerous for Monu to go by himself to visit them, and he was happy that he had now found compatible playmates.

It was 1960 and Monu had reached the age of five when he should be going to school. Schooling was a bit of a problem in Warri, and we had decided to write for a parents-teacher course of teaching him ourselves. My mother had come back and here again she was tremendously helpful in taking over the lessons for Monu. She had been a trained teacher at the age of sixteen because she had been very brilliant at school and had jumped a class which made her qualified for teaching at such a very young age. She loved the profession. She was a born pedagogue who had handled us children and other children with remarkable insight. Unhappily for her, her mother, my grandmother, did not allow her to carry out her profession. My grandmother had a fashion business and my mother was so practical and intelligent that she said she needed her in the business. Her other daughter, my mother's sister, was a romantic person who lived in the novels she read so avidly. My poor mother had always regretted this intervention in her professional life, but now she was happy to teach Monu who responded very well to her.

On Tommy's scene, things were happening. He had been persuaded that it was necessary to own a house in his home town. For the time being he did not have the means to build one but when our Lebanese friend Mr. Khalil offered a small house for four thousand pounds he thought it might be a good idea. Once again my mother was consulted but when she saw the house she vetoed it immediately. She offered Tommy the four thousand pounds if he was bent on buying it so that we would have a refuge of our own, but she did not think the house was a good bargain. When Tommy now asked if he might use the money to buy a Mercedez Benz instead, she readily agreed. At the same time Tommy was being persuaded to come on the Bench as a magistrate. He was told "we need people like you, people who are honest and straight forward, people who are not afraid to pronounce unpopular judgements". Flattered, he thought about it and seemed to like the idea of rising to a more prominent position, although he was doing quite well in private practice.

I too had taken up an office job for a firm of German engineers who had come to live in our road. Their office was at the John Holts beach area, and they offered to take me there by car and bring me back if I would please, please do their German correspondence for them. I took up the challenge although everything within me rebelled against using the German language and being employed by Germans. I need not have worried. The job was easy. The translations were easy for me to do. The money was useful, while Eda continued with the ice cream business when Monu was occupied by my mother. I say I need not have worried because the job did not last long. Tommy had made up his mind to take up the offer of a seat on the Bench.

Within this same momentous year of 1960, I wrote in September to my brother the following:

> The rain is drumming on the roof and I can hardly hear myself think. After the first tap-tap-tap of the advance drops

it bursts upon the zinc like a sack of rice being emptied and now continues to pour in a steady stream. It has been like this for a whole month. No wonder then, that the native Ruler of Lagos, the Oba of Lagos, collected £1000 for the rain doctors to stop the rain for Independence Day, and to appease the gods of thunder and lightning.

With only four days to go before the great day, the atmosphere is charged with anticipation, much as though there were only four shopping-days left before Christmas. New clothes, gay decorations, food-and-drinks-stocks, — no, drinks and foodstocks, dances, processions — and Independence bonus. Those are the things filling everyone's mind, for the real meaning of Independence escapes all but the very few.

Obinu, Tommy's mother, came to ask him for new clothes. "What for?" he asked. "For Independa", she said. And when he asked her, "What does Independence mean? What is it?" she looked very serious for a moment, frowning like a schoolgirl trying to think. "I don't know", she said at last and shook her head. But when he held out a pound note to her saying, "but you know what this is?" she took it with a broad smile, danced a few little steps with pleasure and hurried off to put it to good use.

Her daughter Mewe, Tommy's elder sister, has some views on Independence. "If it doesn't work, we'll call the white man back", and with that she voices a thought that prevails throughout the country. It is as if a child leaves home thinking that if he couldn't make his way in the world, he could always come back to mother.

So the joyful preparations continue, and business is booming. The uproar about the National Anthem has died down. Both the lyrics and the tune, were created by foreigners, chosen during an open contest by a Nigerian committee, and for weeks the newspapers burned with editorials and angry readers' letters on the issue. Since then, the catchy tune of the anthem has come over the radio to us every morning and night at news time, and is now hummed and whistled everywhere.

"I'll teach you the words", I had said to Eda, the nice woman who helps me with my ice cream business. "I know them already," she said and began to sing them in Itsekiri. The enterprising Baptist pastor had translated the anthem into the vernacular of his flock and had practiced it with them, until they were tune and word perfect.

The simple green-and-white flag has been most exploited by business men. Sets of 3 flags, each representing a region, together they make one Nigeria. The market abounds with monstrosities of all kinds in the national colours. Green and white caps, green and white plastic handbags, shoes, balloons and buntings, plates, tablecloths, enamel cups, badges, headties and dress materials. In Lagos, the federal capital, 42 green and white Chevrolet saloons and a fleet of Volkswagen buses have been bought by the government to convey foreign visitors. All these carry IND licence plates, as they zoom under the heavy green garlands that deck the road from the airport to the city.

The celebrations will take three days, Saturday, Sunday and Monday, and perhaps the worst "privilege" the government could have meted out to its employees is the advance of one month's wages, repayable over six months. It is poor moral teaching by the government that encourages a large percentage of the nation to start off with debts life in their young nation.

But who cares? Who stops to think when three glorious days of feasting and merry-making beckon?

We have received invitation (and Car Park Ticket) for the Reception of Princess Alexandra when she visits Benin (73 miles from here and our nearest airport.) We have no desire to attend, but Monu may win the battle. Ever since seeing Princess Margaret's wedding film he has been longing to see a real princess, and vainly we tell him that this one will not be wearing a crown, and will look no different from other welldressed ladies.

To our many friends and family, who with an anxious eye on the Congo, have asked us, "how will Independence affect you?" We can say that it will make very little difference to anyone. For some time now, Nigeria has had her own men as prime ministers, ministers, Chief Justices, and then at the helm of affairs in every conceivable department. The battle cry for self-government and freedom really no longer excites. We expect there to be a little less efficiency and a little more corruption, but people will take these in their stride as countless other young nations do, until slowly, slowly – or softly, softly, as we say here – each generation will be a little more educated than the last, and come to realize their civic responsibilities. There are the exceptions amongst the Nigerians, who have a conscience, a sense of duty and some self-discipline, so that there is hope that their numbers will increase and multiply as time goes on. The Europeans are much to blame for showing an example of good living and much leisure, which is of course misunderstood by the simple Nigerian folk who do not know that tropical climates compel white men to leisure, and who do not understand how much valuable, concentrated and disciplined work can be done during short hours, so that the leisure is well earned.

Tommy's first posting was to Akure in the Western region of Nigeria. There was now the hustle and bustle of packing up our home and transporting everything to Akure. The main problem was the ice cream machine. What was I to do with this giant thing which had to be emptied of the brine, transported to Magistrate quarters and filled again? We did not even know whether there was electricity in Akure and later found that there was none. Painful as it was I decided to sell the machine and found a buyer in our enterprising cousin Mrs. Agnes Esiri.

She was a devout Catholic. She had been brought up by the nuns and had all sorts of skills uncommon among Nigerian girls. She could sew, she could bake, she ran a very good and hygienic home. Not only that she learnt these in the Mission, she was an excellent trader. It was she who imported into Nigeria from Switzerland pure silk headties made by a company called Hayes. It seemed that Mr. Hayes, a big burly Swiss, had lived in Nigeria a long time, always accompanied by his huge Alsatian dog.

At the time most silk headties were artificial silk i.e. they were made of shiny rayon which came undone and had to be tied over and over again because the headties were so slippery. Mrs. Esiri discussed the matter with Mr. Hayes and asked if they could not be made of better material. He then suggested the pure silk headties which became all the rage in Nigeria and must have brought a handsome profit to Mr. Hayes and Mrs. Esiri. This enterprising and very kind cousin, who had often brought me presents of chocolate and other special little things which she knew Europeans enjoyed, was now willing to buy my ice cream machine and all its accessories. The business thrived and as far as I know continued even up to this day although our Aggie died in nineteen hundred and eighty.

I must here mention that it was she who made me buy coral beads. These are the most cherished traditional jewellery of the Itsekiri tribe. It must have been the Portuguese who brought them into the country and who landed on the coast of Warri in the sixteenth century. There is no self-respecting Itsekiri woman or man who has not got coral beads in his possession. They are usually of a light pink whereas we, Caucasians preferred the oxblood darker red. The size of these coral beads is nothing like you have ever seen in Europe. They are huge, almost like cotton reels and heavy. So, according to the wealth of the person he or she will sport two bracelets of huge coral beads and a necklace of course and the women might have three or four rows of coral beads tied on their hips under the cover cloth to make the hips look very full. They jingle when the woman walks, a most attractive feature.

In my own case, Cousin Aggie persuaded me that every woman must invest her surplus earnings in coral beads and gold so that she will never be without means should anything go wrong with her marriage. She introduced to me a goldsmith by name of Ubredi and said he was the only one who made twenty-two carat gold. I regretted at the time that I was so much under her maternal influence, well-meant though it was, that I did buy a set of gold and I did buy these big coral beads. It was a great chunk out of my earnings but in later years I did not regret owning heirlooms. As it was, now Cousin Aggie was happy to take over the ice cream machine from me, and very soon we were on our way to Akure with mother and Eda in tow.

I was pleasantly surprised by the lush green surroundings of our house at Akure. It was a roomy bungalow and Tommy soon put up gas lights and kerosine lamps to make up for the lack of electricity. Every evening at about six o'clock it was his job to clean and light the gas lamps, and only he knew how to handle them. I got used to their hissing sound, and was altogether enchanted with our new location.

We paid a courtesy call on the Deji of Akure as soon as we were settled. He was most welcoming and introduced all his wives to us. If ever I needed any help, he said, one of his wives would certainly be glad to assist me. We also met another European couple who worked in the Forestry Department. They were called Mr. and Mrs. Readhead. Joyce, the wife was a scientist but she was unemployed at the moment and turned all her experience of the natural world to teaching her children. She gladly accepted Monu as one of them even though he was about a year younger than her youngest boy.

Tommy covered Okitipupa and Ondo from his magistrate seat at Akure and was kept pretty busy. There was a little problem of finding enough separate bedrooms in the house so that my mother and I shared one, another smaller one was for Eda and Monu while Tommy slept in the sitting room on a camp bed. It was his own choice, because he often got up in the night to read and study his cases or to fiddle about with the radio. One morning as I was in the garden picking grape fruits from the tree, another European neighbour came to say hello. I was wearing a bright blue and turquoise garment that my mother had brought me from Hawaii. It was called a Mumu, and its loose flowing style was very comfortable in the heat.

The neighbour introduced herself and said: "Ah, I see. We are in the same boat. I am pregnant too." I laughed and said "Congratulations, but I am not pregnant, I am just comfortable in this voluminous gown." I did not know then that the neighbour's predictions had come true. Months later I began to feel sick, very sick, in the mornings. It was the beginning of nineteen sixty-one and I realised that I had conceived a baby on the camp bed.

This happy knowledge was disturbed by an incident which I can never get out of my mind again. Tommy asked our little Monu then six years old, whether he had cleaned the bath after he had been in it. Monu said "yes". Tommy went to inspect and saw that he had cleaned the bottom of the bath but not the rim. He called him out and gave him six vicious strokes of the cane for not cleaning the bath properly. I did not know what to do with myself, I was enraged. Of course, I tried to stop him when I heard the first screams but the same rule applied: "If you try to stop me I'll cane the harder."

After this incident I felt I had lost a large chip of my love and respect for my husband. It was so unfair. The child had never been shown how to clean a bath with Vim and the punishment was so unexpected; it was undeserved when the child had not been warned before. At that moment I hated my husband. He had been unjust.

He then accepted an invitation to spend a holiday in Switzerland with a friend of ours. During his absence of three weeks my hurt gradually lessened, but I was never the same again. I cannot bear injustice, and I had no idea what provoked such sudden anger in Tommy that he had to let it out on the child. Monu was such an amenable boy. He was high spirited, yes and sometimes disobedient, but on the whole, one could talk to him, one could reason with him, and he would not repeat an offence that had upset me. He was a loving child.

When Tommy returned from Switzerland we were posted to Ogwashi-Uku, and once again pulled up sticks and moved to another location. Ogwashi-Uku was a small town this side of the River Niger, and our accommodation left much to be desired. The magistrate's house was a primitive low bungalow with doorways so low that when Tommy entered the kitchen he bumped his forehead so hard that his cigarette was flung out of his mouth. The mattresses were rat-eaten and rotten and the house had practically no ventilation. He cabled Ibadan, then the administrative seat of the Western Region, to say that he could not possibly live in such accommodation they had given him. The positive reply came by telegram. "Move into V.I.P. guest house." This was a good move indeed. The guest house was spacious and clean, even if the bath water which was pumped up by hand every morning was dark brown, and we had to wait an hour before it settled and we could use the top half to wash or to bath in. Other than that there was a beautiful garden and we enjoyed this location once again. Tommy though, did not enjoy his magistrate's office. It was a hovel of a place with a kitchen table not big enough to hold his record books and hardly any chair to sit on. He was disgusted and irate. He telegraphed Ibadan saying "Court accommodation unsuitable for magistrate. I will not sit until better facilities are provided. Ogbe."

Ibadan posthaste sent an emissary to see for himself and to make the necessary improvements, before Tommy would sit. While the improvements were being made, he was, so to say, on strike, despite the rule that judicial officers never went on strike.

Not much later another proposal came his way. His charming cousin Chief Michael Okorodudu, one time Agent-General for the Western Region of Nigeria, to London, informed him that Shell BP were looking for a Nigerian executive in their legal department. He urged Tommy to apply. By this time we had come to the realisation that he could not really afford to be a magistrate. The salary of eight hundred pounds a year was just too small to keep our family and he had used up practically all his savings. So the proposition came at the right time.

Also, I was in my ninth month of pregnancy. Our former plan that I should have ante-natal care in Eku Baptist Hospital, hundreds of miles away from where we were now, was not practicable. Ogwashi-Uku Catholic Mission Hospital it had to be. The car trip there was pure agony. I was very heavy, and even though I held my "bump" with both hands and Tommy drove slowly and carefully, the road was rutted and the peaks and valleys on it made it feel like a roller-coaster ride. It seemed never ending.

On arrival we found sympathetic reverend sisters welcoming us. There was an Italian doctor on seat. He had living with him his youthful though white-haired aunt from Holland. Both seemed pleased to see new faces and served us tea and coffee after I had been examined and pronounced "all correct".

Tommy drove to Lagos in his brand new black Mercedes to see the Managing Director of Shell B.P., Mr. Stanley Grey, who in his affable manner, had a talk with Tommy, then sent him down to Port Harcourt to be interviewed by the personnel manager, because the applicant was to be employed at Port Harcourt.

The manager's first question, "Why do you want to work for Shell B.P.?" Tommy rebutted with "Who said I want to work for Shell B.P.? I only came to find out what you have to offer. Needless to say, the manager reported to Lagos, "Ogbe is unsuitable for the job. Too strict, too disciplinarian. He would not fit in." Mr. Gray held fast to the first impressions he had had of Tommy. He had assessed his potential correctly, and instructed Port Harcourt "Give him a chance."

Tommy seemed to relish his eccentricities. As far back as his secondary school years in King's College, he quoted gleefully: "Ah bad-o, abadere, abadidi, abaditum", so conjugating an imaginatory Latin verb, the "ah bad-o" meaning he was a bad boy. (Not serious! So, maybe just contrary.)

When I first knew him, he gave himself a degree: T.A. Ogbe N.D. (No Duplicate). In later years, when young women continuously robbed him, lied and cheated, he became T.A. OGBE F.O.O.L. (his own words).

He made a sport of being contrary. In the Customs in Port Harcourt, where he worked with T.O.S. Benson and late Chucks Adophy, he annoyed his superior by loudly marching across the wooden floorboards with metal corners attached to the heels of his shoes to preserve them. When he was upbraided for the noise he was making he said "sorry, sir," and stomped all the harder after that.

Now, on the First of November Nineteen hundred and sixty-one, Tommy turned up in the Legal Department of Shell B.P. in his customary three-piece suit, collar and tie plus monocle (for his one good eye.) The open-neck-shirted staff were appalled at such stuffiness, but he over-rode their reservations with his usual breezy manner, with his frankness, not to say charm.

Eager to learn as much as he could (and as fast) he understudied a Mr. Hernandez, a West Indian lawyer, and got on splendidly with him. To his surprise, within days of his arrival in the department, all the staff turned up in collar and tie. "Good man, good man," he would say, slapping somebody on the back.

"We must have discipline in this country. We must have standards. We have no standards. To take the time and patience to put on collar and tie in the morning needs discipline. We must have discipline." One of his many lectures. The other, reserved for a lower cadre of employee, his own or other people's was "Experience is something you gather during your life. You cannot buy it. You cannot buy experience at Chellaram's." Then followed examples of his experiences in England: as a lodger, at the hands of colour bar, as a student, during the war, at the Inns of Court... "You cannot buy experience."

He loved to shock his audience with: "I never sin" (which statement I thought was a sin in itself), "I am always right", "Self first", "I never put up with any inconvenience, unless I must", and "I don't care what people know about me, think of me, say about me". However critical his listeners might have been of him, many, I dare say, secretly envied him for his brazenness and his selfish courage. But it was not easy to live with.

However, Shell BP profited from his unconventional ways. When Tommy retired after ten years with the company, the Managing Director in 1971 gave him a farewell banquet fit for a king. It was attended by the State Governor and by dignitaries from all walks of life. It also happened to be my fiftieth birthday, and, apart from the giant birthday cake I was presented with, I could have wished for no greater gift than to hear the Managing Director's (Mr. Baxendell's) speech during which he said, and I quote:

"Tommy has worked tirelessly to smoothe over difficulties for the company in his own Tommyesque way,... which he would not recommend to anybody else. Tommy has bulldozed over all obstacles with his "Super-super-king-size personality."

As the company was closing down its office in Benin City, it was giving to Hilda and Tommy the bungalow in which the representative had resided.

"For," said Mr. Baxendell, "we have had two for the price of one. Hilda has been an untiring hostess to all our staff who passed through their home, and she has opened our eyes with her enthusiasm for Nigerian crafts and culture. We want to make sure that neither she nor Tommy strays far away from us."

I have now given you the beginning and the end of ten years of Tommy's work with Shell B.P. These were ten magic years socially. The Shell B.P. "Camp" as it was called, stretched for miles alongside the road from Aba to Port Harcourt. Fenced all round with neatly clipped Ixoria hedges, one drove through the gateway into what might be compared to an affluent European suburb. Tarred, smooth roads, kerbs, side walks, street-lighting. Floodlit tennis courts, giant club house with elevated stage, giant swimming pool and spotless changing cabins. Outside the camp there was Go-Kart racing and yachting (sailing) on Sundays.

If an unauthorised visitor came to the gate, the gateman would use the internal telephone for which he had a camp directory, and ring up the person whom the visitor wanted to see. If the householder expected the visitor, he/she would instruct the gateman to direct him to their address. No mean feat, as the whole camp was intersected with a network of streets (all named after the various towns in which Shell Oil wells were located). Within those streets hundreds of houses were placed at angles to each other, not in boring rows, each with its own well-manicured garden surrounding it.

We were assigned a modern bungalow. It was built in the shape of the letter H. The dining/sitting room and the kitchen made one leg of the letter, the bedrooms and bathrooms made the other. The corridor connected the two of them, just like the crossbar of the letter H.

I was busy making curtains. The house was fully furnished and had air conditioning in every room. Such luxury as I had not dreamt of. The only thing we had to provide were the soft furnishings, because the company knew that every housewife had her own taste. I chose bright blue and yellow for the curtains in the sitting room, and despite my big tummy I was still sitting at the sewing machine day after day.

One day Tommy said "come and let me show you the garden. You have been in the house all the time." So I followed him out onto the lawn which surrounded the house. I enjoyed seeing it well trimmed and loved the flowering hedges all around it. As we walked across the lawn, I did not see a small gutter that the rain had made under the grass. My foot caught in it and my ankle twisted sharply. I fell on all fours. Heavy as I was, I stayed on my hands and knees unable to get up. Tommy looked at me crossly. "Get up", he said. "Help me" I whimpered. He then gave me his hand and pulled me up to a standing position, but I was quite unable to put my foot down. It was so painful. I held his shoulder and limped into the house. Straight onto my bed.

Eda and Monu came running to see what was the matter with me. I comforted them, saying I had sprained my ankle, and it was very painful, but it would be better by tomorrow. It had been the evening hour anyway, so Monu had to be put to bed soon. Eda saw to that and afterwards brought me some supper. After Tommy had eaten he said he was going out. Before he left he reminded me of the telephone number of the Shell Clinic where I was going to have my baby and said "I won't be long, Pooppie."

"Can't you stay?" I asked weakly. He looked at me and frowned as if to say "What does this woman want now?" "I won't be long," he repeated.

Monu and Eda slept in a different bedroom from mine with a bathroom in between and there was no communication with me once they had gone to bed. The foot was swollen, hot and painful, so that I began to fear that I might have broken a bone. The evening dragged. I was very tired. I managed to snatch some sleep here and there, until I had to go to the bathroom. How to get there on one foot I wondered. I finally managed to use my bedside table as a support, lifting after every step on the good foot, good foot forward, lift the table, put it down, and make one step. This way I reached the bathroom. When I felt that my waters had broken, I was alarmed. I maneuvered myself back to bed. I reached for the clock, it was 1 a.m. I began to panic, reaching for the telephone and searching for the number of the clinic.

Just then Tommy came back. The relief was indescribable. God was good to me, and to him. How would he have felt, if I had been taken to the clinic while he was out enjoying himself? Now he could take charge, he rang the hospital, the ambulance arrived within minutes, and in a further few minutes I arrived at the clinic with my bag ready packed.

Our lovely baby girl was born at 8.30 in the morning. It was a new experience for me to deliver her naturally because Monu had been a forceps birth after three days of labour. Under anesthesia I did not know when he was born. Now this time I saw this pink baby girl with masses of black hair lying on the table before me, and I thrilled to take her in my arms. We had been with Shell BP only two weeks. Her birth was a beautiful start for me to our ten years with them.

Almost from the word go Tommy became a star, a controversial star maybe, but he made his mark wherever he went. He underwent a series of induction courses within the company, in order to understand fully the workings of the oil production. He needed this information from A to Z, i.e. from management, personnel, workforce, operations, and of course, all the legal aspects of the workings of the company. He was the legal man but he also became their prime public relations officer. Because he was so convinced of the quality of the company of Shell BP he was able to negotiate on their behalf with complete conviction and enthusiasm.

It was now 1961. We had been in Nigeria four years, and this was the first time I saw Tommy happy. At last he was in a disciplined environment. Everybody knew his job. Everybody was anxious to keep it and worked well. People arrived on time at the office on the dot of 8 a.m. and closed for lunch at the dot of 12 noon until 1 o'clock when they resumed, to work again until 4 p.m. Everything functioned. The electricity, the telephone, the plumbing. The roads were swept regularly, and the tennis courts and swimming pool were maintained in pristine condition. For the houses there was a maintenance department to whom one could report any faults. Whether one needed a carpenter or a plumber one just picked up the telephone and the repair crew would appear within minutes. There was also a sanitation department, and the householders were encouraged to report a particular small fly, if it was seen in the bathroom or toilets. It was a pretty, triangular little fly, which indicated that there were some bacteria around. The sanitation men would spray the offending bathroom or toilet and would also spray the whole house and garden against mosquitoes. This was done on a regular basis, so that we could sit outside on the patio and garden without being molested by them. Every garden made provision for children, because there was always a swing and a climbing frame in it.

For the children and their parents it was paradise. There was an excellent primary school, and Monu soon joined it. They had expatriate teachers who taught all subjects. Even botany and chemistry, zoology on a lower level widened the horizon of all the children there. It was not just the three 'R's that were taught, although they were the basis of learning of course.

I had to make regular visits to the clinic for baby's vaccinations, but even that was pleasant in air-conditioned waiting and treatment rooms and it was a medium whereby I got to know other mums and families.

A word about babies' names. Tommy expressed his philosophy of life in all of them except his first born daughter whom he called Shirley after Shirley Temple whom he saw in a film before he came to England. He was so taken with the tap dancing of this little filmstar that he called his daughter after her and her pet name became Ching-Ching because that was what Shirley Temple was called in the film he had seen. Even now, as a grown woman and grandmother, we still call her Ching-Ching.

After her, Freedom was born in 1942. Tommy believed in freedom and used to quote "Freedom is the one thing no man ever grants another. It has to be won in a warfare of perpetual vigilance." When Monu came along in 1955 he gave him the Itsekiri name of Monubarami: "I have faith in myself."

Now our little daughter got the name of Eyewetemi which meant 'the world is what I make of it". I think the European equivalent would be "the world is my oyster". Both our children shortened their long names to something more practical, so they became Monu and Temi, and both children lived up to their names.

The social festivities and sports for relaxation in Shell BP were luxurious. There was tennis and badminton and squash. There was an Olympic size swimming pool. There were go-kart racing and yachting (sailing) at weekends. In between, apart from the many parties that were organised for people leaving or arriving, or high holidays, there was Queen Juliana's birthday.

A large proportion of the staff were Dutch. Their queen was Juliana the Queen of Holland. For this festivity the Dutch children put on amazing shows. There was usually a kind of carnival that went all around the camp with music made by the children, and the children portraying Dutch scenes, all of them flying blue-white and red national flags. Often they wore Dutch costumes, which consisted mainly of wooden clogs (shoes) and the starched wing-bonnets for the girls. The traditional costume was made up of a white blouse, full skirt and a small white apron tied around the waist. I remember vividly one scene in which two boys, dressed as Dutch cheese-makers with black brimmed, flat topped hats carrying, one in front and one at the back, what looked like a stretcher on which was loaded a mountain of the typical bright red Edam cheeses, which had been flown in from Holland for the occasion. One year the whole club was decorated to look like a street in Amsterdam, the capital of Holland. It was a fantastic design of narrow high houses with pointed roofs, windows and

Hilda age fifteen, 1936

Hilda and Mother as domestics in England, 1939

WOMEN'S INTERNMENT CAMP
PORT ERIN
ISLE OF MAN

PHONE: PORT ERIN 3256
'GRAMS: COMMANDANT PORTERIN

All Communications to be addressed to the Commandant
Ref. No. EEL/OE

20th March, 1941

MISS HILDA GERSON, who is a trained teacher of languages, has during her internment given very generous help to her follow internees, by taking large adult classes in both French and English. These classes of which she gave a large number each week, have been among the most popular and helpful of those given in the Camp.

She will be much missed now that she is exempted from internment, and carries with her the best wishes of the Camp Authorities.

Joanna M. Cruickshank
Commandant.

Testimonial from the Internment Camp, 1941

New York. L-R: Hilda, her mother and brother John, 1st March, 1950

Jean Jacoby – Evans, author of several books, 1951

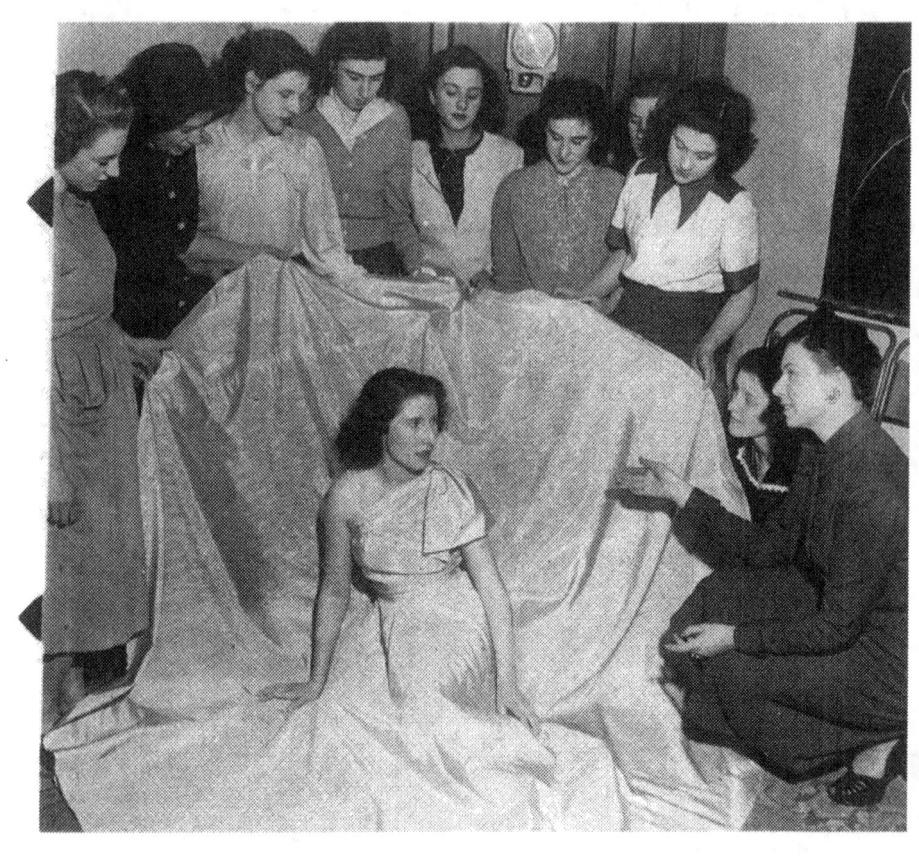

Teenage fashion talk at girls' club in London. Hilda on extreme right, 1951

NOW IN WARRI

At 4, Khalil Road or from shops all over town.

HILLY'S ICE CREAM

7d a cup.

COOL - SWEET - PURE

It's made with boiled water, under hygenic conditions.

Try it today! Offer it to your guests! Store it for days in the freezing compartment of your fridge.

HILLY'S ICE CREAM

A RARE TREAT.

1959

Kagho Industrial Enterprises, Warri.

Hilly's Ice-cream, Warri, 1959

London. Marriage of Hilda to Tommy' Ogbe, 5th July, 1952. Left of Tommy, his friend and best man J.O.B. Omotosho. Next to Hilda: Marlene, her gwn. Next to Marlene: Cousin, Mrs Favour Egbe. Behind Marlene: Miss Doris Prest. Behind Mr. Omotosho: Hilda's cousin Laura, child and husband. On left of male cousin: late Chucks Adophy. Back row: L-R: Philip Lewin, Dr Lasserson and Webber Egbe Esq

NIGERIAN OUTLOOK   Friday, August 7, 1964

NIGERIAN JEWELRY EXHIBITION

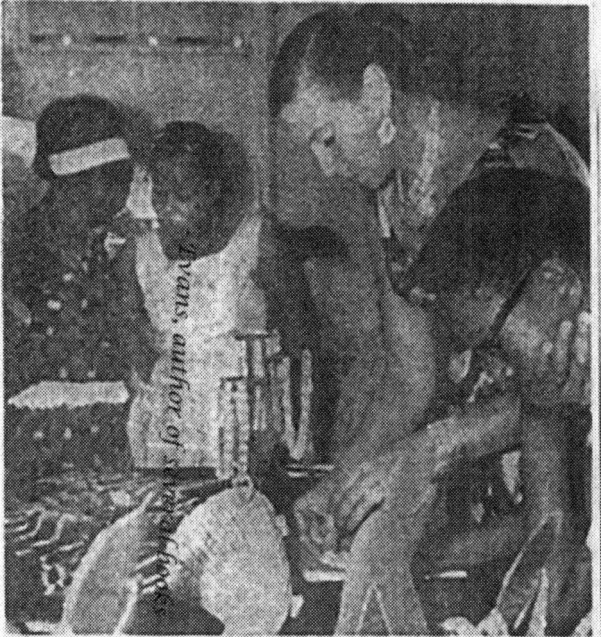

Mrs Hilda Ogbe, a former Chief Fashion Designer to many textile industries in England, and who now helps Nigerian jewellers to improve to proficiency standard, has stressed the need for Nigerians in the jewelry trade to form co-operative societies.

Mrs Ogbe (third from left in the picture) was speaking during a jewelry exhibition she held at the Enugu campus of the University of Nigeria over the week-end.

She said, such a co-operation was necessary to raise the required capital so that Nigerian jewellers could be helped to have ready stock of their locally made ornaments in order to build up a tourist trade in that direction.

She added that tourist trade apart from enhancing the country's economy could also advertise the country's arts to the outside world.

Mrs Ogbe whose exhibition was attended by many American Peace Corps Volunteers and graduate tutors now on a five-week visit to Eastern Nigeria, had assembled more than 500 pieces of local jewelry including necklaces, bracelets, ear and finger-rings, tie-clips, cuff-links and pendants mostly in silver and gold and some with artfully mounted precious stones.

Hilda at a jewellery exhibition in Enugu, Friday, August 7, 1964

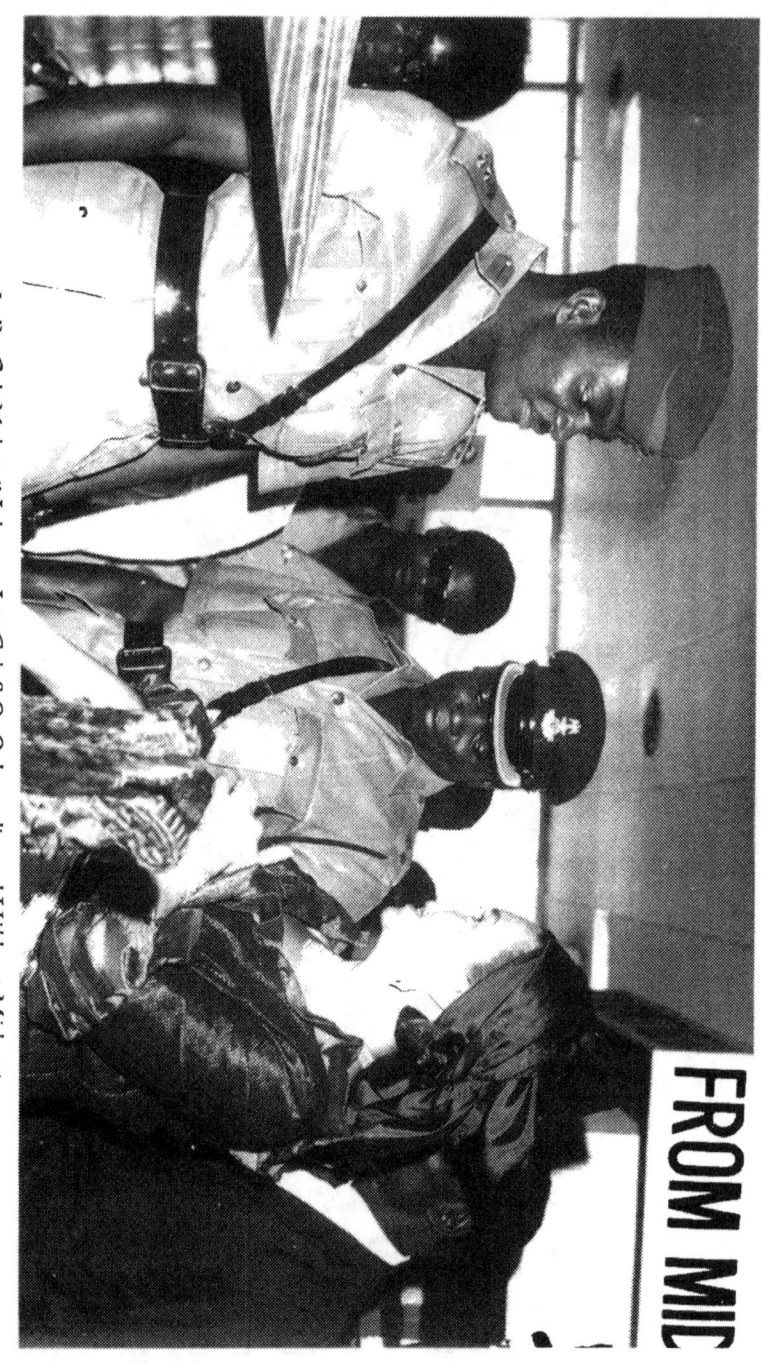

L-R: Col. Mobolaji Johnson, Lt. Col. S.O. Ogbemudia and Hilda at Midwest Crafts exhibition, Lagos, 1968

Pure Sterling Silver Jewellery

Some of Hilda's designs of Silver Jewellery, 1969

*Hilda with daughter Temi making 'Kweke' for the second burial of an Ogbe Chief.
Hilda in all gold, Temi in all silver, 1970*

1972 "Ladies Night": *Hilda and Tommy*, President of Rotary, Benin City

Hilda (centre front) with some Silversmiths and their apprentices at Ubulu-uku, 1973

Family of Tommy Ogbe: Father, Mother, Son Monu and daughter Temi, 1973

1979 Art Exhibition: Hilda – Guest of Honour. L-R: The artist Aghama Omoruyi, Hilda, Mrs R.J. Alli, wife of former Bendel State Governor, and Professor A. Baikie, then Vice-Chancellor of Uniben

Hilda answering questions during an interview with Weekend Observer, 1990

Hon. Justice Victor Omage, Hilda's close friend, 1995

Mrs Christine Omage, Hilda's close friend, 1995

Hilda with Charles Sholepela, discussing healing Herbs, 1999

doors marked on to them and even people leaning out of the windows. No theatre in Europe could have produced a better backdrop for the celebrations. Famous Dutch foods were also flown in for the festivities. There was Dutch Schnapps and smoked eel plus a variety of cheeses for which Holland is famous, and of course, there were masses of freshly picked Tulips, the proud national flower of Holland.

Non-Dutch children joined in the carnival as best they could, rigging themselves out or their vehicles in blue, white and red. I remember threading strips of blue, white and red crepe paper through the spokes of Monu's bicycle, and he enjoyed taking part in everything. There were prizes for the best outfit. I believe that the Edam cheese boys got first prize and a pretty little princess in a fairy tale coach drawn by two boys on bicycles got the second prize.

Add to this June speciality the annual holidays of Easter, Christmas, and of course, Nigeria's Independence, the many private dinners, cocktail parties and luncheons, and you have a hectic social calendar in front of you.

There were also facilities for photography enthusiasts of which both Tommy and I were members. You had to subscribe to the membership of the Photograph Society to be able to use their darkrooms which were housed in containers, fully equipped with electricity, water supply for washing of films and even chemicals for developing and printing. I was a keen photographer myself, but Tommy, aged 18 at the time had been the first commercial freelance photographer in Lagos. At the time he was augmenting his salary with money earned from taking photographs at social functions, like the racing, weddings, or any party of high society. He became very popular because he would rush to the darkroom while the party was still on, develop and print his film and take it back to the guests the same day to take their orders for copies. He was allowed access to the King's College laboratory, where the teaching staff trusted him implicitly.

But now it was my turn. He was my favourite subject to photograph and so of course were my children. When Temi was six weeks old, my mother came back again to see her second grandchild and she adored her on sight. She saw to the feeding of the baby when she began to eat solids. She took her for walks in the pram on those beautiful streets, and she played with her non-stop. Monu was busy in school, so there was no sign of jealousy on his part. Tommy always warned my mother to watch for falling palm leaves when she took the baby for a walk. The streets were lined with palms and he explained to her that these leaves were very heavy and could do great damage to her and/or the baby. He was very solicitous these days. He was happy to be in an orderly environment where his qualities were appreciated.

I had a different new thrill in my life. With the two hundred pounds for which I had sold the ice cream machine, I was able to buy a second-hand small car, a Fiat 600. It gave me such great pleasure and such a feeling of freedom even to drive around the camp on its quiet well asphalted streets. I had not quite mastered the trickeries of driving but Monu was by now seven years old, and it was he who taught me, believe it or not. Sitting beside me he patiently explained the functions of clutching, of accelerating, of changing gear, of reversing and generally minding the kerbs and oncoming traffic. He was a support at such an early age. Like most boys he understood engineering almost by instinct. We had given him engineering toys like Meccano construction kits when he was about five years old. We did not know then that we had hit upon the very thing this boy needed, because he was a born engineer. He was naturally at home with all engines, motors and later technology that his parents could not possibly understand. Now he was my driving instructor in the camp, until I was fit enough to be handed over to a proper instructor who would drill me to take my driving licence.

When the time came, Tommy warned the instructor not to pass me in order to please him, if I was not fit to drive safely in town. Naturally, I had butterflies in my tummy, that is, I was nervous, on the day I took my test. Far from being a smooth ride as I had come to expect in the Shell camp, I was now taken out into the town of Port Harcourt. When Tommy used to drive his Mercedez to take me out for shopping, I had not noticed how rutted and potholed the roads were. It was a fairly smooth run to Leventis stores which was the nearest to our camp, but on this day I was taken further into town around the market area where not only potholes abounded, but traffic was heavy and made me very anxious. As we got nearer the V.I.O. station, there was a row of empty oil drums put up in the road at intervals, so that the learner driver had to slalom in and out between them. That was not all. I also had to reverse in this fashion between the drums, in out, in out. I sweated, but I managed the test without hitting any of the drums. I had passed, and I joyfully waved my driving licence in Tommy's face when he got home that day.

"Well, well Pooppie" he said. "Congratulations, but remember you have your life in your hands when you drive. Remember also that it could be the other man's mistake that may cause you an accident." This was good advice which I remembered all through my life of driving cars of different makes and sizes.

Now I was fit to go into town on my own, but I still lacked confidence so that I used to take Monu with me. Sitting beside me, this little man directed me through the traffic. "Mummy you can overtake now. Mummy somebody behind you wants to overtake. Mummy at a crossroad you must wait. Look left and right until there is a gap in traffic so that you can come out into the road you want." He was such a comfort.

The Shell school was excellent. The teachers were caring. When Monu developed mumps, and Temi, now one year old followed with the same infection, Monu was missing classes at school. In their nature study lesson the teacher had found the cocoon of a praying mantis and had told the children that she would keep it in a glass jar, covered with a paper into which she had made holes so that the baby mantises could breathe when they came out of the cocoon. The day they hatched, the teacher brought the jar of tiny black praying mantises milling around in it. She brought it to the house to show it to the sick Monu so that he would not miss this event. My mother and I thought it so very thoughtful of her.

Another event in Monu's life in that same period was the fact that he began to read books by himself. He had always enjoyed being read to, even though he could read perfectly well. During this month's illness now, I used to sit by his bedside and read to him from Biggles books. He loved those adventure stories of a pilot in a small two-seater plane during the First World War. Biggles was an enterprising traveller who visited many countries with his plane. He also got into many difficulties on his visits, and it was always very exciting to read how he extricated himself from them. During his visits he would describe the foreign country in which he landed, thus giving the young reader an idea of France for instance, France and its people, their habits, their clothes, the food they ate, the produce the country had, and a few sentences of their language. These were informative as well as exciting reading for the young ones.

In the middle of reading to Monu from such a book I was called away to attend to a visitor, so I put the book on Monu's bed and said: "Sorry my dear, I have to go now but you can read on yourself." As the book was so fascinating Monu continued reading and never looked back from that day. He became a voracious reader.

He perfected another skill in Umukoroshe, and that was swimming. We had occasionally visited the swimming pool in Sapele Club when we were living in Warri. Our trips there, however, were not so frequent as to give Monu enough practice. In Umukoroshe, we were able to go swimming everyday and he soon swam and dived like a fish.

Eda too enjoyed the civilized environment of the Shell camp, but we also had a cook now because the entertaining of visitors put quite a strain on any housewife. Peter the cook, a nice old gray haired little man, was unfortunately more often drunk than sober. Tommy once or twice had to drive to the outskirts of the camp to find Peter lying in a gutter. Under these circumstances we had to look for a new cook but in any case we cut down the entertaining for a while.

One aspect of social life in the camp did not agree with me or I with it, and those were the coffee mornings. For housewives who had domestic staff and nothing much to do themselves, it was a way of whiling away the time. It was a good way to meet other women, but I never enjoyed gossip and always preferred a one to one conversation. The talk at coffee mornings paddled on the surface and left me bored. I also found it irritating that the women of different nationalities who had been in Nigeria at least two to three years, knew nothing of the country itself. When I wanted to stimulate their interest with books or artifacts that I had in my house, they showed polite interest at first, but soon their eyes glazed over with boredom.

I had one nice neighbour, a Dutch woman, Mrs. Appleboom who had worked in Indonesia with her husband. She was intelligent, she had an open mind, and what is more, I got a lot of delicious Indonesian cooking recipes from her.

Chapter IV

THE SILVER BUSINESS

For my birthday in 1962, my mother gave me five pounds as a present. It was not enough to buy gold, but I had wanted a pair of silver earrings anyway. I designed them on paper and drove into town with my faithful Monu by my side to locate a goldsmith in one of the narrow streets where few Europeans ventured. I entered one of the dark sheds that had a signboard above it saying "Licenced Goldsmith No..." I showed him my design of big earrings and asked whether he could make them in silver. After some hesitation, he said he would try. I had always coveted the gold jewellery on Nigerian ladies, but not only did the gold not suit my skin as well as it suited theirs, I preferred silver and had been looking for large earrings to complement my rather severe hairstyle. Without earrings, I always felt naked. The goldsmith surprised me by making my large pair of silver earrings absolutely faithfully according to my sketch. I was overjoyed and put them on immediately. As soon as other European ladies saw me they exclaimed "where did you get those from?" because there was nothing like it to be had in any store whether Leventis or Kingsway or UTC, and the Shell wives never went into the market.

When I explained that a goldsmith had made these silver earrings for me, there was an immediate clamour from the women around me to order the same for them or something smaller or could he make a silver bracelet or a chain or ring? I encouraged the women to go into the town themselves describing the street and house number of the craftsman, but they came back to me saying that they did not understand his English, could I please run their errands for them?

I was quite happy to be excused from the coffee mornings now but to be in touch with the women just the same, because they were all eagerly waiting for their orders. It gave me something useful to do, because I reasoned that at least I was providing work for the man in question, and I could use my creative ability to produce different designs. This activity grew. The word went around that here was a craft that the Shell wives had not known about. Every woman likes jewellery and needed presents to take home when they went on leave. The demand became so great that I had to enlist other goldsmiths to produce the silver jewellery as fast as it was needed. I now put a mark-up on what I produced to earn my own money and still the jewellery was very cheap.

This activity was interrupted in 1963 when Tommy was promoted to Shell BP Representative in Enugu. Like all changes, one had to get used to the idea of moving again, sorry to leave behind the known but excited at the prospect of the unknown and of Tommy's promotion. He was very pleased and satisfied that his efforts were being recognised. We heard all sorts of pleasant stories about Enugu which was the administrative capital of the Eastern Region. Tommy was now to liaise with Government at the highest level on behalf of Shell BP. He was to become the Ambassador of Shell BP.

Enugu lay on five hills and had a very pleasant climate. The residence to which we now moved was a beautiful architect-designed storey building. The downstairs part was built around a patio which was open to the sky and which divided the sitting room from the dining room, but it was enclosed by glass doors. Through these we could see the gravel-strewn patio with its lush green potted plants all around it. A cook and chief steward with assistant steward made up the household team. There were three gardeners to maintain the vast beautiful garden from which one looked out onto Juju Hill. Two drivers completed the staff, "one for the Master and one for the Dame." An open highly polished staircase led to the three airy bedrooms and bathrooms upstairs.

We were lucky to be on one of the five hills that made Enugu, so that there was always a breeze and none of the sultry climate of Warri or Port Harcourt.

In Enugu, Tommy was taking over from the outgoing representative, a Dutchman called Mr. Stigter. The outgoing had to hand over to the incoming all past records of his activities on behalf of the company. Mr. Stigter also handed over to Tommy his game of golf!

Tommy had never played this game. He now sensed instinctively that it was part of social life in Enugu, and if he was to be worth his salt as a representative, he would have to pick up this game too. He dived into this new sport with all his usual enthusiasm and ambition to perform well. He mastered it in a short time after buying all the equipment from Mr. Stigter and becoming a member of the Enugu Golf Club.

He also invested in traditionally English golf clothes. A tailor made the 'plus-fours', to his instruction. The bouffant three-quarter length trousers buckled correctly under the knees, joined by Fairisle patterned long socks, golf shirt, golf cap and socks all in the same colour scheme, be it red, green, blue or canary yellow. I could always pick Tommy out on the golf course, he was colour coded for me.

There were as many social functions in Enugu as there had been in Port Harcourt. Now Tommy was not only the legal man but he became 'Ambassador' for Shell BP between the company and the government of the Eastern Region of Nigeria. Port Harcourt had been industrial, Enugu was administrative.

We soon realised that parties were part of his job. The guests always included the many heads of government departments, and when I look at an old guest list now, I wonder how I ever managed to arrange dinners, luncheons and special festivities for so many people. It would have been a diplomatic faux pas of the worst order to leave out one or the other influential person.

I now saw that there were not too many domestic staff. The two chief players were George the cook and Anthony the chief steward. George was quite exceptional. He had been a cook in the navy and had travelled to exotic countries. He was able to make fantastic Chinese dishes including the popular spring rolls, which was an art in itself. He also made a boned chicken that was out of this world. He removed every bone from the inside of the chicken and stuffed it with spiced-minced pork. Talk about gilding the Lily! After stuffing he sewed up the chicken and made it look complete, with only the ankles of the legs protruding. So prepared, it was roasted and it was possible to slice through the whole roast chicken, which drew admiration from every guest we ever entertained. It also got George some handsome tips for this work of art.

Anthony was not only a chief steward, he could have been called a butler. He was the epitome of the tactful, silent, all-observing and all-understanding, discreet kind of butler which used to be found in the best English manor houses of old tradition. We could not have managed without him.

An open verandah ran right around the house, so that we could have luncheons outside, when there was a crowd of guests. Green canvas awnings rolled up on a stick during everyday could be let down on ropes to give shade to the luncheon guests.

Our own parties were always very lively thanks to Tommy's indomitable energy and high sense of humour. He made excellent speeches, but invariably when he told a joke, he lost the point of it. He would then turn to me and ask "Pooppie, how did this story end?" And then he would turn to his audience saying "I kill two things: I kill jokes and drinks". Once, he went on to explain that he was no connoisseur of drinks. It was immaterial to him whether it was the right thing to do or not, when a wine was sour to his taste he put sugar in it. When a beer was too bitter he mixed it with liqueur and/or Coca Cola. This had his audience in stitches, and then he continued: "As you have seen just now, I kill jokes too, because I always forget the point of the story."

People found this frankness endearing and irresistible, so that when he trotted out his well-worn phrases, "I always say self first, I never sin, I am never wrong, he who pays the piper, calls the tune, — people thought such frankness must be a joke and never took him at his word. During cocktail parties he would always have a crowd of listeners around him when he expounded further quotations like "It is better to jaw-jaw-jaw than to war, war, war." Or on the subject of the opposite sex he would say "Nature's laws cannot be infringed with impunity" which was followed by "I love women." Great "ha ha ha" from the men. Or he would grab a lady next to him saying "I love freckles", addressing a freckled lady. On such occasions I would stand by, a frozen smile on my face, because what wife enjoys hearing her husband declare in public that he loves women?

The society in Enugu in 1963 was a great mixture of Europeans and Nigerians. For my purposes it was a rich field of customers for our silver jewellery. I had continued with this hobby as soon as we had settled in Enugu, driving my little Fiat through those areas where I had seen signs of goldsmiths' sheds. I had with me a basket containing a small order book and samples of the silver which I had got made in Port Harcourt. I had realised that here was an industry going to waste. Goldsmiths never had enough money to keep stock of their wares in their shops, and except for the three famous names in Lagos like Hooper, Boulos, and Tabet, most goldsmiths lived from hand to mouth. They might get one or two orders for a bracelet or a ring or a pair of earrings or a chain during the week but this was not regular employment. Most of their income came from washing gold jewellery, but this I will explain later.

I now toured the goldsmiths' sheds on a regular basis to see if I could find more workers willing to make silver. All the senior masters refused. It seemed infra dig to them to make anything lower than gold. After visiting one particular old master and coming away disappointed, I revved my car to drive away from his shed when a young man ran after me. "Madam, madam, I will make silver for you. Where is your house? I will soon get my freedom, and then I will make silver for you." His name was Charles Ezeana, and I will here explain that goldsmith apprentices had to work under a master for five years. After this time they would get their freedom and be allowed to set up their own workshop.

Charles duly called at our house and we began to discuss certain patterns to be made in silver. I found that all the goldsmiths had one catalogue in common, which was a booklet of ink drawings of established Nigerian patterns made in gold and printed for circulation. The other method was for customers to bring something to be copied, sometimes a cheap European brooch or pendant or earrings, and most of these were cast work. That meant the object was pressed into a cuttlefish bone and was cast in that kind of mould.

I did not like copying at any time. I preferred to continue with some of the Nigerian patterns which were very attractive and a novelty to the expatriates. At that time I took over three patterns from that booklet. One was called Pakute, which in translation meant rat trap. Each link was produced in a domed shape and one could imagine a rat running under the dome and the trap coming down on him. The other I named myself as "Chevron" because it overlapped filigree triangles over each other, nothing to do with the Chevron Oil Company. The third I called "Lace". The three patterns are still in my collection now thirty-six years later. Apart from those, of course, I now let my imagination run wild. There was no end to the possibilities of designing, but I had to learn a lot. I had to understudy the silversmith to understand his technique to know what was within the realms of practicability of the filigree work.

When young Charles got regular orders from me every week his contemporaries became interested, and several other young smiths appeared at our house to apply for work. I was thrilled. I was providing employment, which to me was the greater motivation than just making money. I was encouraging these young craftsmen to take pride in their work and pride in their country because their good work would project the image of Nigeria, when it was taken abroad.

Our new life in Enugu was very soon disrupted by the bombshell news that Tommy was to be sent on a three months familiarisation course with Shell Operations in Britain, Holland and the Middle East. This was very exciting for him of course but daunting to our little family who were going to be left alone for such a long time. Again my mother had a brilliant idea. She would rent a holiday home for us in Spain or on the island of Mallorca where we would receive all our friends and relations from Europe to stay with us in rotation. She set about this arrangement with her customary energy and determination and within two weeks had found a bungalow with guest house on Mallorca in the seaside town of Cala D'or. On Tommy's side and our own there were feverish preparations now. The silversmiths were sad to know that I would be gone for three months. I left them with orders for which I gave them the raw silver, so that they would know I was coming back.

Tommy's itinerary was impressive. He would start in England, continue to Holland, from there to Cyprus and then across the Mediterranean to Egypt. From there along the Middle Eastern coast he would go to Lebanon and Syria. I knew gem stones to be reasonably priced in Beirut, so when he asked me what he should bring for me, I asked for semi precious stones like amethyst, aquamarine and yellow topaz. I wrote them all down for him with sizes in millimeters and the quantity of each I would want. I think it was three of each except for the amethyst of which I wanted five.

We all travelled together to Lagos in the Shell helicopter and from Lagos we took our respective planes in different directions. My mother, the children and I flew by Iberia whereas Tommy took off on British Caledonian Airways.

Mallorca was as beautiful as we had been led to believe. But from Palma, the capital, we had a rickety taxi ride to Cala D'or. We found the bungalow enchanting, set in a garden of cypresses and trimmed trees with cacti which were just beginning to fruit. The bungalow was spacious, with green floor tiles all through and kitchen and bathroom facilities that were luxurious. Three bedrooms were plenty, because our expected visitors would be accommodated in the small guest house with its own facilities adjoining our own bungalow.

We really had a wonderful time. My brother and his wife came from America, one cousin with husband and teenage boys came from Berlin, one set of cousins with two daughters came from London, and my guru, dear old Marlene, also came for a fortnight from London. All these came in rotation so that no two parties overlapped, and we always had a breathing space between visits.

Our little Temi now eighteen months old was enchanting. She really was the doll in the family, not I. With her curly top knot and her lovely brown colour and mischievous eyes she drew everybody's attention wherever we went. When we all went to the beach everyday, foreign tourists would follow us and fall on their knees in order to photograph Temi. Click, click the cameras went. One day Temi was dragging behind me holding my hand, when I heard a choking noise. As I turned around it was she who was choking, so I quickly picked her up by the ankles held her upside down and banged her back. Out came a large hard boiled sweet from her mouth. Some well meaning, adoring and stupid tourist had given it to her, not realising that it was much too big for her little mouth and so hard she could not chew it. I thanked my stars for the instinctive knowledge of what to do and was grateful that our precious darling had come to no harm.

On the beach both children were happy as children always are, playing in the sand and Monu frolicking in the sea. Of course I took Temi into the sea with me as well, and later when the two boy cousins arrived from Berlin they enjoyed tossing her from one to the other while they were in the water. Temi was not a bit afraid, in fact she loved every minute of it. Monu was already a good swimmer, and he swam races with the younger boy cousin.

Monu also picked up the Spanish language. I had taught him the rudiments and promised him one peseta for every new Spanish word that he could learn and write down for me everyday. He was quite confident to roam around the small town by himself, made friends and negotiated for me in shops. It was amazing how quickly he learned the language and more amazing still that, when twelve years later he went to study in California, USA he met with many Mexican immigrants there, with whom he conversed in Spanish. He himself did not know where the words came from, he must have stored them in that wonderful computer which is our brain.

A word about my cousin from Berlin. She was the daughter of my father's sister who perished in a concentration camp. Inge came home from school in Berlin one day, and found all her family gone. The Nazis had taken all of them away, and they were never seen again. The terrified girl, then fourteen years old, ran to an old non-Jewish acquaintance of her family and begged him to take her in. This man did so, at great risk to himself, because of course all Germans were forbidden to fraternise with Jews. He was a sports trainer, a man twenty years older than my cousin. He had a small bachelor's flat and hid Inge in that third floor accommodation, instructing her to stay there and never go out. She could not be seen leaving or entering his building without endangering him.

After two years of being so cooped up, Inge had a desperate desire for fresh air and ventured out for a stroll one evening. She was spotted and thought to look un-German so that when she entered the house again, somebody followed her up to the third floor where Ernest, the friend, opened the door to her. Both were arrested and sent to a concentration camp which had one section for women and one section for men. Both escaped, we never knew exactly how, but assumed that since Ernest was a German and knew the German ways, and since he had been a sports trainer he somehow found ways and means to procure two bicycles on which the two of them escaped and fled the concentration camp. We never pressed Inge for detailed information. That time of her life was just too painful for her to want to talk about. She had lost her mother, her junior brother, two aunts and an uncle in one go, while her father had gone to South Africa to prepare a home for his family. It had been too late.

Inge and Ernest had cycled through Germany as fugitives for two years. They had no ration books, no identity papers and must not be seen anywhere during the day. They cycled through the night through countryside, slept in hay lofts or barns and stole from the farmers whatever edibles they could find. Fresh eggs, sometimes cheese, sometimes a drink of milk from the cows. They were always hungry. Often they dug for roots and grass and ate that when there was nothing else. Inge remained with a permanently damaged stomach, but she was glad to be alive. When the Russians liberated Berlin, Inge and Ernest happened to be in that section. When a Russian soldier saw Inge, his eyes lit up, thinking he had found a victim to rape, but Inge recognised him to be of Jewish origin and she stood in front of him reciting in Hebrew one of the most moving and best known prayers of the Jewish religion. The soldier was instantly disarmed, and tears streamed down his face as they do mine now. He gave her and Ernest protection and his food.

Ernest and Inge were married. Their ordeal had forged a strong bond between them, and when life returned to normalcy, they settled down in that same bachelor's flat and reared two sons.

After years of only correspondence with us, here they were now, Inge a fragment of our once large family and still beautiful with her starry dark eyes and her long lashes. Ernest now sixty years old still very sporty and sinewy, performed armstand and other acrobatic features for us. He and his two handsome sons were blue-eyed. Strangely enough, his eldest son was also called Freedom. One can well imagine why, after hearing his story.

My other cousin Laura whom you have met before, the daughter of my father's brother also came with her family. She had married an interior designer, also a refugee from Berlin and the two of them looked remarkably alike somehow. Not only that, but both had the same kindness and helpfulness in their character. They were both born in January and maybe the sign of Aquarius really had the same bearing on their characters. Their daughters were lovely girls of eleven and thirteen at the time. The elder had the same talent for design as her father, and the younger had a passion for dancing, just like her mother Laura had. In fact, Laura had met a Nigerian medical student with whom she enjoyed dancing so much that they became close friends. But Michael had warned her from the beginning that his father back home in Nigeria had already chosen a wife for him, and there could be no future for him with Laura.

Her younger daughter performed ballet steps for us, and both girls of course fussed over Temi who enjoyed the attention from so many visitors to our house. The visitor we most looked forward to was Tommy. As part of his Middle Eastern tour he managed to spend one week with us in Cala D'or. We were so happy to see him and I was glad that he was seeing us in our surroundings. It saved a lot of description and explanation afterwards.

He seemed to be very tired from all his travels, and now glad to relax in the bosom of his family. At this time the cactus fruit had ripened, so that he could partake of this exotic fruit. I did not really know how to handle them because they had very long and sharp barbs. I had to be careful not to scratch my hands when picking the fruits and then started operating on them in order to remove the thick peel from the juicy interior. I did it with knife and fork on a plate. I held the fruit with the fork, sliced the skin open with the knife and then still holding the fruit with the fork I finally managed to get it out of its dangerous covering. The fruit was almost the size of a mango, and tasted similar. Orange flesh and soft pulpy substance strongly reminded me of home where the mangoes would now be ripe. This was an experience for all of us. Tommy's stay was very short but he had nearly come to the end of his course and so we did not mind his leaving again because we would soon all be united in Enugu.

It had been a special joy for my mother and me to see Johnny and Edith. Unfortunately, he could not stand the heat or the warmth because it was not as hot as in Nigeria, but the sun was strong and he had to wear a hat all the time. For this reason he never visited Nigeria to my great sorrow, but I knew that his body just could not bear heat and I did not want the responsibility of urging him to visit me in Nigeria, if it would affect his health. This midway meeting had been a good compromise, because he also had met my children, which was important to me. He and his wife did not have children.

Eventually, laden with souveniors of things made from olive wood, we started on our journey home. Spain and Spanish territory are famous for their olives. The funny thing is that the olive tree is called '*Un Olivo*' while the olive fruit is called '*Manzanilla*'. It is not easy to understand this difference in terminology. One thing I liked about the olive trees was that the under side of the leaves was of a silvery gray. Looking down an olive grove when the breeze blew, one could see streaks of silver flashing in the moving leaves. The olive trees had slim trunks, so that all artifacts made of olive wood were made of small pieces of wood glued together in beautiful patterns.

I had to leave these memories behind now as we were heading for Enugu again. We were received by Eda and Anthony, and George the cook was happy to make our favourite dishes again. The driver had met us at the airport, so that all went well, even though Master had not yet come.

The news of my return had spread quickly to the silversmiths. It did not take long before they clamoured once again to see me, to deliver their work and to be paid for it. As more and more young goldsmiths came, willing to work in silver I had to find new outlets for the work they produced. I could not rely on single private customers any more. The first step I took was to arrange an exhibition of the silver at our house. We had a beautiful guest house with two double bedrooms facing each other and a large sitting room in the centre between them. This was an ideal place for my exhibition as it would not interfere with the regular running of our house. I sent out small invitations to companies and departments in which I knew there were expatriate ladies and on a particular date our guest house was full of visitors who had come to see and buy. My mother was there to help me sell, to watch the customers and to take the money. I also had made friends with a very nice and reliable lady married to an Igbo man. She was Irene Nwokedi who was as thrilled with the silver jewellery as all other expatriates were. She too came to help me with my first exhibition. It was very successful financially and otherwise, and I could now relax knowing that there would be enough work for the silversmiths. I had insisted on good quality work, rejecting anything that was badly made. I now felt an obligation to keep them in constant work.

Not long after this exhibition Tommy returned from his long trip abroad. He had tried to fulfil all my wishes, and I was the lucky recipient not only of the amethyst, the aquamarines and the yellow topaz stones which I had asked for but he also brought me a big 22 carat gold necklace from Egypt, which he had been told was called the Nefertiti necklace. I was a lucky girl, until something later chipped away at my happiness when I learned that he had brought some topaz also for another lady.

Here now starts the saga of Rosa Okpu, a black American woman who looked like a man with square broad shoulders and masculine face. She was married to a Nigerian, but took no notice of her marriage. Tommy told me how she had sat at the bar in the Enugu Club where he was talking to some other people. She had got up, came over to him, held him by his tie and pulled him towards her saying "I want you." He confessed that he was shocked by this behaviour, but also intrigued and flattered. This was the beginning of the story as he told it to me, and I heard no more until some weeks later when he was in a black mood again.

At a cocktail party at our home Tommy played some records and asked people to dance. The fashionable dance at the time was the twist. He was a master at it. Rosa was among the guests and as he sat down for a breather Rosa danced passed him, stopped in front of him and shook her bottom in his face to the rhythm of the music. "Ah", I sighed and knew that Rosa had meant everything she had said to him.

"Pooppie" he said one evening "If I am depressed, it has nothing to do with you." Then he continued "I can now understand why men commit suicide". I had a shock, in fact my heart fell into my shoes. "What was this"? I thought and then said "I hope it is nothing to do with your work?" which he emphatically denied. "Oh no," he said. After a long silence he blurted out: "you see, Rosa told me she wanted to borrow my gramophone, and I took it to her house. She lives with two adopted children, she has none of her own. When I brought the gramophone we played it softly so as not to wake the children and we danced." Mercifully he did not go into further details but then he said when, after some days he asked for the gramophone back she said it had developed a fault and she had sent it for repair. This went on for one or two weeks until he thought he would see for himself. He called at her house when she did not expect him, entered her sitting room and found the gramophone gone. "Has it not come back from repair?" he asked her. And she said "No, not yet". With the intuitive feeling that he used to have he said "Let me look in the bedroom".

"Oh no", said Rosa. "The children are sleeping."

"I shall not disturb them" he said and opened the bedroom door, finding another man in there and no gramophone. This depressed him. Rosa who had, so to say, seduced him and showered compliments on him was now after such a short time deceiving him with another man, who was not her husband, and he suspected that she had given the gramophone to this man as a present.

I never got to hear the end of the story, but eventually the gramophone reappeared in our house. "You see", said Tommy "a wife should be like a mother to her man. A mother to whom one can tell everything and who will understand everything."

This was a dangerous compliment. I was only forty-two years old and thought to be attractive. Where does this kind of relationship leave the wife, a still young wife with her own physical desires and an urge to be appreciated and acclaimed, just like her man? Where does this leave one? I voiced this to Tommy but he never had any understanding for anybody's feelings but his own. If I spoke of emotion he would wave me off. "Oh emotion, emotion" he would say. "Only logic is valid. Everybody must know what he wants in life." He little realised, how emotional he was himself. Rosa's behaviour had mortally wounded his pride. Now he was looking for revenge.

Rosa had a Nigerian friend called Sara. She was a very attractive, well turned-out girl and Tommy, I think, made a beeline for her.

We went to a dance at the Club one evening. Tommy guided me gallantly to a table holding my elbow as always and said he would get me a drink. While he ushered me to my table his eyes kept roving, searching. When he had deposited me he went to the bar to get my drink and I saw Sara hovering there. I never wanted a drink of any kind. I always preferred to eat. I seemed to have something wrong with my thirst mechanism. I was never thirsty even in a hot climate.

So I sat, twiddling my drink whilst Tommy excused himself to go on public relations mission. I sat for a while with a frozen smile on my face, waving to acquaintances here and there when they danced by, but little by little a crowd formed round my table. These were people who were curious about the silver jewellery. I was always wearing some of my designs, and people wanted to know: was it really made in Nigeria? Was I really the one who designed it? Where did the silver come from? Was I a silversmith myself? How did I train the workers? So the questions came fast and furious. I was happy that the news had circulated among the expatriates and explained to them the truth: I had always coveted the lovely gold jewellery which Nigerian ladies were wearing, but somehow the gold looked brown and not as bright as I was used to seeing, and I opted for silver instead. "Why don't you come to my house", I said "and I will tell you more and show you other designs." So, although socially the evening was a dead loss to me, I was able to promote my hobby and my business interest. When Tommy saw people crowding around me he came over saying "come on Pooppie we must go home".

As my reputation for the silver grew, more and more people came to see me. Even people from other towns. At times, it was inconvenient, especially if we were at table. In that case, if a traveller had come from far away, my mother would get up quietly to attend to him, to spare me Tommy's anger. I never quite understood whether he was becoming jealous of my popularity, but if he was it did not deter me from continuing with my project.

On one such occasion we had two lunch guests, two oil men from Canada, who witnessed my husband's irritation at being disturbed at table. He now felt bound to explain to these guests "I really do not approve of customers coming for my wife's silver jewellery at all hours. Do excuse the interruption." Our guests became interested, and addressed themselves to me. "You make silver jewellery?" "No, not I," I replied. "I only design it. Local craftsmen make it." The usual questions followed, and I had to explain how I was developing a cottage industry from scratch, thus providing employment and bringing the skill of Nigerian craftsmen to the notice of the world. I explained my difficulties with techniques and appropriate tools, mentioning in particular the problem of weights.

The goldsmiths were using the old Troy Ounce system, dividing it themselves into fractions of, for instance, a penny-weight which they had fashioned from cutting a farthing coin into half. I had no accurate means of checking their weights. They had never heard of grammes and I had no gramme scales anyway. After lunch, the guests asked to see the jewellery, seemed impressed, bought some gifts and departed. A month later, a parcel arrived for me via Shell BP. Our guests had sent me a finely balanced, accurate set of scales which went down to one tenth of a gramme. I was overjoyed, and that too, I have been using for 34 years.

The first official exhibition I arranged was at the Enugu campus of the University of Nsukka in 1964. Again, as in my London teenage fashion days, I informed the press and briefed them on what they were going to see. A photograph of me displaying the jewellery, with a bored Monu at my side and several Reverend Sisters looking at the display, appeared on the front page of the local newspaper. This created more interest again. After all, silver jewellery was unknown in Nigeria at the time. The Nigerian ladies called it "The White Gold" when they came to ask for it.

I also began to travel with small exhibitions held maybe at coffee mornings among ladies of out-lying towns, like Aba for instance. There I would give a talk and travel with a small selection of gem stones, to also enlighten the ladies about the quality of gold. I had been told and seen that most women sent their gold for washing at Christmas or Easter or for special occasions, so that it would be bright and shiny. During these coffee mornings I explained to the ladies that real gold never needed washing. Its very quality and expensive price lay in the fact that it was completely non-perishable and non-tarnishing. I advised the ladies to get their gold made by only the most reputable goldsmiths so that they would not be wasting their money. In the future, if it became necessary for them to sell their gold, they would get little or nothing for it, if it was of the quality that needed to be washed. I explained that this washing in fact was a regilding by chemical means. I also showed them the gem stones to let them see the difference between a faceted real stone and a plastic button which they often mounted in gold. At the time the ladies absorbed this information with great interest. I also explained to them that the silver was an equally noble metal which did not rust or perish ever, but it had the habit of turning darker with use, especially when it came into contact with the sulphur and sweat of our skin. However, if one took care to dip the silver jewellery into soapy water after each wearing, the sweat would be removed and the darkening process prevented.

Tommy got a bit tired hearing people talk about me now, instead of him. He was so used to being the centre of attention wherever he went. It seemed as though I was becoming a rival. He did not realise the value of what I was doing, helping to develop the craftsman's skills and promoting Nigeria in the best possible way.

Everybody loves a piece of jewellery. Through expatriates buying gifts for their loved ones in their different countries, they were inadvertently exporting our silver to the four corners of the world. The jewellery was so delicately made, and of such perfect standard and purity of silver, that I encouraged our customers to have it tested for quality anywhere they liked. I was so confident that nobody would find fault with it. The feedback I got from one or two customers was that a jeweller had told them that not only was the silver pure, but the quality of the workmanship exceeded that of Indian silver. This was high praise indeed. I passed the information onto my workers to make them feel proud of their achievement, and proud and pleased they were.

I was also still making my own dresses. Their unusual style and fit did not escape the public. One day I was approached by the presenter of a woman's programme on television. She was Miriam Okagbue. She had heard about me and wanted me to give a series of talks and demonstrations on her programme. This was very exciting and a great novelty in my life. So many activities now took my mind off what my husband might be doing. I felt fulfilled and gratified to have won recognition with my efforts.

The first show on television was meant for me to demonstrate evening wear for ladies. I appeared myself in a tight-fitting full-skirted gold lame dress wearing white long gloves and bare shoulders. I had taken with me materials of different weights and designs and showed on television which would be suitable for what type of dress. I remember scrunching up one very light sheer material in my hand and throwing it up into the air from where it floated down gently. This showed its feather lightness.

The second material was a heavier satin which I demonstrated in similar ways, when the television beam which held the microphone hanging over my head suddenly fell down during the show. It did not fall on my head, but grazed my shoulder. I had a slight shock and then remembered the motto "the show must go on". This was the guideline for all actors and actresses in Europe. So I just continued talking while technicians scrambled around to lift the beam away from where it had fallen. It was an amusing experience.

When I got home I asked Tommy whether he had watched the show, but he said "No, no, he had forgotten about it. He had been very busy." My dear mother of course had sat glued to the screen and made her comments about the show afterwards. Several programmes followed. On one of them I was asked to talk about setting a dinner table for guests. The producer wanted me to show the right way to set the cutlery and the plates and what type of glasses were to be used for which drink. It was a good idea and it went well.

My mother had been most helpful again supplying me with tools and books on jewellery-making sent from America. I still had much to learn, and now turned my attention to the setting of stones. This was quite a new technique for the silversmiths. Very few of them mastered the art of making a base the exact size and shape of a gem stone and then devise a 'collar' as it was called to sit around it to secure the stone. My mother sent me also catalogues of gem stones and tools but neither the silversmiths nor I knew what to do with the tools. They were too sophisticated. I always marvelled at the simple tools that the craftsmen used, to bring out such beautiful and well made designs. I always wore my newest design to sustain the interest of the public.

We moved in high society, because Tommy of course had to liaise with Governors and Premiers. At the time the Governor was the most charming Sir Francis Ibiam and his wife the equally charming and capable Lady Ibiam. The latter had heard of me and seen my television programmes. She wanted to get to know me and asked me to a tea party at State House. There I met many highly placed Nigerian ladies, all very fashionably dressed in native dress. The Igbo ladies were not bound by wrappers up and down, they made their outfits in local materials to be highly fashionable. They had excellent dress sense and were consequently interested in meeting a designer of clothes and jewellery. But Lady Ibiam had an ulterior motive for inviting me. She wanted me to become a member of her Ecumenical Society. I did not really know what this meant, but was willing to contribute what I could to a good cause. So, I was roped in to take part in women's gatherings where we made things by hand to be sold at fund raising events. The money so raised would go to churches of different denominations.

My activities with the silver jewellery brought me into the centre of society. People were always grouped around me at cocktail parties and even asked Tommy about this phenomenon of the silver industry which was springing up from nowhere. I used to hear him say: "Oh I don't know what my wife is doing. I never interfere in her activities. You must ask her."

One thing was true, that he never asked for any of my earnings all through our lives. I will give him credit for that. Whatever I contributed, I did of my own free will. I had always thought that money came between husband and wife and resolved from a very early age that I would be self-sufficient and never ask my husband for anything. Maybe it was a mistake. Not only did he have much surplus to spend elsewhere, but he became so confident that I did not need anything that he never anticipated what need I might have. Of course, in the case of his travels he did ask me what he should bring for me and I stated what I wanted.

Now in this new situation where I had become a personality in my own right he seemed to be a little displaced. He was not the only star in the family anymore.

We settled down so well that we were asked to every party or social function like weddings, naming ceremonies, engagements apart from the annual holidays that life became almost too hectic, but Tommy could not afford to refuse any invitation. His golf club activities came into it as well and one Christmas we were so tired of going to parties that we wondered how we could get out of doing our own. In fact, at that time everybody was tired of Christmas and subsequently New Year's parties. To give ourselves a bit of space, I suggested we should wait until the sixth of January and celebrate Epiphany in the French manner. The rules for this were that one would hide a silver piece in a cake of which everybody had to partake, and the person who found the silver piece was made King for the year. He could then choose his queen, and in most cases he would choose his wife of course. For these roles of king and queen, I prepared two red velvet cloaks and a crown of gold cardboard for each of them. A larger crown for the king, a smaller one for the queen, but both were set with what looked like jewelled stones.

For this special event we had invited two hundred guests and the evening party took place in the garden where we had put tables and chairs. The problem of baking a cake so large for two hundred people, was solved by baking two yeast cakes with sugar icing and divided into small portions in baking, so that I knew where I put the silver piece and I made sure that every piece of cake on that tray was eaten. We explained the method of the game before a jubilant crowd. They thought it would be great fun and eagerly reached for the cake. There was another uproar when the person found the silver piece and chose his queen. Great applause and great laughter, because now they were being robed by me with the velvet cloaks and the crowns set upon their heads. When I had so dressed them, I bowed before the 'King' addressing him as "Your Majesty" and the same before the 'Queen', with a little curtsey. For the whole of that year, whoever met the King or the Queen anywhere in town would address him as His Majesty or the Queen likewise as Her Majesty. This created great fun all through the year and people were looking forward to the next Epiphany party where a new king would be chosen. This party was reported in the newspaper as having been very unusual and very successful. "Thank you Pooppie" Tommy would say after each event that took place in our house. "Thank you Pooppie, well done."

Monu went to All Saints School in Enugu where I met Irene Nwokedi. She, an Englishwoman was married to Francis Nwokedi, an Igbo lawyer, she had four children, her eldest son the exact age of Monu, and her last little daughter was born in the exact month and year as Temi. So we had a great deal in common. She was a nursing sister but I heard she was also a trained teacher. Monu was a bit weak in mathematics, because the Shell school had not been as strict in their teaching as All Saints. I asked Irene whether she would coach Monu in mathematics, but she was hesitant. I offered to pay her of course and she, as she later told me, mentioned a huge sum in order to drive me away. Five pounds a lesson. I thought for a moment, but realised that mathematics was so important especially at Monu's young age that it was worth spending money on it. So I agreed, and my friend Irene lost her objections. Monu caught up very well under her guidance and needed no further tuition the following year. He and her son Agha became firm friends and so did our two little girls Temi and Uzo.

Irene became my life-long friend, just as her younger daughter Uzo and my daughter Temi are still friends today 35 years later.

Monu was very close to Agha, Irene's eldest son, and would have remained so, I am sure, if young Agha, age 23 and a qualified lawyer, had not died in a car crash on the Lagos-Benin Road.

It was the greatest tragedy in Irene's life. No one could ever really console her for the rest of her days. Agha had been highly intelligent, sensitive, philosophical and wise beyond his age. Mother and son had similar tastes in art and literature, they were in tune, and Agha was a devoted first son.

Irene Nwokedi did have two qualifications. She was a nurse and midwife as well as a trained teacher. In both professions — as in her private life — she was hard-working, ultra conscientious and ultra truthful. She was heroic and powerful when she needed to be. She was the salt of the earth. When we left Enugu for Benin City, we still visited each other periodically, until the Biafran war broke out. Communication then was impossible until I heard from Irene a year after cessation of hostilities that she was in England with her four children. She was working as a teacher.

On my next visit to England I stayed with her and heard the full story of her experiences on the battle front. She had felt the need to be there when there were no doctors around and she repaired the maimed and wounded as best as she could. There were no drugs other than penicillin powder. She poured this powder into gaping wounds and stitched them up, praying that God would help to heal. On one occasion she carried a wounded soldier to safety on her back, when she broke down under the load. She had slipped a disk in her spine and was in agony, unable to move. She and her children were flown to England in a Red Cross plane. She recovered eventually, but remained in England where, in retirement, she developed her artistic talents by learning to paint in oils, and her paintings won prizes. She died of a heart attack in 1998. I lost a true friend.

I was still involved in Lady Ibiam's Ecumenical activities. During one fund raising bazaar, I had a table displaying my silver jewellery and the table was crowded, to the envy of other stall holders. As we handed over ten per cent of our takings to the organisation, Lady Ibiam was pleased. It also gave our product more exposure. On another occasion we arranged a funfair and I offered to do palm-reading. I was dressed for the part like a Gypsy wearing a large Spanish shawl, a head scarf, heavy eye make-up, huge earrings, and smoking a cigar. There were crowds of people outside my 'Tent' waiting to have their fortune told.

That was a novelty, and my predictions were not as callous as you might expect, because I always asked for the client's birth date and while looking at his palm I could read his character from the date. I did see one ten-year-old boy with an amazing headline that stretched from east to west on the palm. This meant that he was extremely intelligent but his palm had no heartline. I have always wondered what became of this boy. Anyway I collected a lot of money for the Ecumenical Centre.

Whenever things go smoothly there is bound to be some event to rock the boat. Once again, it was the news that we were to be promoted to Benin City. 1965, oil had started flowing in the Midwest, and as Tommy was a son of the Midwest State, it seemed a perfect choice to send him there as Shell BP Representative, to turn on the tap of the flow-station.

We, the family, were faced with yet another challenge. Tommy was transferred to Benin City but there was no house ready for us to follow him. An elegant bungalow would be built for the Representative, but for now he would have guest house accommodation only, not enough for the family to join. So, my mother, Eda, the children and I were sent back to Port Harcourt to wait until the house in Benin City was ready to hold us all. There were many farewell parties in our honour now, and I remember vividly one judge making a speech asking "how is Benin City going to contain Hilda and Tommy?"

The company asked Tommy to select a suitable parcel of land for the Representative's accommodation, and while he was at it he selected an equally large parcel for ourselves next door to the Shell BP compound in Benin. It was located on the prestigious Airport Road, although at that time Airport Road was still bush. There were a few small houses scattered here and there but our own plot had been used as a night soil field. That was the reason why everything that Tommy planted flourished beyond expectation. The soil had been so fertilized!

The building of the bungalow took over a year. In the meantime Tommy used to come to Port Harcourt once a month, and I was flown by helicopter to Lagos to shop for the things we would need for the house. It was my privilege to choose the dinner sets, coffee sets, the crystal glasses, the carpets and sitting room furniture. This I chose specially with regard to my always painful back. It was a beautiful modern set which had a special upholstery built into the very place to support the small of the back. A round black and white Axminster carpet was an unusual choice. It made a circle in the room for people to sit around and make easy contact. While the building was going on Tommy had office accommodation in a nearby street and the office accommodation had a guest house attached to it where he lived.

In 1965 while we were in Port Harcourt awaiting our accommodation in Benin to be ready, Tommy broached the subject of my naturalization as a Nigerian citizen. I had been of the same mind. My husband was Nigerian. My children were Nigerian. What was I doing being a 'foreigner' in my own family? When it came to the crunch though, I had not expected the detail of having to renounce my British citizenship in order to acquire the Nigerian one. It was a very painful moment, as I remembered the kindness and generosity of the British people who had saved me from being stateless. I was eternally grateful for that.

However, I had married into a faraway former colony and I wanted my husband to have the emotional security of knowing, that I had come to stay. I was not going to have one foot in one country and the other in another. I loved Nigeria and her people, and I hoped to make my contribution where I could.

Tommy started compiling the necessary documents for my application. These included testimonials from Nigerians of note, vouching for my character and confirming that I had adapted well. Afterall, I was wearing Nigerian dress, eating and cooking Nigerian food and I even spoke a little of my husband's language. The approval came two years later in 1967. Yes, I had chosen to be a Nigerian citizen.

During that same period in Port Harcourt I had an unexpected visitor. A wholly delightful woman came all the way from Ibadan to find me. She had seen our silver jewellery in Kingsway Stores and was so delighted and impressed with it that on the flimsiest directions she was determined to find me in the Shell Camp at Port Harcourt. She was the beautiful Begum Hendrickse, wife of Professor Ralph Hendrickse, a paediatrician at the University College Teaching Hospital of Ibadan. The couple both came from South Africa where they were grouped among the 'coloureds' of Asian origin. Begum was stunning looking, gentle and humorous to deal with. We had in common our enthusiasm and love for African art. She had opened such a shop in the Premier Hotel of Ibadan and was keen to add our silver jewellery to her stock. Until she saw it at Kingsway Stores she had not known that such a cottage industry existed in Nigeria.

"You are a first." She said to me on parting, "and you must meet another first. Have you heard of Betty Okuboyejo?" I had not, and so Begum described this Scottish young woman who was married to a Nigerian doctor. She lived in Ijebu-Ode. She had introduced colourfast Adire cloth. The local Adire was highly prized by local and expatriate women alike, but it rubbed off on white skins leaving armpits, bras and waistlines navy blue when the weather got hot and the wearers perspired.

Begum and I had bonded instantly. As soon as I could get to Ibadan to see (and supply) her shop, she introduced me to the bubbly, buxom Betty with big blue eyes in her deceptive babyface. Deceptive, because this face hid a powerful personality with an astute and creative brain. I noticed her finger nails which were ingrained with red and blue dye. She carried them like a trade mark and assured me in her giggly manner that the inside of her bath at home, in which she dyed the cloths, sported the same indelible colours. She paid women in the market to tie the cloths she gave them into well known different traditional patterns, but she dyed them with her own hands in her bath.

In those days there were no small portions of dye available. Betty saved long and hard to be able to buy a full drum of I.C.I. colourfast blue which had to be shipped from England. When her fabrics began to sell well she was able to buy a drum of red. Mixing these two dyes she could now make purple as well. So she had red, blue and purple and I am still the proud owner of a purple Caftan with white patterns which is over thirty years old, still good looking and indestructible; as is the friendship between Betty and me.

Our friend Irene and her children sometimes came to see us in Port Harcourt, so that not all ties were broken. It was not too far for them to motor down from Enugu.

The bungalow was being built by an Italian company and was beautifully finished. Before we were ready to move into it Tommy for once suggested that we should go on a holiday together. We never had a holiday as a family and we now chose Las Palmas on the Canary Islands. Monu was then eleven years old and Temi almost five. Tommy really did not like travelling. I believe he was a stay-at-home previously described as a couch potato. This time I had thanked him for taking a holiday, the experience of which would unite us as a family with its memories.

Before we left Enugu of course there were the usual farewell parties given to us by different departments. I was given a farewell party by Lady Ibiam's Ecumenical Centre Organisation. My farewell gift was an impressive large brass tray engraved with the Ecumenical symbols and on the rim of the round tray was embossed: "For Hilda Ogbe in appreciation for her contributions to the Ecumenical Centre." And the year 1965, I had another gift from a high personality and that was the Premier Dr. Michael Okpara and his wife. There too at the State House we were given a dinner which ended with a complimentary speech by the Premier about Tommy's activities in the region on behalf of Shell BP. I don't know how they knew, but my contributions towards giving employment to silversmiths were also mentioned and I was given a parcel of beautiful cloth. Mrs Okpara presented me with a special gift from Calabar. She knew of my love for handicrafts and chose a bag made of velvet embroidered with beads in floral patterns and containing a series of finely carved chewing sticks. She explained that this bag would be a special gift from a woman to her lover. The bag is with me still and has been an inspiration for other carved chewing sticks.

So, our departure became real, and we were sorry to leave the beautiful town of Enugu and the most beautiful residence of the architect designed house and garden on Ridgeway. Before our departure I had gone to see the manager of Kingsway Stores to ask whether he would like to sell our jewellery. It was a bold move, because I did not have a recognised company, I was working with a cottage industry. The manager was doubtful. Even when I showed him newspaper cuttings and photographs of past exhibitions he said he would have to consult head office in Lagos. He also asked me whether there would not be a saturation point, at which the customers would lose interest in our goods. I assured him that for many years to come the silver would remain the most popular gift item in Nigeria because everybody abroad loved a gift of jewellery, and it was so light and easy to carry. It did not have the weight that leather poofs or wood carvings or bronzes have. It would remain a very popular tourist item. I spoke with conviction and I am glad to say that up till now, 36 years later, the jewellery is still selling well. Even so, Lagos Head Office was contacted and they, of course, wanted to see samples. It was not until after our return from holiday that I was able to visit Lagos UAC Head Office.

After all the farewell parties that were given to us, Tommy had to go alone to Benin and the children and I had to go back to Port Harcourt because there was no accommodation for us in Benin. We remained in Port Harcourt until the house that was being built for us was ready in Benin City.

As we were leaving Enugu, and without settling into our newly built bungalow, we dumped our personal belongings in the Shell guest house, packed what we would need for the holiday and set off for the Canary Islands. There in Las Palmas, Tommy found a good and reasonable hotel for the four of us and we began to get our bearings of the town. While I took the children to the zoo, to the beach of course, to donkey-rides, or to see local dance groups, Tommy either slept in the hotel or went out into the town looking for bargains.

In years gone by in London, some scientist friends of ours who had knowledge of Phrenology, had seen Tommy come home from an auction with a taxi load of goods. They had laughed and said Tommy had a large "acquisition bump". Here now in Las Palmas Tommy's bump impelled him to go hunting for second-hand clothes. Whether he always thought of his poor relations at home, or whether he intended to sell them, I never knew. When at home I did not follow up their dispersal.

I was content that he had some occupation which gave him pleasure. The children and I enjoyed our activities and when we had lunch together at a restaurant on the beach we ordered the most unusual fish dishes in order to get to know them. Tommy joined us because he was from Warri/Forcados, he liked fish also. He was a Cancerian, a water baby so to say, and it was natural for him to like fish and the sea (although he did not swim) and ocean going ships. The most interesting dish we had was called "Calamares". These were rings of octopus tentacles. The tentacles were hollow and when sliced made rings which were then dipped in batter and deep fried. We all loved those rings, although they were a bit hard to chew. We also enjoyed a "Sopa De Mar", soup of the sea it was called. It was a fish soup which included all sorts of creatures not only fish but shrimps, lobster, shells and spices which were most delicious.

I hunted the jewellery shops, seeing that the gold was very cheap. I bought a ring and a pair of pendants set with coral beads which I would later make into earrings.

Every time Tommy came home with second-hand clothes and we were already in the hotel room, he would call out "S.S. Independa", in other words, the ship had come home loaded. It was really great fun when he dumped all his bag onto the bed so that we could see what his booty had been that day. He had met several Yoruba speaking traders who had been helpful to him (and lightened his purse).

I was fascinated by the painted pottery of the Island and came home with three candle sticks which could be hung on the wall and a matching vase all painted with flowers. I use all these in my house today, 34 years later.

When we returned to Benin City, life began in earnest. We had not only to settle into our new house, but we had to find schools for the children. Monu was eleven years old and Temi five years. Both were accommodated in the Catholic Primary School of "Emotan", but Monu soon had to sit his eleven plus exams. Both children were bright and active in school and always well liked.

Part of settling in a new town is making new friends and we became members of the social club in Benin and used its swimming pool. There, hanging on the edge of the pool I met another English mother who had a mixed child of Temi's age. The two of them were frolicking in the water, and I approached the mother. I introduced myself and told her we had just arrived in Benin City to settle here. She was shy, or should I say diffident, because when I asked her what her profession was she said she had had many jobs in her life. She had been an accounts clerk, she had been a bookkeeper and a teacher. I was immediately interested and asked if she could suggest some good reading for my son of eleven years. We talked about that for a while until I asked whether she was teaching in Benin now. She then reluctantly told me that she was a lawyer, and had just been promoted to the Bench as magistrate. Wow! Why was she hiding her light under a bushel?

We started visiting each other, and I found her delightful company. She was a very knowledgeable person, although she called herself 'a mine of useless information'. I very much enjoyed knowing her and was privileged to see her advance from magistrate to senior magistrate, to chief magistrate and eventually to Judge of the Benin High Court. She was such an interesting person with many facets to her personality. She had a wonderful sense of humour and maybe, the only thing I did not fully share with her was her passion for animals. I would almost say she preferred animals to humans. She had a special rapport with all creatures, even birds. Kingfishers used to follow her wherever she lived, even when she visited Lagos. Her full name was Joan Aiwerioghene, and we have been friends now for thirty-four years.

Monu was admitted to Federal Government College, Warri. I was really sad to see him go into a boarding school, and I lost forever the years he spent in that school, because his development took place in an environment whose influences I did not know. Consequently, I somehow lost touch with the innermost child in him, and this gap has remained to this day.

His first impressions, although he never complained, were that the food was so peppery. It burned his mouth, so that he needed extra pocket money to cool it with Sprite or 7-Up after every meal. Apart from that he never wrote. He came on mid-term and holidays of course, but somehow there was always a gap between the Monu I had known so well and the Monu who was now a boarder.

Now in Benin City after our return from holiday I set about making a home in the beautiful modern bungalow with its wide open patio which was ideal for giving parties. The thoughtful contractors had even built a bar into it. After I had got used to my new home I involved myself again in the silver business. My workers came from Enugu to deliver the orders I had given them and even the silversmiths from Port Harcourt made the long journey to Benin City.

Chapter V

THE NIGERIAN CIVIL WAR

But that year, in 1966, political storm clouds had gathered in the country. The year before, young military officers had overturned the civilian government. There were cruel ethnic killings in the north by Hausas of Igbo settlers in their midst. Reprisals followed in the south where the Igbos retaliated against the Hausas. Trainloads of wounded and maimed Igbos came down from the north at Ojukwu's order to "come home to their *tents*". Ojukwu, the dynamic young military leader of Oxford education, seceded from the Federation of Nigeria. He called his eastern region now Biafra. I told my silversmiths who worked in Enugu, but who hailed from Midwest Igbo land, (this side of the Niger), to leave the Igbo heartland, as Ojukwu called it, and come home. I felt they would not be safe because they were foreigners in Igbo heartland. It took some time for them to make up their minds to follow my advice, but when they did, they were not sorry. The last man had just crossed over the Niger Bridge when it was bombed and destroyed, to cut Biafra off from the Federation. My silversmiths settled around Asaba and asked me "How did Madam know?" I replied that I just did not think that Biafra would succeed, and I foresaw that the people there would undergo great suffering.

On the 8th of August, 1966 we had heard many rumours on BBC of what was happening in Biafra. They were of the opinion that the Biafrans wanted to colonise Nigeria. One morning there was rumbling of heavy machinery like tanks around our area in Benin City. Tommy drove out early into the town to see what was happening. He told us to close the curtains of our bungalow and stay in the house.

We had many visitors staying with us such as Freedom and Monu on school holiday, a cousin Tunde and two young boys, her son and her nephew staying with us also, there was Mercy, a friend from years ago who had come to visit, there was a little girl, Karen Thomas, who had come for a holiday to play with Temi, there were my mother, Tommy and I plus staff. For the moment nobody could move.

We were sitting behind drawn curtains having breakfast when we heard footsteps crunching on the gravel outside the house. I peeped through the curtain and saw it was Tommy on foot. We let him in quickly and he told us how he had abandoned his Mercedes in Mission Road of Benin City, had given the key to a shopkeeper to hold for him and had come home on foot because there was heavy army machinery everywhere. He saw that people had fled in all directions, throwing their bicycles down, running with their slippers flying from their feet and there was general agitation in town.

We sat glued to the BBC and from the BBC we heard reports that the Biafran Army had overtaken the Midwest of Nigeria and the English reporter somehow joyfully said "We are now at Or", that is the way he pronounced Ore "making for Lagos". In other words, he reported a triumphant march of the Biafran Army towards Lagos.

On that first day when Tommy realised that we were now occupied, he and the houseboys went out to buy large quantities of yams and a carton of frozen fish. He had the foresight that, as we were occupied, there might be a shortage of food in the town soon, because occupying armies usually loot foodstuffs and whatever else they can lay their hands on.

For all those stuck in the house under Tommy's orders it was a busy time. He ordered women and children to stay in the house but he went out with the male staff, continuing to provide food for all of us. The best part of this occupation was that he always stayed at home at night. Every night we had fish pepper soup and yam and every night he sat by the radio relaying the news to us. If I say we were kept busy, it means that Mercy and I were doing a lot of sewing because Mercy knew how to handle a sewing machine. We made children's dresses from materials I had at home, and the children, Karen and Temi had lessons from my mother.

Freedom, the eldest, taught the younger boys. In the evenings we all played Scrabble which was my mother's favourite word game. It was, altogether, a happy period, until Tommy relayed from the radio that the Federal Army was coming in from the North and not from Lagos as anticipated. They were in fact nearing Auchi. His brother Dr. David Ogbe was stationed in Auchi with his Swiss wife and four children. He was in charge of Auchi General Hospital. Irma, his wife was a nurse and was working with him.

Sometime in the early 1950's, Tommy's brother David had qualified as a pharmacist in Nigeria and had completed his first year in medicine. He had done so well, that he won a scholarship to study medicine in England. He looked up to Tommy who was 14 years older and had brought him up from the age of 4 when he took David from his mother who lived in a village. David was studious and intelligent but stood in contrast to his big brother. Physically shorter and of a gentle relaxed nature, he had something naive about him. He met the world with smiles and trust and had none of Tommy's deep furrows etched into his forehead. His patients loved him. While studying in Liverpool he met the petite and dainty Irma from Switzerland whom he married with Tommy's consent. Irma completed her studies as nurse and midwife and was a great help to David throughout their lives.

Now they were stationed in Auchi, not so far away from us in Benin, and we lived in hope that soon the Federal Army would reach us too. On the day they did, there was a strange announcement on the local radio which said "six frogs are swinging". We felt that it was a coded message, and true enough, very soon we heard shelling and bombing of Benin City. When the news got around that the Federal Troops were advancing, many Biafrans had fled already but there was a pocket of them left at the airport. We knew this afterwards. For the moment we could not understand why there was bombing going on in our area. Tommy ordered all of us to lie down in the corridor where there were no glass windows to shatter and hurt us. All sixteen of us were doing so. We were lying down and full of excitement whispering to each other what might be happening outside and when would all this end.

I had the callous presence of mind to bring out my tape recorder to record the shelling which was now getting nearer and quite heavy, because I felt it was a historical moment. The journalist in me overrode the sympathy of a mother for her frightened child because Temi whimpered "Mummy, Mummy" and clung to me. Fortunately, my mother was there to soothe her and later my tape-recording was used by the local radio station to describe the moment of liberation for the Midwest.

As we were lying in some trepidation the shells now began crashing around us, not one, not two, not three, not four. One after the other aimed at the airport. When all was quiet eventually and we were able to come out we saw a huge crater made by a shell in our front garden. It had been close, very close to falling on the roof of our house. But the Almighty was kind to our family and deviated the shell just a little bit from its course. All the neighbours came to see the mighty hole, deep and wide, on our lawn.

There were signs of liberation. Tommy went out into Reservation Road and saw military trucks driving all over the town. The soldiers who came through that road he described as looking very stern, their guns drawn, they lay behind them, not looking left or right, despite the jubilating crowds that welcomed them. They were Murtala Mohammed's disciplined men.

The not-so-disciplined population began looting almost at once. Even in the Reservation where we lived they looted houses that had stood empty when their owners had fled from the turmoil. From our garden at the back, we could see people carrying mattresses, pieces of furniture, lamps, framed pictures, and one even carried fluorescent light tubes on his head as well as a packet of Omo in his free hand.

Suddenly shots rang out and through a megaphone the orders came fast and furious. "Put that looting down on the golf course or we shall shoot." When nobody listened, a few shots were aimed at looter's feet. The shots were so accurate that they dug into the grass beside the looter kicking up earth so that each person knew that these people meant business. The golf course was now littered with furniture and small possessions, then later in the day came the announcement over the radio that the owners of the looted articles should come to the golf course, identify their possessions and take them back.

Tommy was thrilled that the federal soldiers had come. He went out with a basket of beer and food to say thank you to them and take some luxuries to them. As he neared the General Hospital through Reservation Road, he was shouted at: "Halt. Who goes there?" In his charming breezy manner he said, "I have come to thank you. Here is food and drink for you."

"Put it down in the middle of the road," was the stern reply "and go away." He saw soldiers lying on their stomachs on the ground, their rifles at the ready. He too then knew that they meant business. It appeared that the last Biafrans had taken shelter in the hospital and that is why that area was heavily guarded.

The young Lt. Col. Ogbemudia who liberated the Midwest and especially Benin City was the one who had set his shells to be fired towards the airport from the Ikpoba Bridge quite some kilometers away from us. Later, when we got to know him we joked with him and reproached him that he had very nearly wiped out our whole family. But he had done well, and he became a very popular figure.

It was now September. We had been occupied for six weeks. In looking back it had been a short time, but while we were confined to camp, it had dragged, not knowing when it would end.

While all our visitors dispersed now, glad to be able to travel back to their homes, we had a new addition to the household. Tommy had interviewed an applicant for the job of a cook. The man had come with his references on the very day we were liberated, and Tommy had shooed him away shouting excitedly: "Not now, not now. The Federal are coming." Fortunately for us, the applicant came again the following day, when everybody had calmed down, and for me it was another lucky day. Because this applicant was none other than Stephen, my most capable and faithful cook for thirty-three years now. We did not know it then, but he was a gem of a human being. He had standard six education, could read and write very well, could understand recipes, and was so fast in his cooking that sometimes when I wanted to change my mind about a dish he had already prepared it, maybe within half an hour of my giving the instruction. He had had his basic training in an English family in Warri and knew all the standard English dishes, but our household was very cosmopolitan. He and I could read a recipe together and have him carry it out, be it continental or Chinese, or Indian, or Jewish, or Indonesian, — he made them all, tasted them all and mentally noted the ones he thought were awful. But he never criticised. He was discretion itself, and above all, he was and still is a diplomatic and very peaceful man. Almost like another Anthony, but his sphere of work was different.

With Stephen in the kitchen I had no more worries, because Tommy himself taught him how he wanted his native dishes cooked. I knew how to cook them, but my time was otherwise occupied, and I willingly left the kitchen to Stephen. Only when I had a whim of "designing" a different dish, or a dessert, or some cake baking, did I attach myself to Stephen to make sure that my ideas were carried out in edible form. These days thirty-three years later, we measure recipes together, because it was just too much to ask this dear man to switch from long established pounds and ounces to the decimal system of kilogrammes and grammes.

Stephen is as kind to children as he is to animals, a very rare quality in a Nigerian servant. He cooks for dogs and cats with equal care and regularity as he cooks for the humans. Stephen was assisted by a steward or you might as well call them houseboys, who change from time to time. They stayed a year or two and then a new one would come. One of them, Joe was a particularly gifted boy who could draw beautifully. I thought it was a pity not to help him on in life and asked what else he would like to do if he were not a houseboy. He said he would like to be an electrician. So, I introduced him to a friend of ours who was an electrical engineer and asked whether he would take this boy into training. He did so, and Joe, to this day repairs my radios and tape recorders. He had made himself independent, and although he is not earning big money, he lives modestly, and has four very handsome grown up children now.

Young Lt. Col. Ogbemudia was a huge success as Governor of the Midwest. He was a young man full of energy, and a born leader. He applied his intelligence to every aspect of the community. He was interested in trade and commerce, education, medical services, industry, and even small-scale industries. An Englishman had come to Midwest Nigeria to suggest a plan for small-scale industries. It was beautifully bound when he presented it to Lt. Col. Ogbemudia. He accompanied his report with the remark that "Small-scale industries do provide employment and they do pay, as Mrs. Ogbe has shown."

"Who is Mrs. Ogbe?" Lt. Col. Ogbemudia whom I shall henceforth call Samuel Ogbemudia wanted to know. Apparently the man, Mr. Green, told him about my work with the craftsmen, and in the meantime I had already got involved with the carvers and brass casters in Benin as well. Col. Ogbemudia was a man who could not wait. He got into his car and drove up to our bungalow with his outriders, sirens blaring so that I came out of the house worried, wondering what was happening. He unnecessarily introduced himself and asked if I was Mrs. Ogbe. When I confirmed it he said, "I have heard much about your activities with local craftsmen. Can you show me some of the work you are doing?"

"Of course, Your Excellency, please come and sit down." I brought out all the drawers of the cupboard I had had made for the silver jewellery. They were sorted into the small drawers in alphabetical order. I brought out several of these and Sam Ogbemudia asked, "these are made in Nigeria?"

"Yes Your Excellency. Not only in Nigeria but in this Midwest State."

"You mean these are not from India?" he asked.

"No Your Excellency, they are made locally. I can take you to some of the workshops if you like."

"Alright", he said. "Thank you. I shall go to see your husband and ask him to bring you to State House this evening. I have something to discuss with you."

That very evening, my husband drove me to State House and Sam did not waste time in explaining his plans. He had in mind a school in which craftsmen like carvers and brass casters would be trained. But I opposed the idea.

"Your Excellency", I said, "if you do that, you will spoil the typically Benin handwriting of the craftsmen. It is better for the crafts to be handed down from father to son to retain their character."

"What do you suggest then?" he asked me.

And I answered, "what we need is a locally situated crafts shop in which all the talents of the Midwest Region will be shown and sold under one roof. I know the mentality of foreign tourists. They do not like to bargain. I would like to see a real shop with fixed prices which will be fair to the craftsman and fair to the customer."

He listened attentively, then got up. "Alright, I know just the place for such a shop. Follow me to the Ring Road."

He drove himself although it was nine o'clock in the evening and dark and we followed with car and driver. At Ring Road he shone his torch over a football field and asked: "Would this location be alright?"

I was thrilled. It was just the very ideal spot on the central roundabout of Ring Road, a stone's throw from the Museum, and at the back, a stone's throw from the palace of the Oba of the Edo people. I could hardly believe my luck.

"Well, how big should it be?"

I said "I don't know what money you want to put into it." He then scribbled on the bonnet of the car on a piece of paper, while we held the torch for him and said "I think we could afford four thousand pounds and the size would be thirty by forty feet. What do you need?"

I told him I needed a front shop, a small office behind, a store behind that and most important, a flush toilet. He noted it all down and said "My chief engineer and architect will be on your doorstep on Monday morning." With that he saluted and departed.

Monday morning at eight o'clock both engineer and architect did appear at our house. We sat down and discussed in detail how to construct the Midwest Craftshop. It was left to me to supply the locally made parts of the building such as carved doors and artistically welded burglar proof for the windows, locally cast brass knobs for the doors, and flower pots around the outside of the building which would be demarcated by small white posts and looping chains between them.

In the meantime, Sam provided me with transport and a driver to tour every corner of the Midwest Region to ferret out artistic talents. This took me as far north as Igarra and Ososo and south to Forcados.

Five months passed and in this short time the building was fully completed in every aspect and fully stocked with all the best crafts that I had found in the four corners of the Midwest State. There was a ceremonial opening on 5th July, 1968, just barely five months after the inception of the idea. The opening ceremony was grand and I spoke a few words saying that for me and the craftsmen, a dream had come true. And this dream had been turned into reality by none other than the young Military Governor, Lt. Col. Ogbemudia. He was by now known to be an action man because he applied himself, all his personal supervision and energy to any project that he started.

At the time I did not think people realised the full impact this shop would have on promoting Midwest Nigeria and Nigeria in general. In fact, one reader wrote to the Observer "whether it was not a luxury to create such a shop, when other areas of the community needed attention". I replied to that letter in the newspaper saying it was not a luxury, it was trade and recognition for our State.

The fact was that people came from far and wide to Benin City just to visit the Craftshop. It had been well advertised in the newspapers, and on the road coming to Benin City, there were large signboards saying: "When you get to the centre visit the Midwest Craftshop." All the points that I had envisaged, such as fixed prices, decent surroundings, easy access, and the flush toilet proved to be great catalysts for foreign tourists.

We must remember that at that time 1968 there was only one other crafts shop in Nigeria, and that was in Lagos. Lagos always had higher prices and more ambitious works of art that hardly any tourists could carry home, but Benin offered something for everybody, and the tourists were happy to buy Benin bronzes, Benin carvings, local weaving, silver jewellery, local paintings, all under one roof. From Forcados I had brought beautiful miniature canoes and paddles that would be the joy of any teenage boy to put up on the wall of his bedroom.

There was one incident that occurred over and over again which I did not understand. I had placed Olokun pots as flower pots filled with earth and planted with pretty flowers around the building, why was one or the other smashed or destroyed every so often? What did it mean? Who was doing it?

Nobody wanted to tell me, for fear of offending me perhaps. Eventually our wise Mallam, the Storekeeper, explained that he had been told by a Benin woman that the Olokun pot is sacred for the goddess Olokun and serves the women in the community. They must have felt that it was sacrilege to use it for flowers, when it should be used for offerings to the goddess Olokun.

Olokun is the goddess of the rivers and the sea and as I said she protects the women in the community. Where there is any problem in the family, be it sickness or a child badly wanted or loss of job of the husband or need of money, the woman of the house would put offerings of palmnuts, maybe white cloth, and certain herbs into the pot and walk down to the river with it to throw the offerings into the river for the goddess to receive them. She would be dressed all in white and she would be accompanied by other women all dressed in white and by the priestess of Olokun who would be dressed with white and red.

Of course, when I realised the significance of the pot, I respected its meaning and withdrew all the pots to be sold only as artistic objects, but empty of sand and flowers. I replaced them with simple clay pots to decorate the outside of the shop.

I tried to educate myself on the legends of the Benin people so that when a customer asked me "What does this statue mean?" I would know which Oba it represented or which warrior or which soothsayer. I went into the Museum also to familiarise myself with artwork that had been depicted centuries ago and which was still being propagated today by the descendants of the original craftsman. I saw there several soldiers, men with European features and long beards. The curator of the Museum told me that they were the Portuguese who first came into contact with Nigeria on the West coast in the sixteenth century. The joke went around, and I now understood it, that these Portuguese were so flat-bottomed that the slang word for them or for any European person afterwards was "Potoki", meaning that European buttocks were flat and not as well rounded as the African ones.

I learned a lot of amusing anecdotes and legends pertaining also to the work carved in ebony. I visited many workshops and chatted with the carvers. The biggest workshop, which always caught my fancy, was the Edaiken United Carving Industry on Mission Road. They had a vast showroom on the corner of number 40, which I did not find so inspiring. It had rows and rows of lions, elephants, ashtrays, rabbits and the run-of-the-mill objects which were bought by the Hausa traders to be distributed all over the country. What fascinated me was the large workshop behind the store front. As I went around the back of the shop I could hear the cheerful hammering of at least twenty carvers each fashioning his own piece of sculpture. Each man had made his own mallet from ebony to suit his hand in weight and size. This mallet hammered away at the chisels which were used to carve out the object of the artwork. In this workshop I saw not only black ebony statues being made but the carvers also made doors and carved chests from mahogany or walnut planks.

The whole workshop reminded me of Snowhite's seven dwarves who hammered away at their daily job. When I took tourists to see the workshop, I always asked them to pick up a chip of black wood from the floor so that it would be a souvenir to remind them that the statues they were buying were made of purest natural black wood. I also showed them the logs of Ebony that were lying in front of the workshop and pointed out how the centre of the tree was pure black but the sap around it was of a lighter colour.

In those days there were still many huge Ebony trees in the forest, with a girth of twenty or more feet, so that it was possible to make something in pure black. Nowadays, at the turn of the century, the forests are so decimated of mature trees, that many of the carvings have only patches of black on them but the rest is of a lighter brown, because the trees are not mature enough to have the big core of black. I also learned that Ebony is very heavy. When I came across a lightweight black statue I scratched the bottom of it to see whether it was made of light coloured wood painted black. There were many of those in circulation, but not made in Benin. So I enlightened our customers that they were getting the real thing made of black wood and not painted. If the carvers chose to put black shoe polish on black wood, that was their own idea of making the article shine. I did not approve of such methods nor did I buy for the shop these shiny articles. I encouraged the carvers to give them a chisel finish which was an uneven finish almost like pock marks, but it looked artistic and the customer knew he was buying high quality art.

The brasscasting was a hot and long job. If people only knew how much time goes into making a clay core first, of then fashioning the entire statue or the entire face and crown of bees wax laid onto to the core and then the outer layer of mud or clay put over the bees wax minding the sprues at the bottom! These are the channels through which the heated bees wax runs out and into which the molten brass is then poured, to run into all the nooks and crannies, which the molten wax had left behind. Then the whole form is steel-banded, wound around with steel strips. The form is then put upside down into the furnace or hot open fire until it is hot enough for the molten wax to be poured out into a basin so that it can be used again. In the art world this method is called the "Cire Perdue" or literally, the Lost Wax Method.

What is worth mentioning is that with this method every object is an original. There is no casting from a mold. Not many people appreciate this side of the craft when they bargain for the lowest price of a piece of brass.

One of the many functions of Sam Ogbemudia was to open the new road from Benin to Warri. It had been built and finished a long time but it had not been commissioned. We were all waiting anxiously that it should be possible now for us to travel to Warri without having to cross by ferry at Sapele. Action Man that he was, Ogbemudia opened the road and installed toll booths on it so that he would get revenue from cars which used the road. It was a great event.

Now Warri, Tommy's home town, was within reach for all of us. At the approach to his village of Ugbuwangue there was a large signboard showing a chief wearing a waistcoat, a top hat and coral beads around his neck. The signboard read "Yowunren-Agbeje Family Village". Prince Yowunren was the father of Ogbe, Egbe, Okoromadu, Ogisi, who were the grandfathers of Tommy's generation. Princess Agbeje had been Prince Yowunren's sister. Chief Ogbe had been a very powerful chief, who had made himself invincible by cutting his own arm with a matchet and drinking his own blood. He had had fifty wives and two hundred children. No wonder, that Tommy had such a large family. In going through old archives, Tommy also found a letter written by Chief Ogbe to the British District Officer, complaining that all his slaves were running away, and the D.O. should do something to bring them back. This letter had been written for him in 1903.

I realised that I was living in the midst of history, when I was taken to meet the old Chief John Ogbe who must have been nearly a hundred years old. He was helped by two attendants to walk towards us when we arrived. A very thin toothless old man whose loin cloth hung on him, he nevertheless, greeted us warmly and invited us into his house. There he presented me with a bottle of salad cream which had gone dark brown with age, but it was touching to think that this would be a special gift for a European.

Now was the time for Tommy to build a small house in his village of Ugbuangue which was just outside Warri and not far from the Federal Government College where Monu was to be admitted as a boarder. The house was what we called a 'Wendy House'. It had just a bedroom, a parlour and a very small kitchen with toilet and sink attached. Tommy had now satisfied his family that he had made his mark in their village, and he often spent weekends there. At Christmas we the family, he the children and I went to Ugbuangue to stay for two or three days, to join in the festivities and particularly, to watch Umale. These were the masquerade dancers who performed the ritual dances every year. They also went begging in the town, eliciting from motorists money for their upkeep. These dancers were covered from head to foot in raffia, so that nobody would see their faces or know their identity. They wore carved and painted masks on their faces, long-sleeved sweaters and gloves covered their hands and arms. Their stockinged feet had bells around them and a raffia skirt was inevitably tied around their waist. Their dancing consisted of amazing acrobatic feats. Some of them represented birds and would flutter their arms like a bird hop in little steps on their feet and twirl at fast speed. Others turned somersaults and others still performed dancings with a special flavour. Under their raffia skirts they held sticks out in front of them which incited much applause from the bystanders.

Tommy explained to us that these were not humans, they were meant to be spirits from the sea who had come to punish the evildoers in the community. Women were not allowed to watch them. If any woman ventured too near them they would use their whips to drive them back. There was always a crowd of people watching, and it was the highlight for Tommy for which he visited his village on such occasions. It was closely connected with his childhood memories. So too, his relations, his many cousins, half brothers and sisters would come from far away to join in the Christmas fun. It was sometimes incongruous to see glamorously dressed young ladies in high heels and heavy make-up and jewels travel all the way from Lagos to take part in the festivities in their dusty village, but this was my opportunity to meet the extended family and to become friends with many of them. When there was dancing in the village itself, Tommy's eldest sister Mewe was a lead dancer. For me it was difficult to follow the intricate and fast shuffling footsteps to the rhythm of the drums. The drummers were relations also, and I particularly remember Jack who was the head drummer, and who used a wooden drum which was hollowed out from a tree trunk. It had only a slit in the top and I cannot imagine how they hollowed it out through that slit. Jack used wooden sticks on it with amazing speed. Other drums had animal hide stretched tautly across their wooden shape. Sometimes the women used 'shakas' to support the rhythm while they were singing. The shakas were gourds (calabashes) covered with netting into which cotton seeds had been sewn, so that these clattered on the side of the gourd when it was shaken.

I tried to join the Itsekiri dancing. My stiff *oyingbo* back and hips could in no way shake as gracefully as the local dancers did and I felt my feet were clumsy but I tried, and because I tried the family liked me for joining in. I wore my native wrapper of two layers but was never too comfortable, fearing that while dancing, the top layer would fall off. I also held my head stiffly in case the silk headtie would slip or come undone. However, I did so to be part of it all and encouraged my children to join as well. Monu was very self conscious, but little Temi tried her steps in the background where she was encouraged by other children.

I always loved the cool early mornings during those Christmas visits. I used to wake to the baa'ing of sheep and bleating of goats. The cocks would crow and it was no hardship to get up early and to set out our picnic table for breakfast in the open ground in front of the house. The mornings were cool and misty, as the harmattan December mornings often are. By 9 o'clock when the sun rose it became warmer and very hot towards midday. But the air was fresh and I strode out to be in nature, with fruit trees and palms abundant in the village. The front of the houses was always swept clean and weeded of any tuft of grass to keep snakes away. The houses were built higgledy-piggledy on each small piece of land, as it had been allotted to each member of the family. There was no real building plan, it was cozy and I looked forward to spending a weekend in Tommy's village. His little house had a gas fridge and kerosene lamps. In later years, when electricity was brought to Ugbuwangue, electric lights of course were everywhere.

Tommy's elder sister Mewe had her own house in Warri town. She had built a storey building for herself with her own money earned from selling tobacco in the market. She had let the downstairs part to a shopkeeper and the house was not painted outside, but an outside staircase led to her very comfortable, well-furnished first floor apartment. She was always very warm and affectionate towards me, and so were her grown up daughters Lily and Tunde.

Whenever Tommy visited Warri from Benin they would send me a present of fish, or fruit saying to him in the presence of his secretary "Give it to Hilda, to nobody else". It was hard to believe Tommy's statement that his people only accepted me because I was married to him. They showed open hostility towards the secretary, and I often wondered how she could put up with such frequent humiliation. All his relations, who were proud of him of course, who enjoyed his status, his prominence, his elegance and his sense of humour, nevertheless, said of him that nobody could live with Tommy. No wife could stay with him, and they called me a saint.

Chapter VI

THE CRUMBS, THE SLICE AND THE WHOLE CAKE

Now that the oil was flowing in the Midwest, Shell BP began building their large block of offices at Ugunu and later established a camp for their staff, as they had had in Port Harcourt, but not as large and luxurious. This was located on the same road as the block of offices. The road passed Federal Government College and went on to the Ugunu Shell camp. Since there were negotiations about land now, Tommy was involved in the legal aspect of these negotiations and had to spend a lot of time in Warri. So, at least he now had a place of his own in which to stay when duty called him to that area.

Unhappiness made me successful: this is how I started a talk to a Women's Society in Lagos.

I had thrown myself, heart and soul into the running of the Midwest Crafts Shop. Sam Ogbemudia had made me Honorary Chairman and had given me a very nice Co-director in the shape of Mr. Walter Anukpe. Whatever time I could spare from my family, I put into buying and devising crafts for the shop.

Of course the only time I had for quiet reflection and designing was in the evenings. I sat up until late after midnight, drawing, preparing, making notes especially connected with the weavers in the northern part of the Midwest. There was a cooperative weaving industry in Auchi for whom I designed thread by thread table mats and napkins to match. They needed to be woven on a continuous hand loom with two-inch gaps between each mat or napkin so that the gap could be cut in half to make fringes at both ends of the napkin or place mat. I counted out the weaving threads to make irregular squares as a novelty pattern, and I also had to be sure that the Auchi weavers would use colourfast threads, so that the colour would not fade in the wash.

From the hand-woven cloth of Somorika and Igarra I designed trouser suits for girls and ponchos or what we called 'Throw-overs' for boys, and we even made neckties for men and slippers for ladies and men. We also used the '*oja*' which were the strips of thickly woven cloth with which mothers tied their babies on their backs. These came in cheerful looking patterns, and we called the bags 'oja bags'. I had to negotiate with cane weavers who used to make chairs, to make me round cane handles for the oja bags. All this kept me feverishly busy, deliberately occupying my mind, so that I would not notice that my husband was not at home.

The story went like this: My husband had always told me that he did not want a female secretary. "You cannot control them", he used to say. He had a male secretary and a male messenger in his Shell office which was not too far from our house, just across the golf course at the back. Then one day, his secretary had a motor accident and was laid up for weeks with broken bones. During that period a young lady secretary offered her services to him. He then told me the background to this lady's application.

He had been playing golf with a professional colleague of his when a young girl approached the man on the golf course. After she had left my husband asked his colleague "Who was that?" and he replied "That was my daughter."

"She speaks very good English", said my husband; but the father shook his head and said: "I have washed my hands off her. She is wayward, she has had two babies while in secondary school." My husband then said, "It is a pity not to train her, when she speaks good English." But the father said "No, she will not stick at anything. She will not be serious about any kind of study, and I do not want to train her further."

My husband tried to persuade the father that at least he could send her for secretarial training, but the father was adamant. "Well", said my husband "If you won't, let me train her. Let me send her to Lagos to a secretarial college where she will pick up at least some qualification on which to build her life."

And so it was arranged that this young lady be sent for secretarial training. She had now come at the right time to replace the secretary who had had an accident, but my husband told me he tried to discourage her. He had told her he wanted somebody with experience and that she was too young for his kind of work. The girl insisted and persisted, saying she had no godfather anywhere to give her a job and would my husband please put her to the test and give her a chance to show that she could be useful in the office. According to him, he grudgingly agreed, but told her that he was somebody who wanted discipline.

At that time, it must have been about 1968 after the Biafrans had overrun us and then been flushed out, there was still a great deal of animosity against Igbos in the State, even though this girl was a Midwest Igbo, he felt he had to protect her.

He gave her accommodation in the guest house next to his office. Office and guest house, in fact, a duplex bungalow.

Banking on my understanding, as always, he must have felt that I was content with this explanation for his continual absences from home. He told me he was so busy in the office that he asked for his breakfast, lunch and supper to be sent to him so that he could eat while he worked.

Whether, in my heart, I so much wanted to believe that he was telling me the truth, or whether I did not want to know the real facts, my work became my occupational therapy, which drove all other thoughts from my mind. It certainly occupied my lonely evenings so much that I fell exhausted into bed and into sleep.

I also tried to help some of Tommy's relations to establish themselves. Cousin Ethel, wife of a doctor, was baking bread and wanted an introduction to Kingsway Stores who was buying bread. As Kingsway had its own suppliers, it refused hers. When she told me this, I suggested she should bake something quite different and make it so attractive that the store would not refuse. From my cook-book we made Viema Rolls in different shapes. They looked most appetizing with a glossy brown finish, Kingsway Stores could not resist them. That is how she got a foot in the door and later supplied bread as well.

Tommy's daughter Ching-Ching was a caterer and had been given the job of supervisor in a new hotel. Again I told her to offer a different menu from the usual fare; and again from my cookbook we compiled recipes of Chinese cooking which we tried out in my kitchen, found them to be delicious and offered them to the hotel. That is how the first Chinese restaurant in Benin City came into being and Ching-Ching earned herself accolades.

In both cases it was originality which earned them success in a country where all caterers turn out the same type of menu. Sure, the Nigerian dishes are always delicious, but the sausage rolls and the *moimoi* and the *akara* and other fast foods like egg rolls are universally the same, and we all could do with a little variety. This is where foreigners can make a difference because without any formal training in a particular subject, we learn from newspapers and women's magazines, even if we do not study cook-books, ideas are never short. It is the initiative of trying out the ideas and adapting them maybe to different tastes or different ingredients that enables us to create something original. I always felt that I had this advantage and I was keen to share it with whoever wanted it.

The success of the crafts shop led to wider interest in it. Lt. Col. Ogbemudia was friendly with Mobolaji Johnson, the Military Governor of Lagos at the time. The two of them hatched a plan to bring a Midwest Crafts Exhibition to Lagos. In consultation with me Sam Ogbemudia made an arrangement with UTC Stores on the Marina in Lagos to show our crafts for three weeks and if they liked them to continue buying them in the future. My husband never objected to any travelling I did. For one thing, he could trust me to the end of the earth, for another, maybe he enjoyed his freedom when I was not around, although he told me that when I was away things were not the same and he never felt like going out. Contrary?

I stayed in the Bristol Hotel in Lagos for three weeks supervising the exhibition from morning till night, answering questions about our products and generally doing public relations work for the Midwest and its craftsmen. With genuine and full enthusiasm I used to describe the way they worked, and being able to tell a legend behind the work of art, always sold the article. It was the story that sold it more than the article itself. There was much publicity in the newspapers about this Midwest Crafts Exhibition, and Ogbemudia was well pleased. He had pulled off a first once again.

I was glad to get home again after three weeks which were not too comfortable. Back in my own surroundings I continued to attend to all the different sections of the crafts world but I began to get very tired and a bit irritable, possibly, because I was overworked. I had to monitor the finances of the crafts shop as well as its supplies and sales, but I found that the storekeeper was an honest man and our takings always went into the shop's bank account.

The banking had become much easier for him because after we had been in existence for about a year, Ogbemudia had the bright idea of creating the New Nigeria Bank and he needed a central location for the building. Unfortunately, where our shop was located was just the type of location he now needed. So he built the New Nigeria Bank around the Midwest Crafts Shop. To retain our building, he built the bank in such a way that its two wings, like arms seemed to be enfolding our crafts shop.

Stimulated, I think, by our accent on arts and crafts Sam had the outer walls of the bank decorated with local scenes in relief of black on white. For us business went on as usual, until, at a much later date our dear little shop was knocked down and reestablished in the front of the bank building, where it is now.

In the meantime I was put on the Tourist Board and on the International Trade Fair Board of Midwestern Nigeria. There was one drive for tourism but we found that there would be not enough hotel accommodation for bus loads of tourists. However, a beauty competition was set up for the International Year for African Tourism. The selected beauty queen Miss Iyat was crowned at the competition and later fitted out with our locally made clothes and jewellery.

For the international trade fairs I made sure that only the best of Midwest crafts would be put on show in London. I rejected badly made and unattractive cane baskets for instance. They would not have stood a chance by comparison with the dainty and beautifully made Asian baskets which would also be exhibited at the International Trade Fair. I selected only what was inimitably good and Nigerian in quality.

In 1973, a Midwest Arts Festival was organised. It was usual for this festival to portray dancing and drumming and acrobatic skills. This time I interceded and pointed out that the arts included the carvers, the brasscasters, the cane weavers, the cloth weavers, the fine artists, the hair plaiters and the gold and silver smiths. I planned something like a carnival float depicting scenes from the royal court of the Oba of the Edo people. We dressed some royal queens with their coral bead crowns and velvet wrappers and their traditional handmaidens equally dressed for the part, to sit on a trailer decorated with flowers, and preceded by horse back riders. These were fitted out with the traditional helmet and gear, as depicted in old bronze castings. All the different groups of artists were dressed in their different Asho Ebis. They walked behind the float and carried signboards which showed the guilds they belonged to. This procession went around the stadium where the festivities were held, and then marched through the town for everybody to see. It was an unusual show with which Governor Ogbemudia was greatly pleased.

In between I was asked to open arts exhibitions and to judge competitions. It was a full life. Sometime later at another opening of an arts exhibition the present Oba of Benin, His Royal Highness, Omonoba nedo Uku Akpolokpolo, Oba Erediauwa commented in his opening speech that he would call me "the First Lady of Edo State Arts and Crafts".

In 1976, the Midwest Crafts Shop was handed over to the clamouring Arts Council. I had absolved my honorary chairmanship of eight years, and it had been declared that the Midwest Crafts Shop was the only parastatal which had made a profit. We had, at that time, 30,000 Naira in the bank and 14,000 Naira in stock. I left with a happy heart, knowing that I had contributed something worthwhile to the status of the craftsmen and women and to the State. For me, it had been fulfilment, where my personal life had been bleak.

In the interim in 1972, our son Monu had an accident. He was then seventeen years old and mad about motorcycles. Unbeknown to us he had taken training from Ogbemudia's outriders who taught him stunt riding. He was able to jump across obstacles with the motorbike, he could ride hands free, stand on the saddle, ride backwards and could somersault off the motorbike, letting it run forward. This feat was meant for emergencies. He was well known in the streets and young people applauded him whenever he zoomed through the town. Later he was filmed for a Kawasaki advertisement, to prove the power of their machine.

This time now he had broken his arm. It had healed badly so that the bone of the forearm protruded at the wrist. I had to take him to Lagos University Teaching Hospital, for an operation to save the movement in his wrist. We flew down to Lagos, leaving Temi in her Daddy's care, because my mother was not with us at the time. In the evening after the operation I phoned Benin. It was 8 p.m. and Temi came on the line. When she heard my voice she started crying.

"Mummy, when are you coming? I am all alone in the house. I am afraid."

"Where is Daddy?" I asked.

"Daddy has gone out" she sobbed.

I tried to soothe her saying that Daddy would soon be back, and she should go to sleep. I would be back the next day.

Of course, I was horrified. Was this the doting father, who had the heart to leave a nine-year-old little girl totally alone in our big storey building? I hardly slept that night, torn between sharing Monu's pain and Temi's anxiety. When I arrived back in Benin City I found that Tommy had not returned until the early morning. I faced him with the question, "How can you leave a little girl alone in the house all night?" On the defensive immediately he snapped "There's a watchnight, isn't there?"

"A watchnight" I said. "Little children are afraid of dark empty rooms, are afraid of having no one close by, are afraid of bad dreams, what can a watchnight do in such cases? Why can you not stay at home one single night, not even with your child?" He then told me that he had to make sure that his girl in the corner, for whom he carried all expenses and responsibilities, would not admit some nincompoop into her bed in his absence. I reeled from such insensitive logic, and another big piece of my sore heart cracked.

THE SLICE

A few months later Tommy told me he was going to a Rotary Convention in Jos, and since I could not leave the children behind he would take the secretary. I tried to control my voice as I asked "Why do you need a secretary at Rotary? Some years ago you told me that "these girls" in the corner got only the crumbs that fell from the wife's table. This trip is no crumb, it is a whole slice of cake." He denied ever having made such a statement.

I was aghast. "When you told me this I was twenty-one years old. I could never have invented such a declaration, because I did not have any experience of the world. Your explanations that these girls in the corner did not know what love was, they came and went. They came for the money and to attach themselves to a big man for protection, and they would only get the crumbs that came from the wife's table, — I believed you."

He refuted ever having made such a statement and continued: "these girls also make demands, you know." I now realised that I had based all the structure of our marriage and all my sacrifices on an empty promise.

So, this was the man whom I had trusted implicitly for thirty years, the man who had so impressed me with his truthfulness and integrity, the man who was the darling of society, without whom no social function was successful, the man whom everybody admired as the gentleman, the Black Oyinbo. This was the man who was sought after for 'Moot Point' on radio, for speeches at students' clubs, for orations at weddings and burials, acclaimed in court as the eloquent barrister and admired on all occasions for his great sense of humour.

The fault was mine, I realised. I never believed his statement of "self first". I had never seen this kind of promised ruthlessness before, or maybe, I had not recognised it, being blinded by love. I had not believed his relations either who told me on several occasions that nobody could live with Tommy.

A year later in 1973, I took my children to America to visit my mother and brother. There again, I had put up a private exhibition of Nigerian crafts which the local newspaper in Connecticut had photographed and described.

But at that time I was deeply unhappy. I had asked Tommy to come with us on this trip, but he said he had no money. I then offered to pay his fare, but he said he had no time to take off for travel, even though he was now his own master having left Shell BP in 1971 and he was back in private practice as a barrister and notary public. Also, we were now living in our own storey building for which he had bought the land at the same time as he had bought the adjacent piece of land for the Shell BP house. We had not known at the time that we would be given the Shell BP house as a present, or we might not have started building our own place. Now we were established in a beautiful roomy storey building to which I had contributed financially.

After Tommy refusing to join us on our trip to America, a high ranking police officer called at our house to deliver some papers.

In the absence of Tommy he gave them to me saying they were passport application forms.

I stood there wondering. Passport applications? We all had passports. Tommy, myself and the children all had their own passports. And then this stab of intuition told me "This passport would be for the secretary." And he was planning to travel with her.

I trembled in disbelief. Could he be so treacherous? But then, again my better nature took hold of me and whispered "Maybe, it is for a client." All the time though, I was disturbed. We were near our departure for America via England and I concentrated on my packing and organising my workers and craftsmen so that they would be occupied while I was away. But all the time the niggling doubt never left my mind.

I said nothing. I asked nothing. We left on our journey to London to stay with Tommy's relations for a couple of days. His brother Dr. David Ogbe embraced me warmly.

"Where is Tommy?" he asked.

"Oh, are you expecting Tommy?"

He seemed to realise that he had made a blunder.

"No no, I thought he would come with you."

I embarked on the transatlantic flight with a heavy heart.

At Kennedy airport we were met by my mother and brother. A comic situation arose when we were going through customs. I had saved some of our food on the plane, such as bread rolls and cheese for my ever hungry children. One customs officer checked my hand luggage and called over his shoulder "Hey Mike! come here. See what I've found." What he took out of my bag were the bread rolls and cheese, "She's got food in her bag."

"These are from the plane" I said. "I saved them for my children's journey to Connecticut."

"Food is forbidden import and you will be had for this."

"Oh, I didn't know" I said, and with one swift movement I flung the offending bread rolls over the counter into a waste bin at the back. The man was nonplussed. He thought he had caught a criminal, but there was no more proof now, and we sailed through. In a rented limousine we all drove to Guilford, Conn. where my mother had rented a bungalow for all of us to spend a long holiday together.

It was near the sea, but I really had no thought for holiday making. I pretended that all was well, but my heart was heavy. As soon as I could, I got near a telephone and dialed our niece's number in London.

"Auntie", her surprised voice came on the line. "Auntie how are you?"

I was in no mood for social greetings.

"Can I speak to Uncle Tommy" I asked her.

There was a pause "Oh, Auntie he has just gone out."

"Alright then, let me speak to the secretary."

A breathless pause. "Pardon, Auntie". I repeated my request.

"Let me speak to his secretary".

"Oh Auntie, I'm sorry, the line is so bad. I can't hear you", and she cut off.

Her embarrassment was palpable, and my worst fears were now confirmed.

Tommy was indeed in England, — with his secretary.

The few weeks of that holiday were utter misery for me. I tried not to let my mother know what was wrong, but I spent hours in the shower crying my eyes out.

Monu and Temi had a wonderful time. 1973 it was not yet so common in New England to see children of mixed marriages, or any African children. Other children asked Monu who was then eighteen years old some stupid questions like whether people in Africa swing through the trees, which he rebutted with humour and sagacity. Within a short time both, Monu and Temi became quite popular among their crowd. Both of them swam well and won swimming races. Monu became a member of the Auxiliary Fire Fighters. The senior in command said he wished they had more lads like Monu in their outfit. Temi, as usual, with her lively personality made friends with whom she kept in touch for many years afterwards.

They were well adjusted children, as I hoped they would be when I used to tell them from an early age that everybody has prejudices of one kind or another. To Temi I said "You do not like fat girls or boys with pimples. Some people may not like brown or black skins, — but look at us whites. See how we roast ourselves in the sun to make our skin nice and brown, while nature has given you that enviable colour free of charge. We whites pay heavy money for our straight hair to be curled, - while you want to pay that money to have your curls straightened. Is man never satisfied? Besides, have you not heard of the Race of Tan? In the future all the races of the world will be so mixed: black, brown, yellow, white and red, that there will be only the one colour of tan for everybody. You don't have to wait for the future. You've got that lovely colour now."

My mother was very proud of all of us. My brother organised among his friends an exhibition of African arts and crafts, at which I spoke to explain and promote the background of the crafts and the character of Nigeria. It caused great interest, especially as my children and I were all dressed in native attire, and I showed how to carry a baby on one's back. The local newspaper 'The Shoreline Times' printed a two-page article with photographs about this event.

When the time for our departure came my dejected mother and brother sadly bid us farewell. I was dreading my return to Benin City. I was dreading confronting my husband not knowing how I could ever resolve the situation. I felt trapped. I loved Nigeria. I loved the friends I had made, my work and the children's progress. They needed to grow up in Nigeria. They needed to know their roots. Also part of me still loved my husband. What was the solution? The thought raced round and around my mind on the transatlantic flight to England and from there back to Nigeria. In those days the planes from Lagos to Benin City were regular. We took a flight from Lagos home but the nearer we got to Benin the more I dreaded our arrival there. I could not help it, I cried all the way on that flight. Tommy was at the airport to meet us. I drove by his side while he chatted away, probably to hide his embarrassment. When we got home, the children went to their rooms to unpack and I sat in the sitting room with him while he told me every detail of a case he had conducted concerning his family's Ugbuwangue land. He was talking non-stop. He was filibustering, — trying to stave off confrontation.

"I do not want to talk about Ugbuwangue", I said. I want to talk about us".

"Well, what about us?" he asked.

"You have hurt me very badly by breaking faith with me", I said.

"Well, what do you want me to do? I can leave this house for you. I can move out, if you don't like my lifestyle. In any case what are you belly-aching about?"

What was I to say in the face of, again, such insensitivity? I was so tired. I was so depressed. I glossed over it, because there was no real solution at hand at that moment.

"I love you, you know", he finally blurted out. "You are my beautiful wife. I am glad, I married you. Nobody can compete with you. I have told you I feel at peace in my own home. I feel safe with you. You know, I can't trust anybody else. These girls, they lie and cheat and they steal from me. Do you remember that time when money was missing from my locked drawer in my office? I asked the secretary and the messenger about it but both denied any knowledge of it. I then, in the absence of the secretary on some errand, wanted to search her locked bag. I slit open the bottom of the bag and found my money there. You see what I mean? With all that I give her and pay her, she still had to steal from me."

"Why then do you have to sacrifice me to people whom you cannot trust?"

"Ah well, they are all the same. We must have them, whether they are stewards, or gardeners or drivers or secretaries. We must have them. If only you wives will be patient. There comes a time in a man's life when we stop all this woman-nonsense. Anyway, I brought you a present."

He got up, rummaged in his office and presented me with a cloth of blue satin, richly embroidered with silver.

"I do not want it," I said.

"But blue is your colour, and I thought you could wear your silver jewellery with it. I bought it for you."

"I do not want it".

"Oh well, somebody else will be glad of it," and he stormed out of the room.

I did not care. I decided I was no longer going to be manipulated by sweet words. If my husband of thirty years understood me so little that he thought I could be mollified with a present, after he had committed such treachery, there was no hope.

I was at the end of my tether. Emotionally drained. No sweet words, no compliments had any impact on me. I returned to my routine and immersed myself in my work, but nothing I did, no book I read, no radio I listened to, could really remove the pain from me. Nothing made sense. I tried to read but the lines that my eyes focused on were just print, the pages made no sense to me. I could not eat. I could not sleep. I was irritable with Temi, which was unfair I knew.

Several times over the years Tommy had said to me "Poppie, don't be jealous. When wives are jealous they simply give chance to the other woman 'to conquer', to come into the house." Don't be jealous!? No, I did not make scenes. I did not spy on my husband. I did not abuse the girl in the corner. I did not go to fight her. I did not make charms against her nor did I cut off my husband's trouser legs to prevent him from going out. Jealous wives are often caricatured, but it is not a matter for joking.

Oh, but how I hurt inside! Nobody knew how I ached day and night, how, after all we had been to each other, after all the sacrifices we had made to ensure his success, — his total neglect of me rankled. Don't be jealous! It is like saying, don't be thirsty or don't be hungry. One cannot rationalize this powerful emotion. And was not he himself insanely jealous? Not of me: He had no reason to be. Jealousy is a deep searing pain, the pain of seeing one's emotional investment, one's caring and nurturing of a beloved person adulterated or even snatched away. In fact, the fear of losing the lover, — the husband or wife is so great that even in law a murderer's sentence can be mitigated if he or she committed murder, — a crime of "passion" when catching a spouse in the act of adultery. Jealousy is so painful because it affects the ego, — did he know that women also had an ego? He who believed so much in the human rights charter, did he not think that women also had the right to happiness, to recognition, to fulfilment? In Nigeria the word jealousy is often confused with "envy". They are not the same. Envy, — one of the deadly sins, – can be applied to material possessions, or to position or progress of a person. It does not imply the fear of loss of a beloved person.

On another occasion he said to me "The trouble with you is you never put a foot wrong. You are so good. You have a good heart. I will never drive you." His coarse terminology came as a shock to me. I did not say anything but it gave me a start. Drive me? DRIVE ME, HILDA GERSON? Drive me from the house like a goat? From then on I was on my guard. If such a thought could even enter his mind, where was the stability of our married life? Stability which I believed in, stability which was essential to my being. Stability which I had striven so hard to maintain. "Till death do us part". No, I was not going to be driven. I was going to do the leaving! But how? Where to?

After this trip to America, in 1973 Monu entered Ife University to study law.

I continued to cast about in my mind for a solution to the intolerable state of my marriage. I sought the advice of a psychiatrist, who listened to me patiently, prescribed tranquilizers and sleeping tablets and promised to go and talk to my husband. Before I left, he said, "You know, what you are suffering from we call "the second wife syndrome. It happens frequently".

This comment did nothing to alleviate my misery. His prescribed tablets did not help either. The pain was too deep, — not only for myself, but for my husband too. I was disappointed that this man of great intelligence and many interests in his youth, was not developing himself further. He was content with the three G-s: Girlfriend, Golf and Garden.

EAST AFRICAN HOLIDAY

The psychiatrist did come, by appointment. "Ah, my good man, what did you come to see me about?" After many diplomatic gyrations the doctor talked of my depression and advised that my husband should take me on a holiday.

"Oh, yes, yes, yes, — that is already arranged. We are going to East Africa very soon. My bank manager will be transferred to Zambia. He has invited us to visit him there". This was news to me, but the doctor departed, satisfied that he had done well.

The proposed holiday included Temi, so that I had something to look forward to for her sake. She and I both had Sagittarius Ascendants, — the sign of the traveller and we enjoyed seeing different countries and learning.

The trip was planned for Kenya, Zambia and Tanzania. The bank manager had made hotel reservations for us in Nairobi, Kitwe and Dar es Salaam. Although the surrounding mountains in Nairobi were beautiful and the morning and evening very cold and crisp, the town did not strike me as African at all. It was a well constructed place with tarred roads, kerbs and street lighting, houses and gardens immaculate, but one hardly saw any Africans. All shops were owned and run by Indians. The market might have been Convent Garden, well stocked with all European vegetables, and the women traders wore dresses, not wrappers and head-ties. The only African crafts I saw were in tourist shops among many machine-made souvenirs and Indian crafts. There were no native dishes either on the hotel menu, except one fiery hot pepper soup which was specially made for us when we asked for it.

One evening, as we were having our meal in the dining-room, Tommy spotted a group of well suited important looking Africans at another table. Always sure of making an impression and getting a good welcome, he got up and strode over to them, complimentary card in hand.

"Excuse me for intruding gentlemen, but I am a stranger here," I heard him say. "I am from Nigeria, Benin City. I would be glad to make your acquaintance."

I did not hear their reply, but in a moment he came back to us. I knew better than to ask questions. Outside, after we had finished eating, he told me that the leader of them had said "You are not an African. Go back to your table." He was stunned. He had never been so rebuffed in his life. It was clear to me that our mixed marriage had been the cause of their contempt. How could a true African marry a white?

We flew to Kitwe in Zambia where the English bank manager and his family welcomed us warmly. Temi was friendly with their two children of her age. This made her stay much more enjoyable, as she frolicked with them in their swimming pool. We were taken around the town. I made a mental note of the area where the souvenir stalls were, to go back there to browse on my own. When I did, I stumbled upon a street-long row of tables covered with green objects. Zambia had famous copper mines, and this beautiful green gemstone, this malachite, was always found in the earth where there was copper.

The stones had fabulous patterns in them. Here, nature had excelled in forming lines and concentric circles in shades of a bluish green, which no artist could have invented. On the tables lay hundreds of different objects made from malachite. Most of it was jewellery but also masks and ashtrays, all highly polished to show off the beauty of the gemstone, — no two pieces alike. The variety within the material was astounding. The jewellery was often mounted on copper, rough and exotic looking. I spent hours there, admiring and selecting. Even Tommy was intrigued and bought several pieces. I chose some flat backed stones to mount in silver on my return.

In Kitwe town the shops were full of copper plates of all sizes, ash-trays, glass mats and embossed pictures of African scenes. In the hotel there was a gleaming copper hood over the open fireplace, and the ceiling was made of copper squares which shed a warm glow over the room when the lights were on.

The Malachite traders were East Africans, tall and slim with long, narrow faces and lovely, slender hands and feet.

Apart from chatting to the bank manager and getting the BBC news from him, Tommy was getting bored. The Malachite shopping was not enough occupation for him and there were no other bargains to be found. It was with some relief that we started our flight to Dar es Salaam, Tanzania.

From the airport there a taxi drove us through very poor streets, so that we were not prepared for the kind of hotel that had been booked for us on Kunduchi Beach. It was a long white building virtually on the beach, so much so, that Temi could climb over the balustrade of our verandah and drop right on to the sand. The sea was so near that the thrashing waves lulled us to sleep at night. One had to have all confidence in the architect's calculations to believe that, when the tide came in, it would not reach our bedroom.

Our bathroom and bedroom were on two levels. The bathroom was set back, so that from it one could look down into the bedroom and out onto the sea. It was exotic and led to erotic imagination, — if only one had the right partner. The interior was sumptuous, tastefully furnished in modern European style. The long corridors and the dining/ballroom had black marble floors and choice African art work on the walls, and around the many Moorish arches which decorated the inside and outside of the hotel.

Temi and I swam and bathed in the Indian Ocean while Tommy collected shells. These were bargains from nature which cost nothing, and anyway, he loved the sea. Some shells were so big and heavy, they looked artificial, of a bright pink shading into red. He also found a piece of white coral, broken off from its reef and washed ashore. It looked like a tree with sharp-edged branches which cut our fingers. Tommy spent hours collecting, and I felt he wanted to be alone with his thoughts. Temi provided the point of contact between us. He was politely solicitous, but his heart was elsewhere, he was distant, and this was a constant pain to me.

The highlight of the day was the mouth-watering buffet-dinner in the evening. The long table was a feast for the eyes as well as the palate. Here, mountains of red lobsters, of prawns and crabs, of whole fish, interspersed with baskets of fresh tropical fruits and flowers provided a riot of colours. Freshly chilled coconuts were placed among those. They were topped with gay little paper umbrellas and had drinking straws inserted into their coconut "eyes". We had long drinks of cool coconut milk to start with. Sometimes we danced to the live African band which played throughout the evening, but I could not break down the barrier between Tommy and me.

Sometimes Tommy danced with Temi, then thirteen years old. The band leader took a fancy to her, and whenever she passed by on her own he would engage her in conversation. "Where did you learn to dance like that?" he asked. To her it was obvious that where she came from people knew how to dance. Besides, she was dancing with her father.

We left Tanzania laden with sea shells which were our booty from the Indian Ocean. We also carried away memories of the different countries we had visited. It had been a varied and colourful trip from which we learned much.

BACK TO MISERY

On arrival back in Benin City, Tommy dropped us at our house and went out immediately. Apart from checking on his girl, he had also started building some small bungalows on the former Shell BP plot adjoining our compound. He had done his duty by me, and now devoted himself to supervising the buildings and to the three Gs - girl friend, golf and gardening.

Since his retirement he had taken up full time golf and made the secretary his golf partner. Even though he no longer had his meals sent to the office, I hardly saw him because of these commitments. I too continued with my routine, and the memories and hope of the holiday we had spent, faded. In the evenings he would come home from golf, shower and shave. He sat politely in the sitting room to listen to the 9 o'clock news looking at his watch surreptitiously, wondering when I would go to bed, so that he could go out. All this time he kept our cook sitting in the garage on the ironing table swinging his legs. We had finished supper at 8 o'clock and I asked him whether I could dismiss the cook. "No no", he said "domestics have no closing time. I may need a drink of water."

"I can get you the water", I said but he repeated that I should not spoil the domestics. They have no closing time. So the poor man sat until 10 o'clock sometimes. If for some reason, Tommy had stayed home late, he would be in the garage there dozing and waking until almost midnight. I could not bear such injustice, afterall, the man had a wife and family at home and was being kept late for nothing. I thought of a ruse to better his condition. I told Tommy that the cook wanted to work half days at half pay. He would close after we had finished lunch. Tommy was in agreement. "Good. Then I save some money." My arrangement with the cook was that I would pay the other half of his salary. This way I felt happier. It was always the Jewish social conscience which spoke in me. In the evenings after Tommy had left, smelling sweetly of shaving lotion, I stood at the window upstairs seeing the tail lights of his car going in the direction of the secretary's area. I began to pray, "Dear Lord, lift this black cloud from my life. Tell me what to do. Tell me where to go."

The possibilities of moving out of Tommy's reach were slim. I could not see myself renting a house somewhere, because I felt Temi and I would not be safe. We would also be at the landlord's mercy, so where were we to go? It never occurred to me for a moment that I should leave Nigeria.

Our lovely, roguish daughter Temi was often as much an enigma to me as her father. At the time I did not see the similarity in character between the two of them but now I know that much of their similarity consisted of moodiness and contrariness. Both were non-conformists. Monu advised me when he was quite young "If you want Temi to sit down tell her to stand up. If you want her to stand up tell her to sit down." He used this method and it worked for him, but I thought that children should be made to obey. Tommy prided himself in saying that his little daughter was a proper Ugbuwangwe woman. He quoted his aunties as being recalcitrant women who did as they pleased. They did not marry and follow their husbands, they brought their husbands into their houses and when they got tired of them they drove them out. This kind of guidance might have reinforced Temi's willfulness, but she was charming and vivacious and full of humour just like her father.

All the same, I began to feel that she needed greater and more constructive discipline. Shouting at her achieved only resentment and more obstinacy. Her mind needed to be stretched, she needed more diversity in her lessons, and slowly the conviction grew in me that she should be sent to England to do her School Certificate. From several prospectuses I chose a girls' boarding school in West Malvern where she did well, although she complained that they were racist, keeping all the girls of foreign races in the same boarding-house. Nevertheless she made friends with girls of all nationalities. She passed her school certificate and got a prize for literature. She wrote beautiful poems.

DANGEROUS ILLNESS

When the small bungalows were completed next door Tommy moved the secretary into one of them. He blithely explained to me that, as I did not want him to spend nights outside in the town, it was better for him to just cross into the next compound so that I would know where he was in case I needed him. At this final logic which served entirely his own purpose, I broke down completely. As the time had come for Temi to go to England to complete her schooling, I was now totally alone in the house every night. I moved out of our marital bedroom into the now empty children' room. I had to make a statement somehow. "What was the point of sharing my husband's bedroom? I had no husband. I had no one to reach for in the empty bed beside me. I might as well be alone in my own room." Then, a dramatic thing happened. Tommy fell ill, very ill, with what we thought was high fever malaria. But he had such raging headaches that our dear Dr. Garrick, his close friend from King's college days, shook his head and admitted him into the University of Benin Teaching Hospital. There it was found that Tommy had Meningitis. It was a dangerous illness for a man of his age. He was then sixty.

We now had a desperate new routine, taking meals to him twice a day, which I did, alarmed to see his rapid decline, until finally, he went into a coma. When I visited him with a pot of pepper soup, I saw several professors bent over his chart in his private ward and I waited outside until they left, not looking at me nor talking to me. I entered the ward and poured the soup into a feeding cup, when the nurse came back and said "Don't disturb him. Do not give him any food." I ignored her advice. I stood by his bedside, determined not to let him slip away like that. He lay motionless, his eyes closed. I went and touched him. I shook his arm a little and called his name. "Tommy, Tommy, Pooppie is here." He gave no sign. I bent closer and talked into his ear touching him "Tommy I have brought some pepper soup." No sign. Then I used the Itsekiri word saying "Tommy, Igbagba, Igbagba," and miraculously his eyelids fluttered. He pursed his lips and I put the feeding cup to them. He sipped a little, then his eyes opened. His hand reached in a weak and trembling movement to touch his chin. "I want to shave", he said. I could not believe it. He was alive! He was going to be alive! I gave him a little more of the pepper soup and then ran down to the telephone, dialed Dr. Garrick and told him the news. "Tommy says he wants to shave" I shouted into the telephone. He too was overwhelmed. He had come back from travel to hear the good news. He had gone to Warri because he said he did not want to be in town when Tommy died. Now here was the reversal of his illness, the reversal we had been praying for.

Another miracle happened at that moment. Monu came by on his motorcycle from Ife to see his father. "Monu, Monu", I shouted, "Daddy says he wants to shave." Monu not quite aware of the drama that had taken place rushed off to get his Daddy's shaving kit from our house.

The following days were spent on Tommy's convalescence. He was so emaciated, and so weak that he had to be helped from his bed onto the chair beside him. But he was alive! The doctors did not know how to explain his recovery, but everybody was very glad that he had been saved. Eventually he was well enough, strong enough to be taken home, but as soon as we got there without even going into the house he asked the driver to take him to the secretary after they had dropped me. When he was satisfied that he had shown himself to be alive and well he came into the house and stayed on his bed to rest. I kept him company and looked after him for his many needs. I sat with him and on one occasion he said "I suppose you are quite glad to have me ill and weak so that I cannot pursue my usual activities."

No, there was no hope. If he could accuse me of pleasure at seeing him weak there was no hope of his ever understanding my devotion to him. After his recovery Dr. Garrick suggested he should be taken away on a holiday. He, Monu and I drove to Togo into a comfortable hotel by the seaside. It was there in Togo that Monu had his first adult conversation with his father. I had left the two alone on purpose and Tommy discovered that his son was now a man with opinions of his own. Tommy had always prided himself on being a good teacher. He did not know that his lengthy often repeated explanations of a simple point drove us all to despair. We needed so much patience to hear him out when we knew beforehand what he was going to say and what quotations he would bring out to support his points. Tommy was not a teacher. He was a lecturer, who did not allow questions or contradictions. He hammered home his opinions to be imposed on his listeners. This time he listened to his son and realised that his son was worth listening to. The illness had mellowed him. His new tolerance made Monu happy and made him feel for the first time he had a father to whom he could talk. This was the best point of our holiday. Eventually, I sensed Tommy's returning strength and his impatience to be home again. We broke off our holiday to accommodate him and returned to Benin City.

Monu returned to Ife, satisfied that his father was in good hands and fully recovered. I was thrown back into my loneliness once Tommy resumed his normal activities. There was no change in his behaviour towards me, but still I was glad he was alive.

My own miracle happened the following year, in 1976. Tommy in one of his rare moments, when he was sitting with me, said "Would you like to buy a piece of land, which David has bought in Delta Crescent but he has been unable to develop it, and the government want to take it away from him. Would you like to buy that land, so that it will remain in the family?"

"Me, buy land? What for?"

"You could build a house. Many women do. They collect rent from it."

"Me build a house, what with? I do not have that kind of money."

"You do it softly softly. Lay the foundation and as money comes from your business you start making blocks, start building little by little and eventually you will have a house of your own."

The land was a big piece, 200 x 200 feet. I bought it for four thousand naira in 1976. It was a heady feeling to own land. So this was God's answer to my prayers. He had dropped this piece of land into my lap. There was hope now, that I would have a refuge eventually, and my spirit soared.

After I had paid for the land, Tommy drew up the document to change the ownership from his brother Dr. David to me. When I went to look at the land it was all bush, but there were the four pillars with their numbers inscribed which told me where the plot began and ended.

The first problem was how to clear the dense bush. I belong to those fools who "rush in where angels fear to tread" and approached the French construction company of Dumez who were building roads in and around Benin City. I addressed the site manager in his own language and asked whether I could hire their bulldozer to clear my land. He shrugged his shoulders and said "Peut-etre" (perhaps) but he wanted to see my plot. I took him there in my car and as we stood in front of it, he studying the numbered pillars, I asked how much he would charge. "On verra" (we shall see) he answered laconically, and I took him back to his site.

A week later I visited my plot and found to my delighted surprise that not only had the land been bulldozed and graded, but all rubbish from it had been cleared. I rushed to Dumez to thank the manager and to ask how much I was owing, but he, a taciturn man, waved me off saying "C'est rien" (it is nothing). My profuse thanks were barely acknowledged, as he turned to his radio telephone to make a call.

After this lucky beginning I was able to start thinking of a design for the house.

I consulted several friends and one German girl Barbara Atane married to a Nigerian engineer showed me the basic plan for a Ministry of Works house. I thought it looked simple enough for me and that I could eventually afford to build it. I consulted another friend, a Swiss quantity surveyor to give me the approximate cost of that kind of house. When it came to building though I made some alterations, planning for my old age. For instance there was a step up to the dining section which I eliminated. I thought to myself a step is not good for a wheelchair. I also added windows to the bedroom and extended most of the rooms by a few feet, not realising how much this would add to the cost in cement, gravel, window frames, floor covering, rendering and paints. A few months later I began to lay the foundation and as Tommy had predicted, little by little as the money came in the walls of the house rose to roof level and eventually to completion.

The oil boom of the 1970s had made our silver jewellery move briskly. It became the fashion even for Nigerian ladies to own at least one big set of silver for special occasions. I was honoured to think that both Mrs Victoria Gowon and Mrs. Clara Ogbemudia wore my silver, but I knew we had arrived when Swiss lace manufacturers began to make the heavy guipure lace with silver thread instead of gold, which had been the fashion for so many years. It was exciting to think that we had made a difference to the fashion in Nigeria by introducing silver jewellery.

In February 1976, Tommy took me to Leventis Motors who had two Mercedes cars in their show room. "Which colour would you like", he asked me. "The dark blue or the yellow?" I wondered, I said "What do you mean? Are you buying another Mercedes?"

"Yes", he said. "I want to buy it for you". It took some time for me to grasp what he was saying and I was not comfortable with the thought. "I have a car", I said. "My Toyota Crown is still perfectly good."

"There is no harm in owning two cars", he said and finally concluded the sale having the yellow Mercedes delivered to our house and presenting it to me. I felt embarrassed, because it was such a showy car, and I drove it to the back of the house so as not to incite envy from other people. I was just not comfortable with it. "You know," he said, "the Mercedes has a very strong body and is a safe car in an accident. I want you to have it." I was moved by this sentiment more than anything else but then my joy was poisoned when I saw that he had also bought a car for the girl in the corner. Admittedly, it was a Volkswagen beetle, but it stood there in our compound under a big shady tree, a reminder that I was not the only one in my husband's life. I began to see my

Mercedes as a bribe, and I really did not want it. However, Dr. David was staying with us at the time on his return from postgraduate studies in England, and he pointed out to me that I should feel cherished, that this car was a symbol of my husband's regard for me.

But why did he have to make it so obvious that he had also bought a car for the girl in the corner? If really she had remained in the corner I could have tolerated it. But she was out in the open, she was taken to luncheons and golf dinners, as she was a golfer herself and everybody knew of her. At his 70th birthday, the Golf Club gave Tommy a dinner, which I refused to attend. In his speech thanking the members for the honour done him, Tommy said that his wife, Hilda was unavoidably absent, but then he referred to the girl on his right, saying "but you all know my secretary. In fact she is my permanent secretary." Laughter drowned his next sentence.

In 1976, this Mercedes 200 cost ten thousand naira. Today, twenty-four years later, it is still on the road. The price now would be a hundred fold if not more.

Tommy had done well in his practice as a lawyer and notary public, though when he found time to study his cases and type his own documents, — I really did not know. He never wanted to have a clerk. In his youth he had taught himself touch typing, and he said it would only annoy him to have to vet his clerk's typing and discover numerous mistakes in it. These could be costly mistakes in a legal document if they were undetected. Instead of going over his document twice, he thought it was better to type it himself.

Ever since Monu went to Ife University I had opened a shop there which I called Coffee 'n Crafts. It was quite a large ground floor which had been vacated by a travel agency, and I divided the shop from the coffee section by a wrought iron divider with a door in it, so that I could see into the coffee section from the shop and the customers could go and relax with a cup of coffee after making their purchases. It was a lovely place, with cane furniture and round cane tables but when Monu left Ife in 1976 I closed the shop, because the catalyst which had encouraged me to visit Ife, was no longer there.

Monu had had numerous motorcycle accidents with his daredevil riding. I felt that he was frustrated in his studies. He was an Aries action man who could not possibly enjoy sitting down and dealing with volumes upon volumes of law books. He confided in me that he would have preferred to do engineering, but when I broached the subject to Tommy he said "Let him do law first, he can do engineering afterwards." I thought that this was a waste of some years of his life. Eventually Tommy saw this reason with me and allowed him to leave Ife. He told Monu he would finance him for one year but after that Monu would be on his own.

Undeterred, Monu went to America to study computer engineering in Los Angeles. After the first year he had quite a tough time making a living. He started by washing peoples' cars outside their homes very early in the morning. One car owner was very impressed with his efficiency. He offered him a job in his factory where he was making water beds. So, Monu worked as a carpenter in that factory until sometime later he became a security guard in uniform. Fortunately, at that time my mother was in California to visit Lizzie, her old friend from the Internment camp. My mother was in touch with Monu who visited her from time to time and who got financial support from her when he needed it, until she went back to New York where she lived with a cousin.

Monu returned to Nigeria on a circuitous route. Of all the wild schemes that he was capable of, he had bought a Mercedes and drove it through the Sahara desert to Benin City via Kano. He had friends, an American couple, equally adventurous, who joined him on this trip. Monu recalls that they had a car problem on the journey and had to lie low in the shade of the car in the searing heat of miles and miles of desert around them. They were very fortunate to have a lorry come by which offered them help with their car problem and water to drink. They then followed the lorry through the desert until they arrived in Kano. I was glad I did not know of this enterprise until Monu had got home safely. Just as he liked the wide-open spaces and limitless horizon of the desert, so he would, later, when he became a pilot, like the exhilaration of the limitless sky around him.

He had arrived after qualifying in his chosen field and wanted to set up computer business in Benin City. His father discouraged him and said he should go to live in London and perfect his computer knowledge, and to allow Benin to catch up with the latest technology.

Monu left again for England, but came home occasionally, in the days when air fares were not as outrageously high as they are now.

My house was completed in 1978. There had been some difficulties of contractors cheating me and having to be changed. When we got to the floor covering I took the plunge into the expense of buying Italian ceramic floor tiles and that was a luxury which I have never regretted. They are so cool, so easy to sweep and keep clean, and they do not harbour insects as carpets do. At one point Tommy offered me five hundred naira towards the building of the house, but I refused. He wanted to know why, and I told him that this house was a challenge to me, and I wanted to see if I could do it all by myself. The bottom line was, that I did not want him to have any stake in my property.

In the meantime I had met my greatest good fortune. I had asked my friend Joan whether she could recommend to me a discreet and reliable lawyer whom I could consult about my situation. Without hesitation she said "there is only one person in Benin, whom I can vouch for, and that is Victor Omage." Her recommendation brought me face to face with this young barrister of English public school education and law studies in England at the Inner Temple, plus a degree in economics from the London School of Economics.

At first I was disconcerted by his good looks. I fear handsome men and their vanity, but though his features and bearing were aristocratic, his manner was quietly decisive and he was unassuming, not to say shy. When I had laid my troubles before him, he told me that, if I was thinking of divorce, he would not do the case for me. He did not believe in divorce. Later I knew that he was a sincerely devout Catholic.

"Just advise me for now." I said then. "I must save my sanity. I cannot go on like this. What could be the repercussions if I left to live in my own house? How would it affect our children? What would be my standing in the community? Would I have to cope with hostility from my husband's relations?

His first advice was that I should think seriously, whether I could be financially independent. He also asked to see the document pertaining to my house. Was I sure I was secure on my land? The document turned out to be flawed, and he set about rectifying it. He asked me to reflect again on my plans and to let him know if I needed him.

Although it was fashionable for disco youngsters to wear dark glasses, I wondered why this renowned lawyer should be wearing them. I learned later that he had recently lost his wife, and he was covering with dark glasses his tear-swollen eyes.

He was looking after his four daughters himself, mindful of the pledge he had given their dying mother that he would particularly protect the youngest who was just four months old, and be father and mother to all of them. The eldest — Victoria, had not only lost her mother, but she had to live with her own sad problem. She was a Thalidomide child who had been born without her right hand.

The youngest, the baby, Victor fondly called Fifi, while the two middle ones were Toksy and Poppy.

I learned these details by and by, when the lawyer-client relationship turned into a family relationship which filled my life, as my own children were abroad, far away from me.

Victor professed that he never wanted to marry again. He employed several nannies in succession to attend to the children while he was in court or chambers, but none of them came up to his high standards of devotion to duty, and they were dismissed one after the other; until his late wife's family introduced to him a young nursing sister who had just returned from England where she had obtained higher qualifications. She genuinely devoted herself to the children after her working hours. The baby, especially, became her special task as she was often sick with vomiting and high fever. Christine, the nurse, became the only mother whom Fifi knew. The attachment of one to the other became so strong that Victor, in gratitude, made Christine the baby's godmother – and after a while she became mother to all of them It was not easy for the young Christine to jump, at age 25, into a ready-made family of four children, the eldest of whom was only nine years younger than herself. However, she tried to learn and threw herself with all her energy and enthusiasm into running a good home, for Victor, although he continued to grieve over his late wife's death.

There was jubilation, when four years later, he was made a judge in the High Court of Benin City. I acknowledged the honour bestowed on him, but I felt he was too young at 46 to give up his flourishing practice. However, Victor the idealist, wanted to serve his country and accepted the judgeship in 1982. A year later, fate struck him another blow: Victoria, his eldest daughter, died.

When he had hardly got over the grief of losing her too, — there came the unkindest cut of all. After only three years on the High Court bench, and after displaying his most stringent discipline, integrity and impeccable devotion to duty, he suddenly heard over the television news that he, among five other judges had been "retired". Without preamble, without even a letter from the then military government of Buhari, without having the faintest idea of what could possibly be held against him, this vicious and unfounded attack on his honour and good name threw him into an abyss of despair.

He petitioned every conceivable department of the judiciary, but none could tell him that he had done any wrong, — or which wrong he was accused of. Victor was shattered. He could have stood any physical pain, but this unwarranted assault on his integrity was too much to bear. He could not be consoled. We, his friends, wept with him. Nobody found out the reason why he was retired. One could only assume that these were the devilish machinations of an unscrupulous military government who wanted to replace an inconveniently upright man with a yes-man of their choice.

Victor had lost his job, – but he had not lost his profession. The rules were that once a lawyer had been made a judge, he could no longer go to court to conduct and plead client's cases. He could not use his brilliant advocacy. He could, however, act as consultant, and when the first shock and grief had dulled, he showed his quiet strength and determination to survive for the sake of his children, by opening his chambers for consultancy.

Although he was successful, for eight years he never stopped writing petitions to clear his good name. He appeared before several enquiries who, again, found nothing against him, but between appearances, a long time elapsed, which is the way of governments. He never lost his faith though, and finally, his prayers were heard. After eight years, he rose like the Phoenix from the ashes, when a new democratic government came to power and rectified the injustice done to him. Victor was reinstated as a High Court judge in 1993. He rose and shone again, to be promoted to the Court of Appeal in 1998. Since then, his judgements are being quoted in almost every weekly Law Report magazine. Justice had been seen to be done!

These years had been a heavy task for the young Christine. Her own strong faith sustained her and she supported Victor through all his bitter ordeals. When things got better, Victor remained more serious than before but Christine was the bubbling, humorous and competent wife and counterpart to him. I never tired of listening to her talk about her work as nursing sister and matron in the University of Benin Teaching Hospital. I always felt it was a pity that she had not studied medicine. She had such perfect understanding of it and would have been a brilliant doctor. As it was, countless people, as well as myself, benefited from her generous and dedicated way of nursing when someone was sick. I also learned much from her about medicine. I had always had great interest in it, — Christine was also a lively and charismatic lecturer who made learning fun.

I was very fond of the children as well and they liked me, which made me happy. Over the years Victor and Christine drew me into the wider circle of their families and friends.

It was from them that I learned most of what I know now about Nigerian family life, as Tommy had never encouraged me to befriend Nigerians. He had few friends himself. He was a great socializer and the life and soul of every party, but he confessed that he would prefer to be a hermit, which to me did not seem to be in keeping with his personality. He had a few close friends one of them his cousin, Gray Egbe, the other Andrew Sagay, and then Chief Olu Akpata, but sadly he lost all of them before his own demise. With Victor and Christine now I could share all their joys and sorrows as they shared mine. Victor patiently answered my many questions and attended to my problems with untiring patience. If I did not understand a point he would never raise his voice to me or anybody else. Talking to him was balm for my crushed soul. When Christine went overseas for another course of study and he joined her before she returned to Nigeria, I stayed with the children and Christine's mother in their house, and we had a lot of fun. There was a guest room which came to be known as Aunty Hilda's room. It was my refuge whenever I was sick or had some other trouble.

I began to prepare myself for living in the new house. Little by little I took out from our home my clothes, my books, my photo albums and anything that was dear to me. My husband was pleased when I said I would move out all my work equipment from our marital home, because he had complained that our dining room was always cluttered up with cloths and crafts on all the chairs. So, I moved out my sewing machine, my desk and all the soft and hard crafts that I was working on. From Ife I brought down the cane furniture and cupboards from my shop. They were useful, for the time being, when the house was still empty. He never noticed that I had removed my clothes and personal belongings. I left a few dresses hanging in the wardrobe as camouflage.

Now I had to make the difficult decision: Was I really going to leave our home? I was still full of trepidations. Was I really going to move into my own house and live alone? It was the last week of 1978. Just after Christmas I asked my husband "What have you planned for New Year's eve? Where are we going to celebrate?" He turned on me angrily. "You have had Christmas Day, you can't have New Year's eve as well." That clinched it for me. The girl in the corner now had the whole cake.

We had no family life. Temi and I had no father, no husband, to take us to the club to watch the midnight bonfire and to go into the New Year with us. My decision was made. I wrote a farewell letter and pinned it on my husband's bedroom door, then I left our compound for the last time, in my own car, with Temi by my side.

Chapter VII

FREEDOM FROM PAIN

We entered my own little house, where I sat on a stool in the corner. I looked all around me. I looked at the ceiling, the windows, the floor and I said aloud in wonder "This is all mine." I could not believe that I had built a house. "Thank you God, for making it possible."

Temi and I lay low for fear that Tommy might follow us. We need not have worried. He was otherwise engaged. The next morning God gave me another sign. When I opened the front door there were two large black dogs lying on the mat in front of it. They were big valuable Doberman dogs. I did not know their owner. I did not feed them, but they came again the next night and the night after that, and I took it as an omen. I had been sent protection.

Temi had been on Christmas holiday from her public school in England. It was now time for her to go back, and I was left alone to get on with my life.

I was fortunate to have my business activities so that I was occupied and had constant contact with people from the town. After I had settled in Benin, other goldsmiths wanted to join my business; so that I had the trained silversmiths who came from the Asaba area now, and some young Benin silversmiths who wanted to be trained. Business was still good in those days. The Kingsway Stores and also U.T.C. Stores (United Trading Company) were selling our silver, and I put up frequent exhibitions in hotels and other exposed places in Lagos. The silversmiths were prospering.

Many of them were able to run motorcycles, some even bought taxis to run for extra profit and some built houses for themselves. I was very happy for them. As other goldsmiths now saw the affluence of their colleagues in the trade, envy crept up on them. They tried to lure away apprentices from the established silversmiths working for me, such that we had to hold a meeting to decide that we would form a silversmiths union to protect members from losing their apprentices. The rules were these: 'that I was not to employ any silversmith without the consent of the union and the union members were not to work for anybody else except me.' This way they kept their apprentices, who were precious to them because it took some time to train somebody who was used to working in gold, to work in silver. Silver was softer, had a lower melting point, and needed to be handled differently from gold. We founded the Ogbecraft Silversmiths Guild since I had established the company of Ogbecraft Limited.

Stephen, my faithful cook and my driver and his family had followed me from my marital home into my own compound. Stephen lived in the town, but the driver and his family lived in the boys quarters building, which was the first thing I had built in my compound. I had also planted some fruit trees around the house, despite the warning from people that if you plant trees when you start building, the house will never be finished. I lived to disprove this assumption. When I first moved into the house, I had taken a trip to visit relations in Abraka, to tell them I was leaving Tommy, as I had told all other relations whom I was able to contact. On this trip back from Abraka, I told my driver to dig up some seedlings of a particular tree which I had always admired. It was a large tree with leaves that hung down looking like hands, their "fingers" making a lovely rustling sound when the breeze blew. I planted these seedlings in front of my house thinking that if they would grow and thrive, so would I. At that time the house was not yet painted and I had no fence around it. Those were still peaceful days without fear of armed robbers.

One day I had stood in front of my building with a box of paints in my hand trying to decide what colour to choose for the walls. There came, from across the road, a car whose driver stepped out and told me his boss Mr. B.D.B. Watson, lived in the house across the road, and he would like to meet me. I agreed that he could come over, and within minutes B.D.B. (as I was later to call him) stood by my side. He was a young blonde Englishman who introduced himself saying he was an architect working for a Nigerian firm in Benin. He thought he might be able to advise me on the painting of the house and if I needed any other help, he would be willing to give it. How could I refuse such an offer, when I was inexperienced in building and in a dilemma about the colour of the paint? Together we decided on my favourite colour of mustard yellow which was in tune with the lime yellow of my Mercedes and the same lime yellow of my Toyota. I could now go ahead and paint and then concentrate on a fence for my compound.

I had divided the plot, which was too big for me and would be too expensive to maintain, by a metal mesh fence drawn down the middle of it, but with a small gate that led from one compound into the other half. There was this wire mesh all around the huge plot but there was no front wall yet. On this B.D.B. advised me to build the entrance into the drive to the house with rounded corners, so that no car would collide with a corner when passing through the gate. I was grateful for this advice, as it also gave the entrance a more distinguished look. So, the building continued, but I had a problem with the water tank. Here again B.D.B. offered to supervise the plumber so that he would not put the return valve upside down in the pipe leading to the top tank to supply the house. These were details I could not have known about. They saved me a lot of problems later.

I had joined the Field Society, and I met many people, but mostly Europeans. I was invited to various parties, but apart from enjoying a dance here and there, I found them unfulfilling. The void within me was still too great to be filled by superficial entertainment. B.D.B. my neighbour across the road was a cheerful lad whose every other sentence made me laugh. He was breezy company and sometimes invited me to share his evening meal. If I did not feel like leaving my house, he would bring his food and come over. He cooked delicious Indian food because he lived in England with an Indian friend with whom he had travelled to India many times. On one occasion, the Indian friend, Dave, visited him in Benin City and cooked a truly splendid meal of several daintily spiced dishes to which I was invited. From him I learned much about cooking tasty vegetables like spiced courgettes or curried beans or highly spiced cauliflower and potatoes, in other words, he brought to Benin City part of his exotic world. I in turn invited the boys to Nigerian food and we spent our time exchanging cooking recipes and discussing our respective countries. I had always been intrigued by the Asian continent, especially India. Dave promised me that one day he would take me to India to meet his family, but I thought it was a vague, polite promise.

INDIA

To my surprise, not long afterwards Dave made good his promise. He invited me to join him and B.D.B. for a holiday to see his people. Could I travel with them? Wow, here I was given a journey to Asia on a platter. Dave was working for Air India and got reduced fares. This time, I would be included. I made up my mind in a hurry, for fear that no such opportunity would come again.

Dave had arranged with all his family and friends to give me accommodation, he had also planned an extensive tour of the vast country, saying that within the country there were cheap air tickets for round trips, with which one could hop from one city to another, never mind the distance. It really sounded quite perfect. I accepted with relish. I was told it would be the cool season in India, this month of February, and I would have to bring some warm clothes. It was the best time to travel, before the intolerable Indian heat set in.

We landed in Bombay where Dave's family lived. I met his father, his senior brother and his sisters, all of whom were very friendly and generously hospitable. Of course Bombay is not a tourist place. The eye and the heart take in sad scenes of poverty stricken people living on its pavements, covered in rags or newspapers, and then there were the everlasting swarms of beggars accosting our vehicle as we drove through the town. Haggard mothers with a sucking baby under their arm were the most pathetic, but later I learnt that these babies were handed from woman to woman if she did not have any of her own with whom to elicit pity and receive better alms.

I was most attracted to the flower sellers who sat on the pavement making garlands of flowers heaped in their baskets. The women themselves, mostly elderly, sometimes white haired, were dressed in simple cotton saris in brilliant solid colours. There was kingfisher blue and crimson red. There was bright yellow and orange, and these colours spoke to me. The women themselves wore flowers in their hair or wound around their long plaits at the back.

What I enjoyed most was the after dinner snack of digestive herbs. For this we went out into the warm night to a particular paan seller who had a little kiosk in the street, which was filled with shiny brass receptacles and ornaments. They were polished so brilliantly that that alone was a feast for the eyes. On a few small benches outside his kiosk we sat and munched the mixture of spices which he had carefully selected and wrapped in a beetle nut leaf. One bit into this packet of leaf and chewed the aromatic content which was to help the digestion after a rich and oily meal. I swear I tasted mentholatum in this concoction, but good traveller that I am I ate it all and did not feel any the worse for it.

Our next trip was to Udaipur where we were accommodated in a Maharaja's palace. The Maharanee, named Annabel was an English woman, a friend of Dave and BDB. I had heard much about Annabel from my two friends, so that when I met her I said "It is so nice to meet you Annabel." The boys looked at each other and hastily added "Yes, It is very kind of your Highness to invite us to your palace". I had not realised that the formality of her title was observed in private conversation. After making this mistake I felt I had no right nor opportunity to ask about her private life, although it interested me very much, as she seemed to be one of us, a foreigner married into a different race and culture.

Some time after we had left India we heard that the Maharaja had died. Annabel returned to live in England and died there some years later. She had had no children.

The Maharaja was away on tour but she, dressed in sari and with complete Indian make-up and sandals, was a most gracious hostess. The palace was on the edge of a lake, wonderfully romantic with its ornate arches lavishly furnished rooms and corridors. I slept on a big brass bed under a cover of pure silk velvet. The Maharanee encouraged us to visit another palace in the middle of the lake. It could be reached only by boat and when we got there we found that it had been turned into a tourist hotel. Again, I marvelled at the decorations everywhere on walls, doors and windows.

The view out onto the lake from both, this palace hotel as well as our own Maharaja's palace was spectacular. The lake was surrounded by a mountain chain which shimmered sometimes, purple, sometimes indigo in the mysterious distance. It was hard to believe that we were standing in the world of the twentieth century.

Anabel had made it her vocation to relieve the suffering of animals. She canvassed in the country, that the slaughtering of animals should be preceded by stunning the animals with a blow from a wooden hammer on the forehead, to spare them anxiety before their throats were cut.

Her concern for animals was evident, not only in this project, but there was the story of the rat. I had reported much rustling noise in my room and Her Highness concluded that there must be a rat in it. This seemed to be no unusual occurrence in the palace. She put a rat trap, made of cane and looking much like a bird cage, into my room and the following night a big rat dutifully entered the trap attracted by the bait in it, and the trap closed. The following day Her Highness took the wicker cage out into the open and set the rat free.

I most enjoyed a trip to the market at Udaipur. There the transport system was that of three wheeler taxis. They were driven by motorcycle engines and were open at the sides. The daring drivers managed the haphazard traffic with the enjoyment of mischievous youngsters. At times it seemed to me that they deliberately caused near collisions as though they were in dodgem cars at a funfair in England. We got to the market unscathed. There I feasted my eyes on lavish Indian trimmings and decorations for ladies wear, and jewellery upon jewellery. I fell for the most exotic and largest pair of earrings littered with gemstones and dripping with pearls. A matching necklace and pendant were too short for me but the vendor assured me he could lengthen it while I waited. Wait I did, and watched him deftly adding pearls each side of the necklace to make it longer. I came away with my treasure, jubilating that at last I had found something so decorative and rich looking that it might have come right out of Aladdin's cave.

After the market we drove to the Women's institute where one could buy hand-woven pure cotton towels and embroidered table linen and napkins. I opted for the towels which have served me well ever since. Their weave is a little rough, just enough to massage one's body when one is drying it. The return journey to the palace was hilarious, because this time we did not get into a three wheeler taxi, but took a bicycle rickshaw. I had my arms full of packages and BDB was getting in on the other side of the rickshaw, hardly able to help me. After several attempts to climb onto the hanging step into the rickshaw I nearly gave up, I was laughing so hard at my clumsiness. We got back to the palace quite safely and looked forward to our trip the following day to

Anakpur. What awaited us there I do not think I have the words to describe.

We drove in the Maharaja's Mercedes through bush on either side where we saw varieties of monkeys leaping through the trees and chatting among themselves. But our destination was further on, deeper and deeper through the bush on a tarred road until we reached the Jaine Temple of Anakpur (Jaine are an offshoot of the Buddhist religion). The outside was a work of art of myriads of carved grey marble columns reaching in conical shape to the top of the temple. We entered, having left our shoes outside and now I was struck with such awe by the surrounding whiteness of the marble interior of the temple, the carved marble columns, the carved altar, the many shimmering white marble gods and goddesses smiling down on us, that I held my breath. I was not quite sure whether I was dead or alive, until the biting cold of the marble floor cut through the soles of my stockinged feet, and I realised I was alive. If I was to stay alive, I had to leave this holy whiteness with its bitterly cold floor to save myself from an internal chill.

I stepped out into the warm day once more, looked for my shoes, put them on gratefully and then sat on a stone bench, waiting for my friends to join me. In the meantime I watched the stone masons at work. They were untiring in their effort to chip away at columns of marble, to make new works of art.

It had been a literally breathtaking experience which stayed with me throughout my life. I saw some Jaine nuns dressed in white with face masks over nose and mouth lest they should accidentally inhale and swallow small insects. So strong was their belief that one must not kill any living thing, that they all walked bent forward, a broom in hand with which they swept the path in front of them so as not to tread on an ant or other creature. When my friends rejoined me I was apologetic about not staying longer in the temple, but I think they understood. On this same trip we also visited a sacred place which retained some of the water of the holy river Ganges. I sat under a tree looking at the muddy water, while monkeys played about me or in the top of the tree above me. Another place we came to offered elephant rides. One would climb up onto a raised platform from where one mounted the brightly decorated elephant, but for once I declined the offer of this adventure. On return to the palace we thanked the Maharanee for her gracious hospitality and regretted that it was now time for us to move on.

The next day took us to Jaipur, the Pink City it is sometimes called. There are still remnants of gone-by splendour in the red buildings of which only the latticed fronts are still standing. Behind their screen work the women in purdah used to sit to watch the passers-by in the town without being seen themselves.

From Jaipur onto Delhi the capital, in the heart of India. There we stayed in a sumptuous hotel with a peacock room which was decorated in the turquoise blue colours of the peacock feathers. From there we ventured out into the night to watch the light and sound show at the Red Fort. This historic place cast a shadow over me, I do not know why. We sat on seats in front of the fort, and although I had brought my fur coat, the night was cold, and I had not thought of covering my head. Eventually, the show mesmerised me, as we heard over the loudspeakers the history of India unfold. At intervals, parts of the fort were picked out in light to mark their importance and sound effects really enveloped us in the history of the country as we heard the hooves of galloping marauders invading it. According to the commentary, these were the Mongols and the Turks, the Persians, and long ago, the Egyptians who left their mark on Indian culture.

I contracted the worst cold of my life during that evening. In the hotel I could not eat anything, I felt so ill. I was plied with hot orange juice and whiskey, which would not normally pass my lips. It eased my condition sufficiently for me to enjoy our next trip to Aggra the famous stop for the even more famous Taj Mahal. The train ride to Aggra was intriguing. Dave had bought first class tickets which meant that we each had a seat to ourselves with a table in front of us and a foot rest which was most comfortable.

We consumed some refreshments, but it was not long before we reached the stop for this most famous palace of all, the wonder of the world. I approached the fabulous building with awe. From a distance I could see it reflected in an artificial lake in front of it. This lake was bordered by flowering shrubs, it was rather like a very large long swimming pool. When we got nearer the building I discovered that it was not only made of white marble, and I wondered how the strong white marble could have been fashioned into the graceful rounded onion dome. The building was inlaid with floral mosaics made of different semi precious stones. There were petals of lapis lazuli, of red agate of mother of pearl, and the stems and leaves of the flowers were made of green aventurine and malachite.

It was a pity that our visit coincided with a group of school children who ran about in the sacred hall of the mausoleum, their laughter and shouts echoing from the walls. For me it disturbed the atmosphere. I wanted to linger over the romantic story behind this magnificent building. It was the Mogul Emperor Shah Jahan who built it in the 17th century as a mausoleum for his favourite wife, who died in childbirth. The tragic story culminated in the Shah's being taken prisoner by an opponent, and being locked in a tower not far from the Taj Mahal by the side of the Jumna River. The Shah at the time pleaded for only one thing, and that was to be allowed a room in the tower from whose window he could look out on the resting place of his beloved wife, until he himself died.

For me it is love that makes the world go round, and a true love story always affects me deeply, because I know from experience that true love, — not lust or infatuation, — true love never dies, however many blows it receives from fate.

I was silent as we retraced our steps to the town of Aggra. I was not really in the mood for looking at gem stones in a jeweller's shop, but since my companions thought it was in my line of interest, I did not want to disappoint them. What I cherish to this day are two marble coasters (drink mats) made of the white marble of Aggra each one inlaid with the same kind of gem stones forming a flower as I had seen on the walls of the Taj Mahal. These are my treasures and bring back memories of that Wonder of the World. The gem stones also were fascinating, but my modest means did not allow me to buy diamonds or ruby. I settled for a small faceted garnet, blood red like a ruby, which a goldsmith in Bombay later set into a gold pendant for me. It was made to my design, reflecting the ornate Mogul arches of India. I have now given this pendant to my daughter. The jeweller entertained us with strong sweet tea and sat patiently with many white paper parcels in front of him, each holding varieties of glittering stones. Aggra was a memorable place, but our schedule urged us to move on.

From Delhi we moved on to Bangalore in the south. It was the home town of a young Indian doctor who had been doing his housemanship in the Central Hospital of Benin City. He had gone on to England for further studies but he had begged us that if ever we got to India we should visit his parents. Dave had written letters in advance to announce our coming, and it seemed that the parents were pleased to welcome us.

Bangalore was of particular interest to me because it harboured the hand-loom weavers of the most beautiful raw silk which I had already been given as presents by my friends in Nigeria, and which I used as headties. They were the right thickness and stiffness to be used for that purpose.

We did not know exactly where to find the weavers but we were told of a certain quarter in the town where they lived. A taxi took us to that quarter, but from then on we were left to our own devices. We walked through the streets not getting much help from passersby but I began to hear clattering noises. From all sides they came click-clack, click-clack, click-clack, and in my experience of looms, I thought this might be the noise their shuttles were making while they did the weaving. We did indeed approach one of the low white washed houses and peeped inside the open door. There, to my great joy, I saw the weavers at work, and it was the most amazing sight.

Two men, one each end of the loom, were standing up to their waist in trenches dug into the ground. Across the floor at waist level, their work was drawn thread by thread onto a wooden beam which had slots cut into it to hold the threads. A shuttle of silk thread was passed from left to right, right to left, in quick succession making the most beautiful patterns in either stripes or squares. There were of course many shuttles, each filled with a different coloured thread, and at the other end of the 'loom', the second man would roll the woven cloth when it was finished. We stepped across a low wooden "bridge" which protected the warp. I had never seen or imagined such a novel way of weaving, and I was really thrilled to now know the story behind the headties that I wore with such pleasure. We thanked the men with a small gift of money and then went back to our host.

Father host, took us to the Bull Temple to watch a ceremony. I was intrigued to see in front of the temple a short cement wall about waist high, fashioned into a sharp edge at the top. It was like a peaked roof, and I saw that each person cracked a coconut on the sharp edge, and let the milk flow over the structure before entering the temple. I was told that this was an offering to their gods when the coconut milk flowed over the structure. We entered the temple ourselves and, after taking off our shoes we rang a gong above the door to announce our arrival. Everybody hit the gong gently before entering. We did not stay long, as I was unable to sit cross legged on the floor and I did not wish to stand out as a foreigner in their midst. We returned home to do our packing for next day's flight, but to my amazement, I found that all my luggage had been disturbed. Everything was in a different place and I wondered who could have searched it and for what. Dave and BDB had the same experience. We were puzzled until we told our hostess of our experience, thinking that the maid would have been the one to ransack our belongings. But it transpired that the hostess herself had gone through our things which she talked about openly asking us now how much did you pay for this and how much did you pay for that, disapproving of each price that we had paid. We were glad to have planned to leave the following day, when our next flight took us to Goa, the one-time Portuguese colony in India on the west coast. We criss-crossed India from south to west and landed in a veritable paradise on the seashore. Fringed with palm trees, built up with picturesque small houses and gardens and what was best, Dave's friends were a delightful family who really rejoiced at our visit. They could not do enough for us when cooking, asking all the time what we would like to eat. I remember a fantastic dish in which a whole fish was slit open both sides behind the gills then stuffed with grated coconut and fresh coriander and then fried crisp on both sides. The coriander plant is of the parsley family. It has the same serrated leaves but a much stronger and different flavour than the parsley. Coriander seeds are also used in cooking, when they have been ground to a powder. Dave and BDB went swimming in the ocean, but I stayed behind sitting in the shade of a palm tree.

Because of the influence of the Portuguese colonizers, the people of Goa were Catholic, which was very unusual in the otherwise mostly Hindu and Islamic religions of the country. We wandered about the pretty town admiring the churches and the small cozy shops which had not been reached by modern civilization.

All too soon, it was time to leave, back to Bombay from where we would fly back to England and to Nigeria.

This time in Bombay, it was the New Year festival. While Dave and B.D.B. stayed with Dave's family I had been invited by a millionaires's widow to stay with her in her magnificent house on the outskirts of Bombay. She seemed to enjoy my company, and especially my Nigerian dresses. She thought that Europeans in their short flowered summer dresses did not make the most of their femininity. She liked my long two-pieces and the jewellery I wore and said to me "With your dress and hair style you could pass as one of us." We had dinner together in her richly decorated dining room at a long polished table with white uniformed servants bringing in the tali dishes. The tali trays were of pure silver. Each person had her individual tray, on which was one pile of rice and numerous small silver bowls of different curries. Curried shrimps, curried fish, curried potatoes, curried dhal, a dish made of lentils, cucumber and condiments of all kinds, some so hot that I did not dare touch them but others deliciously spiced. There was also the indispensable bowl of yoghurt which cooled the palate after the hot food. I was given spoon and fork but my hostess ate in her native manner with her hand. Although I was used to seeing people in Nigeria eat like that, it was an incongruous sight to see her heavily ringed hand dip into the curry and rice with diamonds sparkling on her fingers glittering among the rice and sauce. We enjoyed a lively conversation followed by tea and eventually she accompanied me up her marble staircase into my guest room.

She had four guest rooms, each in one corner of the square building, each with its own big bathroom attached and richly furnished. When she saw my dressing gown and gold embossed slippers laid out on my bed she repeated "Yes, yes, you like beautiful things. You are a woman, you could be one of us." With this compliment she bade me goodnight, and I snuggled into the big bed hoping for a good night's sleep. I had not reckoned with the crows outside. These big black birds swarm all over Bombay in the day time, and even do not settle completely in the night. One or two of them must have perched on my verandah to keep me company. The outcome was that I did not get much sleep with them cawing outside my window.

The next morning was designated for me to shop for jewellers' tools. I wanted to take back with me something for each of the silversmith's workshops. My hostess Rajni kindly gave me her car and driver with whom I picked up Dave and B.D.B. who guided me to that part of the city where I would find the kind of tools I was looking for.

There again, I was distracted by the crows overhead, but once I got inside the shops I could concentrate on what I had come to buy. I had extra luggage allowance and was able to buy ring sizes to measure customers with, ring mandrels on which to fashion rings to their correctly marked size, and sandpaper sticks with which to smooth the inside of the rings when they were ready. The tool shops also sold jewellery, and I enjoyed seeing the showcases full of gold sets of which the necklaces were so large. They were like bibs. Happy with my purchases I returned to Rajni to share another splendid meal with her. She then told me that at New Year all the principal buildings in the town would be lit up at night and she gave me her driver again to take me around the town so that I could enjoy the spectacle. We drove through the dark streets to be suddenly confronted by a fairy land of illuminations. Each public building and its gates was outlined in closely placed small electric bulbs all in white. There must have been millions and millions of them. It was a fantastic sight, and I was grateful that my hostess had given me this opportunity to see them.

I had also been taken around very many temples some of which had steps perhaps a hundred or two hundred leading up to them while the temple stood serenely at the top. Alongside the steps were walls painted with scenes of past battles all in colour and all accurate history to tell the tale. Other temples of course had the carvings of the famous Kama Sutra, the book of love-making carved into the walls. The fame of Indian love-making has spread across the Western World, so too has the knowledge that Indian women are literally taught how to make love and are desirable wives and mistresses. For me the pictures seemed to be full of acrobatics which in my opinion might well extinguish the flame of desire with the effort of achieving satisfaction. My own satisfaction must always be borne out of love and affection and the total desire to cherish with my body. I daresay many tourists are turned on by these pictures, or at least given ideas for a more varied love life. In any case, the postcards and video films of the Kama Sutra are a source of wealth to their manufacturers.

Before we left Bombay we had another ceremony to perform. Dave's family urged us to go to a temple on an island across from Bombay to pray for his younger sister Anu, a beautiful tall slim girl with thick black hair hanging down her back in a heavy plait. She had not been able to have a child. We all boated across the Arabian sea to this island where there was a delightful small white temple. Before entering, the sister and I were decorated with flowers. She had a garland around her neck but I had a circlet of blossoms fastened around my bun. It was a moving ceremony of which I do not remember the details but I remember the reverent atmosphere which seemed sacred, and I hoped the lovely girl would yet have a child of her own. After the ceremony we were served local snacks by a family of friends who lived on that island. There were the tasty samosas fried in hot oil and other tidbits fried by a very old woman who squatted on her haunches beside the low fire and the pan of oil.

It was time to return to the city.

SINGAPORE

Our departure from Bombay was a bit chaotic because I had much overweight luggage. The silversmith tools made my luggage very heavy. But fortunately the airport officials discovered that I had some luggage vouchers which would pay for the overweight.

At the airport BDB, Dave and I parted company. While they went back to England, I continued my flight in a different direction. I had arranged to meet my cousin from Australia, whom I had not seen in thirty years. We had agreed to spend one week in Singapore, and he had made reservations for our rooms from Australia. The reunion was quite emotional. My cousin who was also called John had the title Johnny number two in the family whereas my brother was Johnny One.

Johnny Two was a lonely man. He had lost his mother, his sister and her two babies during the holocaust in Germany. His father was nowhere to be found and his favourite Uncle Fred, had already emigrated to South Africa. There was no one to arrange immigration into another country for him. In despair, aged sixteen he had stowed away on a ship bound for Holland. At arrival in Holland, he was put in prison by the Dutch authorities, for illegally entering their country. Eventually, he had worked his way from Holland to Britain. In Britain, my mother, my brother and I were reunited with him. He married a very lovable English girl, Peggy, with whom he emigrated to Australia. They had one daughter, but, sadly, Peggy died quite young when her daughter was only a teenager. Ever since then Johny Two had been writing sad and nostalgic letters to me, in which he expressed his loneliness as well as his bitter sense of humour. He had failed to replace his Peggy with any other suitable woman, and his daughter lived far away from him. For the moment, his meeting with me seemed like a shaft of light in his life, reuniting him with a member of his family.

Therefore, my memories of that trip were mostly personal, although I did not fail to take in the extreme cleanliness and orderliness of the town of Singapore. The small country was well run by its lawyer-leader, President Lee. Everybody seemed to be well disciplined, traffic was beautifully regulated, and I had no hesitation to eat meals in an open food market. It was situated in a large square of the town, 'roofed' with white awnings letting in daylight. Under them various food stalls were set up, each one serving its own speciality. We went from stall to stall choosing rice from one, Chinese pork from another, Bombay duck from yet another, Chow Mein from the next, crossing over from one to the other to see what else was on offer. When we had assembled our menu, (of course we had paid for each dish) we sat down at one of the many cleanly washed white tables and chairs to eat our inexpensive meal in a jolly and lively atmosphere. Finally we ended with a piece of fruit, again from one of the stalls, and I made the acquaintance of the delicious, juicy, Jackfruit.

On a more elaborate scale we had a fish dinner in a hotel garden by the seashore. I was shocked when we were each presented with a big whole baked fish on a platter decorated with fresh vegetables cut in the shape of roses and lillies. The fish stood on its belly, its fins standing upright along its back, and it seemed to look at us malevolently from its dim eyes. Of course, I could not even eat one-quarter of the fish although it was delicious, and the hotel was too elegant for us to ask for a 'doggy' bag in which to carry home the leftovers. I just hoped that the hotel had many cats around.

Wherever we went, and whatever we did we chatted nonstop, reminiscing over our common childhood and trying to keep at bay the deep sorrow which my cousin felt over every memory. When the short week came to an end I tried to look for souvenirs from Singapore, but everything was too orderly, too civilized, too manufactured, to be of any real interest to me. The one item that held my longing glances were the delicately made artificial flowers. They were so real, so lifelike, that the customs of Lagos airport wanted to confiscate them. "You cannot import live flowers into Nigeria."

After returning from such a long exciting trip, I might have felt lonely, coming back to my empty house, had it not been for my adopted family. Victor and Christine had kept a check on my itinerary, and they and the children would be expecting me. So, during the boring four hours drive from Lagos, where my plane had landed…, I had something to look forward to. They lived at the near end of the town when one came in from the capital, while I lived at the opposite end, twelve kilometres away.

The warmth of their welcome soon made me feel at home again, and I slipped back into the old groove with ease. In those days, in the 1980's I did a lot of travelling, always combining business with the pleasure of seeing family and friends.

Whilst I continued with my silver industry, I had also become a director in an all-women's travel agency. To get a better understanding of this complicated business, I spent three months in London in 1982 to take a course on Travel Agency functions, prescribed by IATA, the International Association of Travel Agents.

Curiosity had driven me, but I might have known that it was not at all "up my street". I hate figures and abbreviations. They have no soul. They do not speak to me, yet… the course was all of those and more, fare calculations, flight schedules, time zones, town abbreviations flew at me from all sides. The only living and interesting part was world geography which taught the capitals and major towns of all the countries which had flight connections. I managed to pass the course and escaped the tedious lessons with the requisite diploma.

There was one bonus though on this trip. On my way from the underground to my lodgings at Holland Park, I passed a French butcher and delicatessen shop. There I bought what I had never seen before, a smoked chicken, to eat for my supper. One bite of this tender, succulent smoke flavoured meat sent me into ecstasy. "Out of this world" was my verdict and when my departure date for Nigeria came due, I bought another chicken to take back. Once at home, I sent half of it to Tommy. This made a rod for my back, because he became so enamoured of this delicacy that he belaboured anybody who was going abroad, to bring him back a smoked chicken. Tommy was then sixty-seven years old, and the idea struck me that if he learned to smoke his own chickens, he would not only satisfy his craving, but it could become a little business and something for him to do in his retirement, although he was still going to court.

I gathered information from two continental chefs who were working in Nigeria, — one in Kaduna, the other in Ajaokuta, with the construction company of Berger and Bilfinger. We learned which kind of wood to use for the best flavour, but before the smoking, the chickens had to be marinated overnight in water with spices and preservative, the length of time for smoking depended on their size and weight. Tommy was fond of cooking anyway, so we built a red brick smoke-house in the back of his vast garden and he not only ate happily ever after but sold to affluent customers as well. I was one of them.

In the 1980's I made several trips to Israel, where our unpredictable daughter Temi had chosen to do her A-levels in an American High School. Without any prompting from me, who had enlisted her in an Oxford Tutorial College, she had got herself a place in that school on the outskirts of Tel Aviv and was adamant that she would study in Israel. I had been annoyed, thinking it was one of her whims and told her I would not lift a finger to help her. If she could make her own arrangements, well and good.

For two days, she had sat in the office of an Israeli Engineering company in Benin trying to get through on the telephone to the school in Israel. When she finally got the connection on a difficult line, she shouted her request through several interruptions to ask if they would accept her. She mentioned all the subjects she had passed in her school certificate, mentioned her family background... and came home jubilant. "Yes, they would take her into eleventh grade and would she please come soon with all her credentials and the requisite (high) fees for the semester".

It was 1979 in the days of strict foreign exchange control in Nigeria, and it was a hassle to get permission for dollars for education. Tommy readily gave his permission for the school Temi had chosen. He was a great admirer of the disciplined Israelis, their hard work and ingenuity. "Lucky girl" he said to his daughter "I wish I could go with you". He helped us to make the financial arrangements, and his wish to go to Israel came true two years later, when we all converged on Kfar SHMARYAHU to, attend Temi's graduation ceremony from that American High School in Israel.

My mother, my brother and his wife came from New York, Tommy and I came from Nigeria and Monu came from London. We stayed in simple Kibbutz hotels which were clean and the buffet-style meals plentiful, all made of home-grown fresh vegetables, fish, chicken and cheese. Meat was rare and very expensive. Besides, leaving it out of the menu, it was Kosher and safe for orthodox visitors, because meat and milk would never be cooked together or served at the same meal. Fish and chicken were neutral and could be eaten with anything.

For her first trip I had of course, taken Temi to her new school to see her settled and to find foster parents for her.

Later, I visited twice a year in that fascinating small country, to supervise her progress. It was amazing to me that my African child should have brought me to Israel which I had never visited before and without her, never might have done so. In a rented car she would drive me all over the country from the sea of Galilee in the north to the Red Sea at the southern tip. On my first trip, my heart nearly stood still when we passed a signboard pointing "To Jerusalem". This was real! This was history come to life!

Yes Jerusalem, Bethlehem, Nazareth, Capernicaum, they were all there. We floated in the Dead Sea. We lay on top of the water in which it is impossible to sink because of the thick salt content. It feels oily, and we had to sluice it off under powerful showers on the beach. It made our skin feel soft and supple for weeks afterwards. The hardest part had been to wade into the water, as our feet bled, walking over the sharp rocky salt ground. However in the concentrated salt, the wounds healed almost immediately. Where pillars of crusted salt rose out of the water, I could well imagine one of them being Lot's wife.

Temi was happy in Israel, whose warm, hospitable, boisterous people reminded her of Nigeria. The sub-tropical summer heat suited her as did the abundance of luscious fruits and flowers which the hard-working people were growing in the desert. She brought her brother Monu over from England to share her enjoyment and the many new friends she had made.

I was glad that brother and sister were always close, now that Temi had outgrown her nuisance little sister act, during which she would needle Monu incessantly, teasing and disturbing him to gain his attention. This was not easy in the early years when the seven years age difference did not make her a suitable playmate for him. In the 1980's when Temi was 24 and Monu 31 years, the three of us could reminisce over the journeys we had made together. When I had taken them to America, Monu then 18, had said "I know what you are doing, mummy you are making a bridge for us."

I marvelled at his sensitive insight, for that indeed was my aim. A bridge to countries and people, so that my children too might embrace the world citizen idea in which I had believed all my life. If one can enjoy other people's culture and customs, other people's food and clothing instead of criticizing them, then one can adjust to anywhere in the world. I had always thought that, if one had any surplus money it was best spent on travelling, for "what the eye has seen the heart never forgets". I was in that lucky position as my silver business grew so that the children and I visited Austria, Switzerland, Spain, Germany, France, Egypt, Israel and America.

Temi had visited Rome with her class when she had been in boarding school in England. Monu and his guitar had spent a summer course of learning German in Vienna, while we were in East Africa. Needless to say that he came back with the amusing, but un-German Vienna pronunciation of that language, but he had had fun.

On a flight to Mallorca, we had made a night stop at Madrid, where in few hours we had not only eaten real paella, visited the Prado to admire the royal gilt coach, shopped for fans and Spanish hoop earrings and taken in a fun-fair where Monu enjoyed Go-kart racing. We loved the warm night air, the brightly lit streets and small shops which seemed to be busy all night and it was fun to be part of the crowd which thronged the streets. Wherever we visited, I encouraged my children to make a simple diary of events, using post-cards, bus-tickets, receipts, hotel stickers or whatever, — to remind them in future of what they had seen and done.

Chapter VIII

SICKLE CELL COUNSELLOR

It was now three years since I had left my home. By and by I had some furniture made by a carpenter. I had curtains sewn for all the rooms, and my days were full, but my evenings lonely. There was still a vacuum in my heart which could not quite accept the fact that I had parted from my husband after thirty-five years. Every time I drove into town through Airport Road, I averted my face, when I passed my former residence. I just could not bear to look at the home I had left.

About two weeks after I had left, Tommy drove up to my house announcing himself with his loud and dominating horn which he started blowing from the beginning of the street, for all to hear that he was coming. My heart beat wildly, not knowing how I would handle a confrontation with him. I stepped out of my front door closing it behind me and walked towards his car. He did not get out of it. "Well", he said "haven't you had enough?" "Enough of what"? "Enough of playing house." "I am not playing house. I came to live here." "I see. Well, that's alright then," and he drove off.

I was relieved, but two weeks later he came again asking me to accompany him to a Kings College Old Boys dinner at a certain hotel. I declined with thanks, thinking to myself he had a companion whom he had been taking around, let him take that one. Sometime later he came again asking me to a Rotary convention in Tokyo, Japan. Knowing my love for travel he must have thought this would be a sure pull. "If you pay your own fare, you can come with me." I did not accept this invitation either but he brought me a large red silk fan from Tokyo as a souvenir.

The next time he came with a plea which I could not refuse. As always, I received him outside my front door. There we sat on the verandah and discussed his sister's problem. Her daughter Bridget was ill and in and out of hospital. "She is suffering from sickle cell disorder," Tommy said. "Do you know anything about that?" I did not. He continued saying that Mewe was at her wit's end. She could no longer afford the hospital fees but also she could not bear to see her daughter in such pain all the time.

I thought for a moment, and then something rang a bell in my head. Since living on my own I had become a member of the Nigerian Field Society. I was interested in all aspects of the environment in which I lived and found the lectures there very interesting. I now remembered that one lecturer had taken us to a botanical garden of medicinal herbs. There he had pointed to various plants, saying "This is for asthma, this for pregnancy, this one for cough, this is for eye trouble, this one for sickle cell, this one for tummy trouble..." Now the word sickle cell came back into my memory. I offered to take our niece to the kind botanist who had given us the talk. He was Charles Shokpeka who was renowned for his study of snakes in Nigeria. When I took Bridget to him he took us to a field, uprooted some small plants and gave them to her. "Grow these near your house and break off a piece, chew it and swallow it twice a week. You will have no more serious crises after that."

And so it was. Bridget was relieved of the recurring excruciating bone pains. She lived happily ever after and is now over forty years old. She has had two healthy children, and I remember forever the help she had got from Mr. Shokpeka. At the time, when I saw the recovery of Bridget, I was amazed at the efficacy of the simple, modest looking herb. Although I knew nothing about the sickle cell illness, I thought I should plant this herb in my garden. Maybe I could help somebody with it some day.

I started talking to doctors and doctor friends about the astounding recovery of our niece, but that was my mistake. Doctors who practice orthodox medicine, cannot really mix it with herbal treatment, but at least they gave me information about the blood disorder and one of them lent me a book to study. I made copious notes and studied them, but of course, no one can catch up with six years of medical training just like that. I also wondered, why was I driven like this, driven to learn about a disorder I had never heard about before? It was a compulsion to gain knowledge with which to be able to help.

Around the 1980s there was not such awareness of the sickle cell disorder. People seemed to be resigned to the misery of constant pain, malaise and weakness and did not expect young patients to live out their time. B.D.B. had been transferred to Jos, and when he came down for consultation with his employers and a visit to me, he brought me my first patient. His driver's wife had given birth to a baby boy, but when I congratulated the driver, he was downcast. His baby was sick. The tops of his hands and feet were swollen and painful to the touch. He cried incessantly, and the hospital, after taking a genotype test, diagnosed him to be a sickle cell sufferer. Instantly, my mind went to the herb in my garden. But how could a four months old baby chew and swallow a herb?

While B.D.B. stayed in Benin for a few days, I dried and ground the herb and then asked a young doctor friend what dosage of this powder he would suggest for the baby. "One quarter teaspoon in pap" he answered. I also gave the driver some plants to propagate in his garden. Within days of his return to Jos B.D.B. phoned me to say that the driver's baby was now well. The swellings had gone down, there was no more pain, the baby had stopped crying and was eating and behaving normally.

My gardener brought me my second patient on his bicycle. A twelve year old boy, the size of an eight year old. The boy shuffled into my house, listless, weak, thin, with jaundiced whites of the eyes. He also had a mildly enlarged spleen and was in poor shape.

He went away with enough of the herb-powder and instructions and I told him to see me again in a month's time.

I hardly recognised him when, at the appointed time, he strode briskly into my house, his eyes clear and a big smile on his face. "I can now play table-tennis" he announced and made a sharp movement with his right hand holding an imaginary bat.

Not long after that, my friend Christine Omage introduced a junior nurse. She brought her and her twelve-year-old daughter in her car. They entered, the nurse carrying her daughter on her hip, because the girl could not walk. Her painful legs were dangling when the mother sat her on my settee.

The girl had not been to school for nine months. She could not bathe herself, nor carry anything. The mother had gone for alternative medicine to a practitioner who charged her twenty thousand Naira to "change the girl's blood." She had paid down three thousand, but despite different potions and massages, there had been no improvement. I gave her a month's supply of my powdered herb and got the feedback that after two weeks the girl could carry her bucket of water and bathe herself. After three weeks she could walk down the road to buy something, and after one month she went back to school.

I felt joyful, — and humbled at the same time. Who was I, a medically untrained person, to be able to bring relief to people? I had not even known what the sickle cell disorder was, as it did not affect Caucasians, but I now felt that God had made me His instrument. He had put this herb into my hands to be able to help people. He did not censure me for not going to church, — or synagogue. He knew that He lived within my heart and that His Ten Commandments were my guide throughout my life. He gave me a chance to redeem myself, — that is, I could show gratitude for having escaped the holocaust in Germany, and I hoped I was justifying my existence.

As the news spread that there was a remedy for bone pain crisis in sickle cell sufferers, more and more people came for help. I started a regular "clinic" in my house every weekday from 6-7 in the evenings. I also began to keep records: attendance and patients' medical records, albeit in layman's fashion.

At the time of writing, in this new millennium my greatest goal is to find a pharmaceutical company which will encapsulate the powdered herb to achieve wider distribution and to bring relief to millions of sufferers, more than I ever can.

Chapter IX

A FULFILLED LIFE

I had settled down well into a routine of business and private life, until my long standing driver caused a great upheaval. He had been with me for eighteen years. I had taken him and his family of six children to be my responsibility, helping them in whatever way I could. I had sent all their six children to nursery school in town, so that they might have the opportunity of early learning. I had employed his wife as well so that they had two incomes, and in the beginning I lent them my car to take the children to and from school and to church on Sunday until the driver bought his own car. To cut a long story short, the driver organised an armed robbery attack on me in my house during the night of the 14th February, 1992. The case took four years in the High Court to be judged, and he was convicted of armed robbery. That night when the robbery happened, I was shaking with terror. After the robbers had left I phoned Victor at 3 o'clock in the night just to have the reassurance of his voice and by 7 o'clock in the morning, he and Christine arrived at my house to see in what way they could help.

Tommy showed solidarity during the years of investigation, by going to court for every hearing even though he was then in quite some pain with a hip problem. I appreciated this help and support.

After I had first left our marital home, Tommy continued to visit or telephone me at odd intervals. On one occasion, about two years after I had left, he told me that nobody had slept in my bed all this time and that my slippers were still in front of it as I had left them. Two years further on, the girl in the corner who had caused us so much misery left him. She had become tired of her gilded cage and its possessive owner. He was alone in the house, fending for himself for another two years, until his relations in Warri decided that it was not seemly for a man of his status, to live alone and they sent him a young girl from the village to be his 'small wife.'

The small wife produced two children, first a boy and then a girl, two years apart, but Tommy did not seem to be happy. On occasions he asked my advice saying that he did not know why the small wife was always moody and bad tempered. He had bought her all the things that he thought a girl could wish for, but I dare say, she had other dreams. He found his money missing continually and eventually discovered that she had duplicate keys to every one of his rooms and cupboards. The day he discovered her purse of keys she snatched it from him and ran away, never to be seen again. She literally left him 'holding the babies!' Later he learned that she had made her way to Italy.

I was very sorry for the small children, but there came a great and wonderful change over Tommy. The boy was four years old, the little girl two. I visited them from time to time, to see if I could comfort them in any way. On these occasions I saw how tenderly Tommy looked after them, bathing them, dressing them, shopping for them, cooking for them, because he never wanted any househelp. He did have a series of nannies but could not get on with any of them. It seemed to me, that he was now fulfilled. He was in his element, looking after helpless little beings, who would not argue with him but obey his every command. The boy grew up to be very intelligent and helpful to his father. He learned at an early age how to deal with television, video and CNN, how to serve his daddy beer and soft drinks, how to find missing articles, and Tommy in turn taught him a lot of incidental knowledge. The little girl obviously missed her mother or a mother, because she snuggled up to me anytime I went to visit them. Both children jumped up and down at the window shouting "Aunty Hilda, Aunty Hilda" when they saw my car coming into the drive.

Tommy would then be in the kitchen frying dodo or frying fish or he would be sitting in his rocking chair in the sitting room peeling boiled breadnuts. He treated me with wistful affection. One day, as I was leaving, he said "You have been loved you know." I noticed the past tense. In fact, it was past perfect. Yes. Perfect.

He had previously told me of a dream he had had before I left our house. He had been driving his own car but saw me in front of him sitting in a taxi. The taxi caught fire and he shouted "Pooppie, Pooppie", but could not rescue me. When the fire subsided only my headtie was left of me. He was quite an intuitive man, and it was not surprising that some premonition had crept into his dreams.

When the children began to go to nursery school, he took them there himself for eight o'clock in the morning and collected them when school closed. Fortunately, the school was not far from his house. I sensed that Tommy had a new kind of respect for me. I had found my feet, - without him. I had made friends, - without him. His relations still were fond of me, - without him. My business was well established, and well known. When he consented to give an interview about me to be shown on television, he talked at length about himself first, recalling his days as captain of the Nigerian football team against Ghana, as freelance photographer in Lagos, and his war years in England. When he remembered that the interview was about me, he said "Hilda is a wonderful woman. She made me (a Freudian slip) well, she didn't exactly make me, but she taught me many things. Yes, Hilda is the wonderful woman in my life."

In these series of interviews Sam Ogbemudia also spoke about my work with the craftsmen. Walter Anukpe, my co-director in the Midwest Craftshop days contributed, and so did various craftsmen who were interviewed in Benin City as well as Igarra and Somorika. I have a copy of this film, but to my knowledge it has never been shown.

My love for languages never died. One day a young man appeared on television, introduced by the presenter, and appealed for help from the public. He told his story, - he was an orphan but had been educated by his relations to reach School Certificate. When I heard that he had been admitted to the University of Benin to study English but that his relations could not afford to educate him further, I contacted the presenter of NTA and asked to see the young man at my house. His name was Lucky. He struck me immediately as being open and truthful. "What do you want to do with English?" I asked him. "You can only teach when you are qualified." "No", he said. He wanted to be a writer and poet. I remarked that that would hardly earn him a living in the beginning but he insisted that he would like to be proficient in English.

"If you really want to speak good English, I will support you on the condition that you will take elocution lessons from me in addition to your university curriculum." He agreed to this and truly, for the next four years he came to my house on Sunday afternoons punctually, to be taught English pronunciation. He was very appreciative of the chance he was getting and tried to keep his boarding and feeding expenses as low as he possibly could. He was never demanding. He applied himself to his studies with great tenacity, and he also desisted joining the trouble makers in the university. Half way through his studies, another English student was added to my Sunday lessons.

I had discovered that in my street, adjoining the other half of my compound, there was a school for Mass Communication. Bearing in mind that they were training amongst other subjects, broadcasters and television announcers, I went in one day and offered my services to teach English pronunciation to the students. The director regretted, saying they could not afford to pay me, but I said that I did not want any salary. I just wanted to help. He accepted, and once a week I would walk down from my house to theirs to give an hour's lesson in pronunciation. There I noticed an outstandingly diligent student. He would be the first in class. He was the one who brought me a chair. He was the one who cleaned the blackboard. He was the one who made sure there was enough chalk. I noticed his eagerness to learn. He was the most attentive student in the class, the one who asked the most questions, the one who was always cheerful. I asked him what he wanted to do after qualifying from this school and he said he wanted to be a journalist. I invited him to join the Sunday lessons I had with Lucky.

He came punctually, and when I asked him to write me some essays, he wrote prolifically. Unfortunately, his writing did not make sense to me. He seemed to be stringing many 'big' words together without any structure to their sentences. Eventually I found out that he had no knowledge whatsoever of grammar. I bought him the five basic books of grammar meant for primary school and set about teaching him the meaning of nouns, verbs, adjectives, adverbs, personal pronouns and so on. I was angry with the school who had passed him with flying colours in all the exams he took for journalism giving him a false sense of achievement. He studied the grammar very hard and made good progress but I feared that he would never be a good journalist. I suggested to this boy, called Emmanuel, that he would have a better future taking up computer training. I offered to sponsor him through weekend courses at the University and in the meantime I would employ him in my office. I also gave him accommodation and he seemed well pleased with this new idea. As he began to learn to handle a computer he was able to work on mine with the help of my then secretary, Margaret Obeahon, an English Nigerwife. Emman, passed the Ordinary National Diploma and the Higher National Diploma. He sponsored himself through the postgraduate Diploma and is now teaching in a school for computer science.

NIGERWIVES

The new term Nigerwife was forged in Lagos in 1979. It was an organisation of foreign women married to Nigerian men. There had always been this feeling that we, the foreign wives, were vulnerable in Nigeria. We had no family to back us up. We were sometimes isolated and lonely in faraway towns where there were not many of us. At first, the Nigerian husbands viewed us with suspicion. Were we going to cluck together about our husbands? The organisation soon dispelled such fears by declaring that we wanted not only support for each other, but we wanted to help to integrate newcomers into Nigerian society. Therefore many lectures were arranged, which taught Nigerian history, traditions and culture. Of course, these varied from place to place, but as each section of the country established its own group of Nigerwives they taught what was relevant to their area and their husbands' tribe. In Benin City we formed our first group in 1989. We canvassed among our friends and sought out those mixed couples whom we met while shopping in the big supermarkets or at parties. Most wives were doubtful, not knowing what their husbands would think of the idea and whether they would allow them to attend.

Eventually, we held our first meeting at Joan Aiwerioghene's house, which had a large enclosed verandah with its separate entrance, so that her husband, Prince Ayo Aiwerioghene, would not be disturbed. He, on the contrary, sometimes walked in on us and listened to what was going on. This was our opportunity to thank him for his hospitality.

At our first meeting we all introduced ourselves in turn. It became clear that I was not only the oldest in our midst, but I had been in Nigeria the longest. I was proposed to be president of our group, but though I appreciated the honour of being nominated I declined. I promised to give our group all the support and all the co-operation behind the scenes, but I could not accept any post on the committee. I did not have any surplus energy. I was then 68 years old and needed all my strength to survive in my single existence.

The point was taken, and Joan became our first president, with other members supporting her as vice president, secretary, financial secretary, treasurer and member. We had members from Hungary, Sweden, Germany, Britain, USA – from Mexico, Russia and the Philippines, from Austria, Italy and Spain, not to forget the foreign wives from East Africa, Ghana and Sierra Leone. There did not seem to be any corner of the globe which Nigerian students had not penetrated.

Although we had introduced ourselves, it was difficult to retain all the different names, how many children and what profession each had, not to speak of understanding each person's country of origin. There was also some shyness about asking each other questions. The more often we met and the more often we smiled and nodded at each other without remembering the person's name, the more embarrassing it became to now ask, "Where do you come from and what do you do?"

I felt it was necessary for each member to know the other in print. I offered to write a profile on each member of our group, which would then be included in the monthly newsletter. I think it helped to get the story of each of us eventually, even if it took a year or more to do the whole round. In the meantime we also organised members to talk about their country and to bring some display aids, if possible, or some of their national food. It helped if the speaker would wear her national costume. This was great entertainment which brought us all together, and here was an opportunity to ask questions which had long been saved up. As the years went by we really developed that sisterly feeling amongst us all, so that we felt we could call on somebody when we needed help.

Of course, some people are more forthcoming than others, but one of them stood out in the crowd. She was of Hungarian origin and at first hardly ever took part in conversation, because she felt her English was wanting. But in readiness to help and comfort others she surpassed everybody else. Her name was Reka. At the time of our first meeting she was heavily pregnant. She had five sons and her husband badly wanted a girl. She got that girl, a much deserved daughter who is now almost a young lady already. Reka never changed. She had and has great empathy for all, and her profession of nursing is the ideal for her. But we had and have other most helpful sisters one of whom is Reka's next door neighbour, a Scottish lass who, although she trained years ago as a computer programmer in Scotland, became our master baker in the University community. Her cakes are truly works of art. She is probably the most popular mother on the campus. Whatever the occasion, a birthday, Valentine's Day, Easter, Christmas, graduation, exams passed, — all can be celebrated with a special cake from Eileen Uku. Special in design and inscription, special in colour and originality.

Well, Reka Okonkwo learned to speak English, and we learned to understand Eileen's Scottish accent. Mexican Manuela's torrent of "Spanglish" was another matter. In her most vivacious manner she would eloquently describe events and activities that she had been through, but we would look at one another and later piece together the few words each of us had understood. What needed no translation was her very warm, hospitable and loving attitude to everybody. We admired this dynamo of a woman who had lived in the husband's uncle's house in one room for five years with all her children, but who had in the meantime worked like a Trojan, cracking palmnuts and earning enough money to buy land and build a house for the family. Her husband Dr. Patrick Iyahen was a gentle medical practitioner working at the University of Benin Teaching Hospital (UBTH) and like so often, opposites attract he found this dynamic woman to be the right counterpart to his retiring self.

Gradually, we all got to know each other, got to know our weaknesses and our strengths, and we embraced each other as our sisters in our self-imposed exile. It was a comforting feeling, because not everybody had a surrogate family as I had. We also hoped to help in the Nigerian community wherever possible, although our finances were very tight. We arranged means of raising funds and conscientiously put into the kitty our tea money and raffle money which was raised at every monthly meeting. Volunteers would bring cakes and tea and the person who won the raffle would bring a present the next time to be raffled so that the takings could go into the kitty. As for lectures we arranged not only speakers on Nigerian customs and traditions, but we included the environment, the flora or fauna around Benin City and Nigerian recipes and tips how to adapt Nigerian produce to European tastes. There were creative suggestions from all sides. We also arranged an annual picnic at Abraka, where the families could bring their children to swim and play in the sand. Abraka had a very cold and fast flowing river, but canoes and rubber tubes were at hand to keep safe those who were not strong swimmers. The enterprising Chief McCarthy had brought white sand to pour on the shore of the river and provided thatched huts and umbrellas, deckchairs and tables, so that one really had the feeling of being at a seaside resort.

Another popular event was the annual Valentine's party. This was a grand affair on the 14th of February, held in the garden of Prince Aiwerioghene's house. All the members rallied round to decorate, provide food and drinks, provide blocks of ice to cool the drinks, and husbands were designated to attend to the music and or the bar. Naturally, admission for couples was charged, raffle tickets were sold and a profit was made on food and drinks. The food was provided by members and consequently had a very international flavour which the husbands enjoyed. They were now quite happy to be members of the Nigerwives circle and enjoyed the fun provided by our extremely talented MCs. One of them was Pat Uddoh who is fondly invited to every possible function to liven up the party, as she is a born comedienne who never fails to make people laugh. Her greatest asset perhaps is her ability to bring to life her Jamaican background, in using the accent and terminology of her home country. She also invents hilarious games to be played by husbands and wives while dancing, thus bringing people together with laughter.

If there was any serious problem in any Nigerwives' family, we would consult over it and help out in whatever way we could. The monthly newsletter always had an editorial, news about members of the group whether in Nigeria or abroad, a column on health, one on topical subjects, another had tips on gardening and cooking or child care, members' birthdays were mentioned and on every page there were snippets of humour inserted here and there. For many years, my wonderful secretary Margaret Obeahon and I were joint editors. After Margaret left to take her handicapped child to England for better training and a better future, I could not continue the editorship on my own. Dear, funny and brilliant Sue Iyoha from the U.S.A. took over.

Chapter X

WIDOWHOOD

When I began my story it was the new millennium, January 2000. I had been connected with Tommy for fifty-two years. After the initial break-up we had become friends. He was like an old familiar relative to me, and possibly his regrets were greater than mine. He continued to look after the small children with all his heart, but young women regularly visited his house and ended up by making a fool of him. They always came in twos, and the story that they came from his village of Ugbuwangue was always the same. Parochial considerations did not allow him to send them away, he told me. After each visit he confessed sheepishly that once again he had been robbed by these girls. It became routine for me to hear that they had stolen a radio, or an electric shaver, a telephone or a teapot, or cutlery, and plates and dishes used to disappear at regular intervals. They always knew too where to find his money. It did not matter the clever hiding places he devised in our big house, the girls always made away with lots of money when there was any. Of course these incidents no longer affected me but I was always sad to see how the mighty had fallen. I was reminded of the story of the cock's comb which Tommy used to tell me and the children.

"Everybody feared the proud cock because they thought the red comb at the top of his head was made of fire. Nobody dared come near the cock or touch him, until one day the cock fell and broke his leg. There he lay on the ground helpless, and now the other animals took courage to go near him and found that his red comb was not of fire after all." Tommy, the proud one, was victim to his weakness and he was the first to admit it. That is when he attached the letters F.O.O.L. to his name.

I was often concerned that if anything happened to Tommy in the big house nobody would know about it, until the little son Wojolomi, grew tall enough to open the bolted door of the garage to let himself out to call for help. I impressed on Tommy that he must take very good care of himself for the sake of the small children who had no mother. They must not lose their father also. "Ah well," he used to say, pointing heavenwards. "It's all written up there. You know I believe in Destiny."

Even so, I hoped fervently that he would live into his nineties as my mother had done, so that the young children would at least be in their teens when he had to leave this world. He was still so strong. He seemed to have an iron constitution, still driving his car at nearly 84 years, still shopping and cooking and attending PTA meetings at the children' school. He was always extremely independent. "If I can't, I won't", regularly accompanied his refusal to accept help.

When the end came I wrote in my diary: "It was all so quick, quite without warning. My driver, whom I had sent to Tommy, phoned me to say that Tommy was very weak and could not get up from bed, so I asked him to come and collect me quickly. Just then a young doctor friend of ours called to say 'hello'. I asked him to come with me to see Tommy. Together he and the driver carried Tommy to the car and took him to the mission hospital where the doctor works. In a cool, clean private room he was put on drip and all routine tests were done. Tommy was in no pain, had a little temperature, but said he was feeling better already. He smiled to reassure us all that nothing was wrong with him. We sat with him until the evening. His young children had come with us and when it got late I took the little girl to my house to sleep with me. I left the boy of ten with Tommy in case he could not find the bell to call the nurse: they chatted until midnight, Wojolomi said later, until he told his daddy that he was tired and wanted to sleep. 'Not a bad idea,' said Tommy.

An hour later he was dead of cardiac arrest. The following morning I got up early to go to the hospital when two of my close friends came to break the news that Tommy had died. Shock. Disbelief. 'Why?' I asked stupidly and burst into tears. Only a few hours before I had wiped his mouth in the hospital and squeezed his arm, saying I would soon be back. The old rascal had become my friend and 56 years of attachment are not a small thing in one's life.

When I had composed myself, a great warm peace settled over me, almost like happiness: Tommy had had an easy and dignified death. He did not have to suffer, did not have to be dependent on anyone — and I had been there when he needed me.

He had gone through a divorce because of me. He had brought me to this country where I could fulfil myself. He had broken my heart, but I had not forsaken him. This thought was a great comfort to me.

In August I, had collected myself sufficiently to be able to write an account of the burial ceremonies to my relations and friends overseas. This account went as follows:

> Tommy died on the 23rd of June, 1999.
> You cannot imagine the horrendous preparations for a "big" (great) man's funeral. Everything had to be done in grand style. It is not a matter of arranging with a funeral parlour to wash and dress the body, provide coffin, hearse, music, and sandwiches for the mourners who come sombrely dressed, pay their condolences, drink their tea and depart.
> When a man dies at 84 there is cause for feasting and rejoicing that he had lived a full life to the end of his days. Three cows were slaughtered, continuous cooking went on days before the events, to feed all the relations who had come and spread themselves over Tommy's house. A platform was erected in the garden on the big lawn, for different dancing groups to perform on the night of the wake-keeping which

preceded the burial in Tommy's village outside Warri. There were countless canopies erected for different groups of friends and drinks and food (cooked food) had to flow. My children and I hired a cooling van stored with chilled drinks. It stood by for two days to supply my group of revelers. We had also cooked. I, the widow, had to stay in the house where people would come and go to pay their respects to me. I was graciously allowed to lie on a settee to receive them instead of lying on the floor, as is the custom for widows. My Nigerwives "sisters" turned up in force wearing our identical uniforms of red and silver hand woven head ties and shoulder shawls over long-skirted white two pieces. They looked truly glamorous, and two of them sat by my side throughout the night, assisting me with food and drink and anything else I required. The others joined the multitude of guests under our canopy where lively socializing and feasting went on, as it did in all other canopies. There must have been near to one thousand guests.

The really dramatic and honourable event was the lying-in-state of Tommy in the High Court of Benin City. He lay in his barrister's regalia in an open coffin lined with ruched white satin. He lay tall and straight and elegant as he had always been. He had been embalmed.

The Chief Judge spoke first, enumerating Tommy's qualities and the great contribution he had made to the Bar and the Bench, when he was a Magistrate. She also told us that she had to get special permission from the Chief Justice of Nigeria in Abuja, because this lying-in state in the High Court was a privilege granted only to judges. It was the first time in Edo State (our State) that an exception had been made for this "Inimitable elder statesman of the Bar". A great honour for the Ogbe family.

Other speeches followed. Monu was the last, and my heart swelled when he stood there, immaculate and relaxed in his black suit, impressive in stature. He told us in his cool flowing English the story of how his father, two years ago, after a hip replacement operation in London, had discharged himself from hospital and gone to visit his old Inn, Gray's Inn. He did not know it then, but it was a symbolic "Thank you" and "good bye" to the beloved institution which had given him his profession, and, Monu said, his pride in it. Temi, the true "chip off the old block" wore Tommy's bowler hat and flitted about, taking photographs, while people in the crowd whispered "Little Tommy".

We had brought my specially upholstered chair so that I was able to sit through the ceremony but I did not join in what happened next. The coffin was closed and carried back by the barristers into the ambulance that had brought it. The crowd now followed it to the Benin Social Club where Tommy had been President several times. There the fun began. All his friends and club members vied with each other in telling anecdotes about his eccentricities and his frankness, to the point of rudeness, but he always got away with it. It was a jolly affair, and Monu and Temi were surprised to see how well his friends knew their father.

From the Social Club the coffin was then carried to the Golf Club. There it was laid on the turf at the first tee of the rolling green and a special round of golf was played in Tommy's honour. His ten-year-old son, Wojolomi, already a novice golfer, played the first ball to a round of cheers. Later, a tree was planted on the golf course, in honour of Tommy. "Daddy liked that", remarked Temi later about the whole show. She was specially attached to her Daddy and he to her. "We have such wonderful children," Tommy used to say every time he saw me.

The following day was the day of the wake-keeping which I have already described. Tommy lay in state again in the open coffin whose sides folded down. He lay in our sitting room on the same satin-covered podium, while the whole room had been decorated with masses of flowers and artistic wreaths, some on high pedestals near the head of the coffin. The walls of the entire room were draped in white lace from ceiling to floor with a deep purple satin frill overhanging the top edge of the lace all around the room. Some relations sat silently near the coffin, others filed in and out until, finally a group of drummers and dancers clapped and danced around the coffin singing praise of the deceased and rejoicing over his life well spent.

I was escorted home at midnight, but Monu and Temi stayed until the early hours of the morning, only to leave again a few hours later to escort their Daddy to his village near Warri where he was interred after the customary ceremony of prayers, breaking kolanuts and firing several canon shots. Only close relatives had taken the trip to Warri in a few cars, for a quiet family burial, as there had been dangerous ethnic violence in that area against Tommy's tribe, the Itsekiris, and we did not want to draw attention to ourselves.

We had again prepared cooked food, jollof rice and meat for the villagers and also took three gallons of locally brewed gin which was received enthusiastically by the headman. As is the custom these days, different members of the family distribute all sorts of gifts to deserving guests. These could be plastic bowls, trays, souvenir note-pads, mugs or glass plates — all of them inscribed with the name of the donors and their place in the family. Temi and Monu had printed white T-shirts with a photo of Tommy in wig and gown and a text which said:

> "He stood for
> INTEGRITY
> EFFICIENCY
> GENEROSITY
> ELOQUENCE
> WISDOM and
> HUMOUR
> "We'll try to follow his ways"

Needless to say that the shirts were a hit and demand by far outstripped the 150 pieces that had been printed.

The interment finally took place in a grave which had had to be cemented because of the swampy ground in Warri. In fact, even while prayers were said in the family open hall, the bottom of the grave was filling up again with water until finally, Tommy was laid to rest. The exhausted mourners returned to Benin without delay to beat the 6 p.m. curfew which had been imposed on Warri, but the memory of all these events will take long to fade.

The friends and most of Tommy's cousins, nephews and nieces have shown me love and affection. They continue to call me or visit, to ease my loneliness, now that my children have gone back. So, let no one ask me "What are you still doing in Nigeria? Won't you come home?"

Nigeria IS HOME.

Chapter XI

ASTROLOGY, MY CRUTCH

You, the reader, must have noticed my several references to people's zodiac signs in this book. I am no astrologer. I have no technical knowledge of how astrology works, I only know that it works in relation to people's characters. I am born under the sign of Leo. Leos are frank and gullible people who think that everybody is like themselves. Therefore, they are not good judges of character. During my life I have often been at a loss as to how to understand other people, when it turned out that they did not behave or think like myself. I even had difficulty understanding my daughter from childhood, because she was so very different from myself.

My interest in astrology dates back almost thirty years. It was by chance that I picked up a book on the character of Leo only and found it so apt a description of myself and other Leos whom I knew that I began to read more and more about all the signs of the zodiac. The zodiac signs, as you probably know, derive their names from the animal patterns which the stars make in the sky at the time/date of your birth.

I say I have no technical knowledge, but I can give you a little insight of how the constellations under which we are born affect our basic character. It affects anybody on earth anywhere, whether black, white, brown, yellow or red in complexion. It does not make any difference. Of course, the environment influences a person's character, and so do his parents' genes and the education he has received, but the basic traits are always there. To the basic traits we must also add the influences of other planets on the sun sign at the moment of birth. Each planet, and there are ten of them, has a character of its own which adds or subtracts from the sun sign of the individual. Some planets have a softening influence, others can make a person more belligerent than the basic sun sign would have contributed.

	DATES	SIGN	ELEMENT
Aries	21/3-20/4	(Ram)	Fire
Taurus	21/4-21/5	(Bull)	Earth
Gemini	22/5-22/6	(Twins)	Air
Cancer	23/6-23/7	(Crab)	Water
Leo	24/7-23/8	(Lion)	Fire
Virgo	24/8-23/9	(Virgin)	Earth
Libra	24/9-23/10	(Scales)	Air
Scorpio	24/10-22/11	(Scorpion)	Water
Sagittarius	23/11-21/12	(Archer)	Fire
Capricorn	22/12-20/1	(Mountain goat)	Earth
Aquarius	21/1-19/2	(Water bearer)	Air
Pisces	20/2-20/3	(Fishes)	Water

The twelve signs of the zodiac are also divided into the signs of the four elements of earth, water, fire and air. The earth signs are basically solid, dependable, and security conscious. The water signs are basically emotional, intuitive, caring, and malleable, because water takes the shape of the vessel it is poured into. The fire signs are extrovert, enthusiastic, passionate, often colourful and leaders of men. The air signs are of the mind. They bring intelligent and swift thinking and sometimes wavering personalities to the scene.

When studying compatibility with other signs, it is logical that earth and water go together, fire and air go together because the water makes things grow in the earth and the air fans the fire. If you combine water and fire for instance, the water may quench the fire. Earth and fire means that the fire may scorch the earth. Air and water would bring a bubbly relationship as the air whips up the water. Air and earth obviously make dust. However, when people work at a relationship it can always be managed whatever the combination.

In this way the relationship is not only between lovers or husband and wife, but it extends to parents and children, to friends, to business partners and colleagues, in fact, wherever there is a relationship, even between employer and employee these astrological factors count. They sometimes explain why one cannot 'get on' with a certain person. The zodiacal make-up of the two people may be just too different, too contradictory to produce harmony. When people are of the same zodiac sign they will understand each other completely, but there will be a kind of rivalry between them or a power struggle.

I gave a few examples in my life story of people close to me. My son, an Aries, was no problem to me. He was a fire sign like myself, exuberant, outgoing, creative and smiling – a happy person.

My daughter was born under the sign of Scorpio, a water sign, and she presented from babyhood the same enigma as my husband did. He too, being Cancer, was a water sign. It was not until I delved into astrology that I understood in my husband the cancerian qualities of caring and yet dominating, and often the indecisions and wavering opinions of the water sign. Cancer, the crab, has a hard outer shell but a soft vulnerable underbelly. Cancerians have the moon as their leading planet and the moon stands for femininity, making very good loving, caring wives and housekeepers, good at cooking and gardening and always willing to nurture and protect the weaker ones. In the case of my daughter I read much about Scorpio. This made my daughter, also a water sign, very intuitive and analytical, producing astute judgement of any situation from an early childhood. But so too, she had the qualities of a scorpion who lives in the dark under stones or hidden in the sand, so that she would be found reading her books lying on the floor in a darkened room. All my admonitions failed, my warnings that she was damaging her eyes, why did she not put the light on? She persisted reading in the dark. On the other hand, she was fiercely loyal to her friends and doted on animals. The fierce loyalty is typical of scorpios who either love or hate with a passion.

My mother, born on the cusp, that means on the exact date between one zodiac sign and the next, was born a Taurus on the cusp with Aries. She could not have been more typical. She had all the solid dependable, sensible qualities of Taurus, an earth sign, and yet the impulsiveness and adventurous attitude to events which are characterized by Aries, the fire sign. When a person is born on the cusp, or within five days of the neighbouring sign, he can take on some of the qualities of the preceding or succeeding sign.

CHARACTERISTICS

The "Key" words for the qualities of each zodiac sign are:

1. **Aries**
   Impulse, anger, courage, energy, leadership, wit, versatility, creativity.

2. **Taurus**
   Art, possessions, money, property, beauty, singing, gardens.

3. **Gemini**
   Letters, books, stories, reports, radio, telephone, dexterity, handicrafts, art.

4. **Cancer**
   Memory, home, antiquity, motherhood, ties, wood, gardening, cooking.

5. **Leo**
   Kingship, jewel, gold, vigour, warmth, fire, happiness, command, courage, breadth, generosity.

6. **Virgo**
   Work, diet, natural, animals, health, teaching, precision, details, analysis, criticism, perfection.

7. **Libra**
   Beauty, art, partnership, tact, charm, affection, relaxation, compromise, diplomacy, laziness.

8. **Scorpio**
   Creation, birth, death, sex, regeneration, passion, research, secretiveness, analysis.

9. **Sagittarius**
   Travel, philosophy, religion, tolerance, working, space, freedom, aspiration, idealist, optimist, justice.

10. **Capricorn**
    Aspiring, responsible, cold, prudent, self-contained, persevering, methodical, plodding, modest.

11. **Aquarius**
    Clubs, revolutionary, waves, telepathy, eccentric, averse, intuition, freedom, protest, reform, destruction.

12. **Pisces**
    Rhythm, liquids, fluidity, escape, mystic, pretence, sleep, unworldly, acting, meditation.

The Zodiac Affects the following Parts of the Body

1. Aries: The Head

2. Taurus: The throat
3. Germini: Lungs/arms
4. Cancer: Breasts, stomach
5. Leo: The heart and back
6. Virgo: The nervous system and intestines
7. Libra: The kidneys and lumbar region
8. Scorpio: The sexual organs
9. Sagittarius: The liver, hips and thighs
10. Capricorn: The skin and bones
11. Aquarius: The ankles, calves and circulation
12. Pisces: Feet and pituitary gland.

These are the rudiments of how the zodiac sign under which we are born affects us.

If you look around in your circle of friends and family you will observe how the characteristics fit each person provided you know their birth dates.

Astrologers also ask for the time of birth, in order to calculate the sign rising at that hour. This determines the Ascendant, which shows the kind of face you show to the world. It can be very different from your basic sun sign. To take the hour of noon on the day of your birth is not accurate enough, but some astrologers suggest it when the client does not know his hour of birth. The result can be very misleading as to the character of the person described.

One can see now why the generalizations of the horoscope indicated in newspapers and magazines are not to be taken seriously, but I know from personal experience that the character studies I made of my friends and family have proved very helpful in understanding them. In the case of our son Monu, who wanted to leave his law studies and take up engineering, I consulted an astrologer by post. I wrote to him in England, giving him our son's birth data and asking him to do an aptitude analysis, telling us which profession would best suit his character. The reply I got was for engineering and aviation which was exactly what our son wanted to do. On the strength of this analysis Tommy agreed that Monu could change from Law.

When I look back further into my family there were my two grandmothers. My mother's mother born under Taurus was a solid dependable business woman who sold model gowns from foreign cities and who kept the whole family financially. My father's mother born under Gemini was the delightful, witty story teller of my youth. My brother and I used to listen to her every day, telling stories, some invented, some authentic of whatever came into her thoughts. She had imagination and a quick mind. My father, himself born under Pisces, was subject to the moods that assail most water signs. He was moody, but very artistic without ever having been trained in art or for the piano. Yet, he could draw delightful, funny sketches and without reading music he could play the piano by ear, with full chord accompaniment in both hands, and never hitting a wrong note.

Allow me to repeat that what I have written about astrology is by no means an exhaustive study of the subject, but these guidelines are enough for entertainment and also for understanding the people you associate with. There are schools of astrology and in the U.S.A., I believe one or two universities have offered it or are offering it as a discipline. In detailed studies and analysis much more consideration must be given to the planets in each horoscope, to the houses they fall into and to the aspects which the planets make to each other. There are many more considerations as well but I assure you that my own guidelines have stood me in good stead during my life.

EPILOGUE

Readers may wish to know what became of some of the 'players' in the drama of my life.

Obinu
Tommy's mother the gentle frail Obinu died in 1972. She was so slight that her white coffin looked like a child's. I was given the honour to decorate it with flowers all over. Bearing in mind the hot and humid climate in which we lived I bought masses of artificial flowers, which I knew would last a long time. They covered the whole coffin.

Mewe
Tommy's sister Mewe was four years older than he and she is still going strong. She is living with her daughters Tunde and Lily in Lagos. They look after her most touchingly but although she is physically well she does not understand now much of what is going on. Nobody has told her of her favourite brother's death.

Tunde
Tunde, whose doctor husband left her a widow almost 30 years ago, lives in a large house in Lagos. It is a storey building, but on the ground floor she has built an attachment of a small restaurant called The Golden Egg. There, people eat not only eggs but full Nigerian meals as well as consume plenty of drinks of all kinds. Tunde has a son and a daughter and is a grandmother. She has lost none of the sweet smile of her youth.

Lily
Lily became a very efficient secretary in England where she was married to an Itsekiri man by whom she had three sons. When she became homesick for Nigeria she came back to live with her sister Tunde, and the two of them seem to be happy in each other's company.

Freedom
Freedom was not only very intelligent but also ambitious and studious. He took his first degree in geology at Ibadan University. His second degree, the M.Sc. he took at Ife University, and then went to England to do his Ph.D. He worked very hard in England, be it as dish washer, taxi driver or any other thing, his mind was set on his goal and he did not bother about what kind of job he was doing so long as it gave him a living and the ability to further his studies. He now has a very successful company called GEO Consults in which he deals with oil companies for whom he drills the soil to examine it for oil. He has a laboratory in which the drilled cores are analysed. He also has a bore-hole from which his company sells water to tankers who supply areas of Benin City that have no water. He has four children, two boys and two girls who are all doing well. It is Freedom who has taken over the education and welfare of Tommy's small children, as is the custom in Itsekiri tradition. The eldest always looks after the younger ones.

Ching-Ching
Ching-ching lost her husband, an electrical engineer, with whom she had three strapping sons. She was a caterer and also had trained for nursing. She lives in England where she is now a health visitor for old age pensioners. She is a very kind step-daughter to me who sends me bacon, cheese, chocolates and other things which I crave whenever somebody travels from Britain to Nigeria.

Monu

Monu, our son, did extremely well after we had asked the astrologer's advice. He has combined his engineering instinct with flying. He trained himself through aviation to become a private pilot and flying instructor. He combined this with his computer knowledge to become a systems analyst and now an Internet specialist. He built his own company called Aviators Network which was a very unusual business ten years ago, as he concentrated only on internet enquiries about aviation. He has two boys and a charming Scottish wife. They live in England. Monu and Moira are supportive, loving children to me.

Temi

After her eventful stay in Israel, Temi settled in England and also became a computer trainer. She calls it a softwear trainer. On one of her assignments she worked for a huge firm of engineers, where she trained small groups of engineers in computer literacy. She married one of her students, a Scottish engineer. Both our children accidentally married partners from Aberdeen, Scotland, who did not know each other. Temi has a baby boy at this moment and a girl of four and with her Scottish husband, who is an oil and gas platform structural engineer, lives with him and her children in the United Arab Emirates. They have spent some years in Abu Dhabi and are now in Dubai.

Temi has developed several hobbies which earn her substantial pocket money and give her an interest in life other than that of motherhood and housewife. While in England she trained herself in dancing Salsa, the now fashionable Latin American dance which has swept the world. With her natural rhythm and love for dancing she has made herself into a 'Salsa Missionary' teaching groups of enthusiastic couples to dance this latest craze. She has also discovered a talent for making beautiful greeting cards with a method of embossing and decorating them, such as I had never seen before. She is a loving, caring daughter to me.

Stephen
Stephen, my faithful cook, is still looking after me to this day. He is like a mother to me making sure that I get my favourite fruits, my daily garlic and honey and a piece of Aloe Vera which I grow myself and eat everyday. I cannot imagine what I would do if he were not around any more to cook my favourite dishes.

My Mother
My wonderful mother spent altogether twelve years with us in Nigeria. She used to come for a year or two and then go back to see my brother in New York until her next trip to Nigeria. The last time she came was in 1982 when she was ninety years old. She enjoyed staying in my little house but unfortunately in the early part of 1983 we had three months of power cuts that is, no electricity at all. Something major had broken down, and at that time I did not yet have a generator. The heat was unbearable for her so that she spent most of the days in a friend's house where there was a strong generator day and night. Eventually she decided that she had to return to New York if she wanted to stay alive. I let her go with great misgivings. She died just before her ninety-third birthday when I had already got my ticket to fly to be with her on that day. It was sad that I now had to fly out for her funeral instead of for a celebration.

Johnny and Edith
My brother and his wife had qualified with honours from their studies of interior design. They had both been working in New York but at weekends they used to go to the country where they had built a house for themselves. They were both very successful in their field. Edith became a colour consultant and Johnny became well known for his outstanding wall hangings, which grace many an important building in New York to this day. One of them is in the Rockefeller Centre, another in the World Trade Centre. So, although he had no children, he left behind his brain children

to the world. Unfortunately, he died at age 74. He was given a place in the War Heroes' cemetery outside New York.

My Cousins, Laura and Guenther
They are still living in Golders Green. Also in their eighties now, the husband is still carrying out interior design projects and my cousin Laura is a superb cook and 100% mother, and grandmother to her three grand children, after retiring from her career as nursery teacher.

Marlene, My Guru
Marlene had been four years older than my mother. She died about ten years after I had left for Nigeria, but I often feel that she is still around in spirit, still connected with me, as her teaching lives on in me.

Jean Evans
Jean Evans is widowed now, but she continues to write funny stories and she is forever planning new stories or jokes to write. When her husband died, their three big sons took over looking after their mother.

Joan
Joan Awerioghene is also widowed. She lives with her daughter in England, and I miss her witty company greatly.

Betti-O
Betty is still buzzing with ideas. Her husband too died. She has three sons and a daughter who is following in her creative footsteps.

My Adoptive Family
My adoptive family of Victor and Christine and their three daughters are as close to me and I to them as we have been these last twenty-two years. The eldest daughter is married with two

children. She took a university degree in English. Poppy and Fify are both lawyers and very handsome they look in their professional garb.

Nigerwives
Our group of Nigerwives has shrunk somewhat. As the recession in Nigeria is biting harder every year, many of them have gone back to their countries, some of them with their husbands, in the hope of finding greener pastures. Although we are few, maybe ten or twelve, we still meet regularly and enjoy each other's friendship and support.

The Silver Business
Talking of recession, this has affected our business adversely. There are fewer customers now who can afford the luxury of jewellery. I continue to tempt them with new designs, but the turnover is just not what it used to be.

The Sickle Cell Project
After this book is published my last foreseeable goal will be to produce the sickle cell herb in large quantities. So far my attempts to introduce it to a pharmaceutical company have failed, but I have not given up hope. I am still gratified and encouraged by the happy faces of my patients who now do not fear pain anymore. They have the remedy.

As I am now in my eightieth year I have only the one regret: that wisdom comes so late. Just as I begin to understand life and people, it is almost time to say goodbye.

Index

A.T. & P. (African Timber and Plywood) Sapele, 116
Adophy, Chuks, 142
African
— crafts, 92, 215
— laws, 43
— market, 104
Afro-American community, 79
Aiwerioghene, Ayo, 266, 269
Aiwerioghene, Joan, 183, 266
Ajemijereye, Thompson, 42-49, 52, 56
Akpata, Olu, 232
Alexandra, Princess, 136
American Baptist Hospital, Eku, 133
Anderson, Mr., 9
Anukpe, Walter, 200, 263
Appiah, Joe, 46
Appleboom, Mrs., 153
Arts Council, 206
Arts exhibitions, 205
Awokoya, Stephen, 67
Asaboro, Mr., 93
Astrological factors and Atane, Barbara, 224
Attlee, Clement, 46-47
Auchi General Hospital, 186
Awolowo, 85

Ballroom dancing, 91
Baxendell's, Mr., 143-144
BBC, 184-185
— News, 217
Beier, Ulli, 86-88
Benson, Bobby, 85
Benson, T.O.S., 84-85, 142

Biafran
— Army, 185
— War, 175
Buckingham Palace, 99
Chamberlain, Prime Minister, 8
Chevron Oil Company, 159
Ching-Ching, 91, 93, 108, 113, 115, 127, 147-148, 203, 286
Churchill, 55
Coff 'n Crafts, 226
Colin, Mr., 59-60, 75
Concentration camp barracks, 15
Concentration camps, 2-3, 57, 162
Cooperative weaving industry, Auchi, 200-201
Coral beads, 138
Cowan, Mr., 37
Cripps, Sir Stafford, 46

Deji of Akure, 139
Donkin, Miss, 4, 8
Doodle bugs, 53
Dunn, Miss, 4, 8

Ecumenical Society
— membership of 172, 175
Edaiken United Carving Industry, 194
Editti, 164, 288
Egbe, G.B.A., 91, 232
Eku Baptist Hospital, 141
Empire State building, 65
Epiphany Party
— celebration in French manner, 173-174
Esiri, Agnes, 107, 137-139

Ethel, 202
Ethnic killings, 185
European brooch, 159
Eyewetemi (Hilda's daughter), 148
Ezeana, Charles, 158-159

Field society, 236
Free legal aid, 58
Freedom, 108, 113-114, 127-128, 148, 163, 185-186, 286

Garrick, Dr., 221-222
German Jews, 2
German schools, 1
Gerson, Mrs., 120
Goddess Olokun, 193-194
Goldberg, Miss, 21
Goldberg, Mr., 31-33, 36-37, 58-62, 64, 67, 71, 75-76
Gowon, Victoria, 225
Granny Obinu, 104-105, 122, 127, 131-132, 135, 285
Green, Mr., 190
Grey, Stanley, 142

Hammersmith Hospital, London, 75
Hayes, Mr., 138
Hendrickse, Begum, 178
Hendrickse, Ralph, 178
Hernandez, Mr., 143
Hilda
— application for British citizenship, 58
— as a British Citizen, 73
— as First Lady of Edo State Arts and Crafts, 206
— as member of International Trade Fair Board of Midwestern Nigeria, 204
— at Croft Home, 8-9
— at Industrial Training Centre, Acton, London, 39
— at Isle of Man, 15-16, 25
— at Singapore, 249-251
— in India, 237-249
— married to Tommy, 78
— member of Field Society, 236
— naturalisation as a Nigerian, 177-178
— now land owner, 224
— undertaking a course on Travel Agency functions, 251
Hilda's activities in Ecumenical Centre, 176
Hilly's Ice-cream, 117-118
Hiroshima
— bombing of, 56
Hitler, 8, 22-23, 43, 57, 87
Hitler's oppression, 4, 6
Home Guard, 54

Ibiam, Francis, 172
Ibiam, Lady, 172, 175
Indian crafts, 215
International
— Association of Travel Agents (I.A.T.A.), 251
— Trade Fair, 205
— Year for African Tourism, 205
Internment camp, 227
Itsekiri
— dancing, 198
— table manners, 102
Iyahen, Patrick, 268
Iyat, Miss, 205
Iyoha, Sue, 270

Jacoby, Jean, 74
Jardin des Tuileries, 87
Jeux des Paumes, 87
Jewish
— citizens, 1
— officials, 1
— welfare committee, 3
— welfare organisations, 2
Johnny, 164, 288
Johnson, Mobolaji, 203
Jones, Mrs., 28
Jones, Sir Elwyn, 68-69
Judaism, 49

Kensington Palace, 100

Khalil, Mr., 134
King's College, Lagos, 43, 63, 142, 149
Kingsway Store, 116-118, 132, 178, 180, 202-203, 234
Kubeinje, Lawyer, 129

Labour
— exchange, 17
— Party, 46
Lagos University Teaching Hospital, 206
Lawson, Ben, 119-120, 130-131
Lee, President, 250
Levitas, Mr., 65
Lewin, Philip, 85-86
Lily, 91, 93, 108, 113, 127, 286
Lucas, Canon, 122

Mama Rosa of Forcados, 113
Marlene, 47-48, 289
Marshall, Miss, 28-29, 34
McCathy, Chief, 269
Merogun, Uncle, 96
Middlesex Hospital, London, 81
Midwest
— Arts Festival, 205
— Crafts Exhibition, 203-204
— Craftshop, 192-193, 200, 206, 263
Mohammed, Murtala, 187
Mongul Emperor Shah Jahan, 241
Monubarami (Hilda's son) [Monu], 82, 90-92, 98, 103, 108-109, 111, 116-118, 120, 123-129, 133-134, 136, 139-140, 145, 147-152, 154, 161, 169, 174-175, 179, 182-183, 206-207, 210, 214, 220, 222-223, 226-228, 253-255, 274-276, 284, 287
— as member of the Auxilliary Fire Fighters, 210
— at All Saints School, Enugu, 174
— at Federal Government College, Warri, 183, 185, 197
— left for America for Further Studies, 227

Nagasaki
— bombing of, 56

Nature's laws, 158
Nelson, Mrs., 31-32, 38
New Nigeria Bank, 204
New Year Festival in Bombay, 246
Nigerian Field Society, 257
Nigerwives, 265-270, 290
Nigerwives Sisters, 274
Nkune, Mrs., 107
Nnoka, Barbara, 133
Nosound ear plugs, 20-21
Nwokedi
— Agha, 174-175
— Francis, 174
— Irene, 165, 174-175, 179
— Uzo, 174

Oba of Benin, 205
Obeahon, Margaret, 265, 270
Obinu, Madam, 91
Obiogun, Mrs., 122
Ogbe
— David, 186, 209, 223-224, 226
— Edema Brick, 114
— Hilda, 190
— Irma, 186
— John, 196
— T.A. (Tommy), 142
Ogbecraft Limited, 235
Ogbecraft Silversmiths, 235
Ogbemudia, Clara, 225
Ogbemudia, Samuel, 188, 190-192, 196, 200, 203-205, 263
Ogwashi-Uku Catholic Mission Hospital, 141
Ojukwu, 184
Okagbue, Miriam, 171
Okonkwo, Reka, 267-268
Okorodudu, Michael, 141
Okpara, Michael, 179
Okpu, Rosa, 166-167
Okuboyejo, Betty, 178-179
Olu of Warri, 99
Omadukpe, Uncle, 105
Omage, Christine, 259, 261, 289
Omage, Victor, 228-232, 251, 261, 289
Omotosho, Mr., 63-64

294   Index

Ovie-Whiskey, 115

Prest, Arthur, 108, 122-123

Quota system, 2

Readheads, 139
Refugee Committee, 22, 25
Refugee immigrants, 2
Religious instruction, 49
Rockeffeller Centre, 65
Russian revolution, 3

Sagay, Andrew, 232
Second-class citizens, 1
Second wife syndrome, 214
Service exchange, 17, 20
Shell BP, 200, 208, 218
Shell Operations, Britain, 160
Shokpeka, Charles, 257
Silver exhibitions, 165-166
Silver official exhibitions, 169
Silversmiths Union, 235
Social
— behaviour, 102
— greetings, 102
Solankes, 83
Stephen (the Cook), 189, 235, 288
Stigter, Mr., 156
Sylvester, Victor, 91

Temi (Hilda's daughter), 148-151, 161, 164, 174, 179, 182, 185-187, 198, 206-207, 210-211, 213, 215, 220-221, 233-234, 252-255, 275-276, 287
— at American High School, Israel, 253
— schooling in England, 221
Thomas, Karen, 185-186
Thomas, Oritsejolomi, 67, 75
Tommy, 61-64, 67-68, 70, 73, 75, 77-78, 81-83, 85-86, 89-93, 99-103, 105, 107-114, 116, 118-129, 132-134, 137, 139-157, 159-160, 164, 166-168, 170-174, 176-177, 179-181, 184-189, 196-200, 203, 207-210, 212-213, 216-227, 232, 234-235, 252-253, 256-257, 261-263, 271-275, 277, 284
— as member of Enugu Golf Club, 156
— as Shell BP Representative, Benin, 176
— as Shell BP Representative, Enugu, 155
— at Shell BP, 142-148
— down with meningitis, 221
— on admission at UBTH, 221
— on familiarisation course, 160
— relations of, 91
Tropical Diseases Hospital, London, 120, 124
Two, Johnny, 249-250

Uddoh, Pat., 269
Ugunu Shell Camp, 200
Uku, Eileen, 268
Uncle Merogun, 119
University
— community, 268
— of Benin Teaching Hospital (UBTH), 231, 268
— of Ibadan, 86
— of Nsukka, Enugu Campus, 169
UTC (United Trade Company), 234

Valentine Party, 268-269

War effort, 38-39, 52
War of Pearl Habour, 56
Watson, B.D.B., 236-237, 240, 245-247, 249, 258
Wendy House, 197
Wenger, Susanne, 88
West African Students Union (WASU), 83
The White Gold, 169
Williams, Vaughan, 26
Wojolomi, 272-273, 275
Women's territorial army, 38

Yoruba
— drummers

— language of, 86
— literature, 86
Yowunren, Prince, 96, 99, 196

Zik
— visit to London, 83-84
Zodiac signs, 278-279
— qualities of, 281-283